IF WE CAN WIN HERE

The New Front Lines of the Labor Movement

FRAN QUIGLEY

ILR PRESS
AN IMPRINT OF
CORNELL UNIVERSITY PRESS
ITHACA AND LONDON

First published 2015 by Cornell University Press
First printing, Cornell Paperbacks, 2015
Printed in the United States of America

Library of Congress Cataloging-in-Publication Data

Quigley, Fran, 1962– author.
    If we can win here : the new front lines of the labor movement / Fran Quigley.
      pages cm
    Includes bibliographical references and index.
    ISBN 978-0-8014-5367-0 (cloth : alk. paper)
    ISBN 978-0-8014-5655-8 (pbk. : alk. paper)
  1. Labor movement—Indiana—Indianapolis. 2. Labor unions—Organizing—Indiana—
Indianapolis. 3. Service industries workers—Labor unions—Organizing—Indiana—Indianapolis.
4. Working poor—Indiana—Indianapolis. I. Title.
    HD8085.I53Q46   2015
    331.88'11640977252—dc23   2014042069

Cornell University Press strives to use environmentally responsible suppliers and materials to the fullest extent possible in the publishing of its books. Such materials include vegetable-based, low-VOC inks and acid-free papers that are recycled, totally chlorine-free, or partly composed of nonwood fibers. For further information, visit our website at www.cornellpress.cornell.edu.

Cloth printing   10 9 8 7 6 5 4 3 2 1
Paperback printing   10 9 8 7 6 5 4 3 2 1

Portions of the introduction and chapters 1, 3, 6, 8, 9, 10, and 17 were previously published as the following, respectively: "We Deserve Better: Local Hotel Workers Talking Union," Indianapolis NUVO, November 18, 2012; "The Battle of Indianapolis: Workers Win Gains despite Right to Work Laws," Working In These Times, December 14, 2012; "Low Wages Mean Two Jobs in One Day," Indianapolis NUVO, November 16, 2012, and "Local Janitors Pushing for Living Wages," Indianapolis NUVO, July 31, 2013; "Workers Pushing for Unions May Pay the Price," Indianapolis NUVO, November 16, 2012; "Butler Food Workers Fight for Improvements," Indianapolis NUVO, June 21, 2013; "The Caregivers' Dilemma," Indianapolis NUVO, July 10, 2013; "Security Guards Seek Training, Health Care," Indianapolis NUVO, December 19, 2012; and "Workers Brave Cold for Medicaid Expansion Rally," Indianapolis NUVO, January 23, 2014.

Printed with Union Labor

To Ellen

CONTENTS

ACKNOWLEDGMENTS

The working people of Indianapolis are the heart of this book. Both the workers named in the book and many others who are not named taught and inspired me. They were patient with my many questions and my presence as a witness to their struggles. My deepest gratitude—and admiration—goes to them.

I also thank the organizers, whose idealism and persistence provide an example I will strive to emulate. Like the workers, they took time from overstuffed schedules to explain puzzling situations and new concepts to me.

When I get it right in this book, the workers and organizers are to be credited. When I got it wrong, that is on me—because they certainly did their best to keep me on track.

Special thanks goes to Yasmina Bersbach, who spent many hours transcribing interviews and offered insightful comments throughout the process. Early readers of portions of this book helped guide its development. Those readers include Ellen Quigley, Florence Roisman, John White, Steve

Early, and Bob Healey. Fran Benson at Cornell University Press provided very welcome encouragement even before a full draft of the manuscript was complete. Along with the Press's anonymous peer reviewers, she delivered several much-needed suggestions for improvement.

My colleagues at the Indiana University McKinney School of Law clinical programs were supportive at every stage. My thanks go to Ginger Smallwood, Jasmine Coombs, Carrie Hagan, Joanne Orr, Fran Watson, Novella Nedeff, and Cynthia Baker. The students in the Health and Human Rights Clinic have traveled this workers' rights journey with me, and often taught the professor quite a bit as they fought for justice for our clients.

All my love goes to Ellen White Quigley, and to Sam Quigley, Katie Quigley, and Jack Quigley, who have provided me joy beyond anything I could ever deserve.

IF WE CAN WIN HERE

Introduction

"Why Can't I Do That as a Housekeeper?"

It is October 2012, the first cold morning of the year, and Keisha Johnson shivers as she walks out the front door of her home a few dozen yards from Interstate 65. The near-Northside Indianapolis neighborhood is quiet enough that she can hear the birds chirping. It is Saturday, and most of her neighbors are still sleeping. But Keisha Johnson is headed to work.

A trim African American woman of thirty-two, Johnson is wearing her work uniform, a gray polyester blouse and matching slacks, with her hair pulled back and held by several pins. She starts off walking at a brisk near-trot to the bus stop two blocks away. Johnson has lived at her current house, a small rent-to-own with white aluminum siding, for just a month. She is still learning the IndyGo bus schedules and is worried she will be late for work. She arrives at the stop, steps off the curb, and nervously scans the horizon north on Capitol Avenue. Johnson moved here in large part for its access to more bus routes—her previous home on the northwest side of town did not have any bus service at all on Sundays, a workday for Johnson. Finally, the Number 4 comes into view. Sighing with relief, Johnson boards, finds a seat, and begins to put on her makeup.

As the Number 4 enters downtown, the streets are deserted. Since it is a weekend morning, the lawyers and accountants and state government employees who usually crowd these sidewalks are not here today. No one has arrived yet to eat at Oceanaire Seafood Room or to see a show at the Indianapolis Repertory Theater. But as the bus pulls up in front of the Indiana Statehouse, a crowd awaits, huddled close together under a plastic shelter and stamping their feet against the unseasonable chill. Some wear nametags around their necks, while others wear reinforced safety boots and heavy jackets. Like Johnson, most are wearing a work uniform.

As Johnson descends from the bus, she hears one woman greet another. "What are you doing this morning?" the first woman asks. The second woman looks down the street. The #4 is not her bus, and she can't see her bus in view yet. "Trying to get to work, if they let me!" she replies.

Johnson flicks her sweatshirt hood over her head and walks across the lawn of the Statehouse toward Washington Street. As she approaches the sweeping stone and glass front of the Westin Hotel, she veers past the main entrance and walks in the rear door.

Johnson's parents were in the military, and she spent most of her childhood in Germany. After returning to Indianapolis and graduating from North Central High School, she worked in factory jobs and in restaurants. In 2007, she started as a housekeeper at the Westin. Her husband is a delivery driver but is between jobs right now, so they have taken in a roommate to offset the rent. Johnson knows Spanish and a bit of German and has a bright and ironic sense of humor. ("I get to spend another weekend at the Westin," she laughs, feigning anticipation of a grand adventure.[1]) But a recent attempt to earn a nurse's aide degree was not successful. Her school loan required her to take a full load of classes, but Johnson could not pay the bills unless she worked full time, too. She was perpetually exhausted, and her grades suffered. She hopes to enroll in online courses soon.

Johnson's title at the Westin is room attendant. She starts her workday with a list of assignments for the rooms she is expected to clean, up to eighteen in a day. A cart stocked with clean towels and sheets waits for her in the hallway of her assigned rooms. She lugs the 120-pound cart down to the room entrances—no mean feat in thickly carpeted hallways—and knocks on the door. "Housekeeping!" she calls.

Johnson is expected to complete a "stay-over" cleaning in just ten minutes. She will make the bed, change the towels, and ensure there is a full supply of soap and shampoo. Johnson's managers expect the process for a "check-out" to be accomplished within thirty minutes, but even an experienced housekeeper like Johnson often takes much longer to clean a room. Johnson tells of rooms with gum stuck in the carpet, melted ice cream welded to the bottom of a trash can, a room where a child vomited in the bed. "It's kind of the luck of the draw; you never know what you will get behind that door," she says.

The housekeeper's nemesis is hair in the bathroom, where it tends to stick to shower curtains and sinks. Not surprisingly, it is no fun using a scrub brush to clean a stranger's toilet. "There are crevices in the porcelain, so disgusting things can get into those crevices," Johnson says.

The Westin housekeeper's arsenal does not include a broom or a mop or a pail. The cleaning is done on hands and knees. Some of the hotel mattresses Johnson and her colleagues must maneuver weigh more than one hundred pounds each. Johnson was a gymnast in high school and is still very physically fit. She takes care to stretch her back and hamstrings before she goes to work. But she still wakes up sore most mornings, and she has suffered leg cramps in the middle of the night. The U.S. Bureau of Labor Statistics reports that hotel workers have the highest injury rate of any service industry workers, and a recent study reported in the *American Journal of Industrial Medicine* showed housekeepers are at greater risk for injury than other hotel workers.[2] Johnson talks with pride about the attention to detail and people skills she has mastered in her work, but she acknowledges the need for speed, too. She has seen newer housekeepers get fired after they failed to clean their assigned rooms quickly enough. She refers to Rip It energy drink, just ninety-nine cents in some stores and packing more caffeine than Red Bull or Rockstar, as "the housekeeper steroid."

The mythology of the American Dream would suggest that all this hard work must be allowing Johnson to move up the economic ladder. The American Dream would be wrong. Johnson started at the Westin earning $7.50 per hour and just received her most recent raise to $9.27 per hour. She is never assigned a full forty hours per week. Tips are unpredictable and often meager or nonexistent, and Johnson cannot afford the premiums for the cheapest health insurance that Westin provides. She has not had health insurance for over ten years. Although her wages easily exceed the federal and state minimum wage of $7.25 per hour, they are far below the $17 per hour estimate of a "living wage," the minimal cost of supporting a two-person family in Indianapolis.[3]

That leaves Johnson in the most vulnerable position in the U.S. economy: too poor to pay all her bills but with a reliable paycheck for her creditors to garnish. A fall at home last year led to an emergency room visit, five stitches, and a hospital bill she has not been able to pay. Johnson has been evicted for being late on her rent, leading to court judgments that tacked on attorney's fees, court costs, and interest. She receives bill collector calls every day. Her student loan debt was eventually collected out of her paycheck, week after week, for more than a year.

Johnson has supported an effort to organize Indianapolis hotel workers into a union, and she testified about the use of temporary workers in the local hotels in front of an Indianapolis City-County Council hearing in June 2012. Wearing a bright red "UNITE HERE" union T-shirt, Johnson spoke briefly and clearly into the microphone. But she admitted later that she was rattled by the unexpected sight of her Westin general manager sitting in front of the hearing room. "I was shaking like a leaf," she recalls. "All I could think of is that 'I am going to get fired, fired, fired!'"

She did not get fired, and she continues to support the union campaign. Johnson knows housekeepers in unionized hotels get paid significantly more than she does and have more affordable health insurance. But it is not just about the money. "I have always seen housekeeping as a noble profession," she says. "Someday, I want to be one of those moms who can send kids to college and have all the bills paid. Why can't I do that as a housekeeper?"

During the first weeks of 2012, on the same side of the Indiana Statehouse where Keisha Johnson gets off her bus, thousands of union members and supporters from across the Midwest crowded together in angry protest. The occasion was the Indiana General Assembly's consideration of anti-union "right-to-work" legislation, a law that allows workers to opt out of paying union fees even when they benefit from collective bargaining. For weeks, labor advocates held rallies outside the building and in the hallways separating the legislative chambers, chanting "Kill the Bill" and singing "Solidarity Forever." But the Indiana Senate ignored the clamor and passed the right-to-work law on February 1, 2012. The vote paved the way for Indiana to become the twenty-third state in the United States to adopt

Figure i.1. Tired of earning subpoverty wages as a hotel housekeeper, Keisha Johnson joined the union movement in Indianapolis. "Someday, I want to be one of those moms who can send kids to college and have all the bills paid," she says. "Why can't I do that as a housekeeper?" Photo by Mark A. Lee.

the law, and the first in the country's Rust Belt, where union-staffed manufacturing once was a dominant feature of the economy. Later that year, Michigan governor Rick Snyder cited Indiana's example as his motivation for reversing course and supporting right-to-work legislation in his neighboring state.

The right-to-work setback is just the most recent and dramatic of several blows inflicted on Indiana workers in recent decades. As recently as 1989, one in every five Indiana workers belonged to a union. Today, barely 9 percent of the Indiana workforce is unionized.[4] In 2005, Indiana's governor eliminated collective bargaining for state employees. At a national level, income inequality is at its highest since before the Great Depression. The Center on Budget and Policy Priorities reports that Indiana's wage gap has grown faster than those of all but five states.[5]

Yet, on the very same day in early 2012 when the Indiana Senate approved the right-to-work bill, food-service workers at Indiana University–Purdue University at Indianapolis (IUPUI) gathered less than a mile to the west of the Statehouse and took a step in the opposite direction. Away from the glare of the television cameras focused on the legislative debates, new members of UNITE HERE Local 23 voted to approve their first-ever collective bargaining agreement with the IUPUI contractor Chartwells Dining Services.[6] Fifty-year-old James Meyers, a lead food-service worker at IUPUI, was thrilled with the new contract's wage increases, improved health benefits, and recognition for seniority. But what meant the most to him was the intangible benefit that came with finally being treated as a partner at his workplace. "I felt like I had won a million dollars," Meyers said. "I got to tell the manager, 'You are the boss, I understand that. But I am a man, too, and we can respect each other.'"

Meyers is not the only Indianapolis worker to feel the strength of a new union affiliation. Despite a state political climate that proved inhospitable to labor activism in the right-to-work debate, service-sector workers are launching union organizing campaigns across the state's capital. At Marian University and Butler University, two private colleges located on the north side of Indianapolis, maintenance and food-service workers for the contractor Aramark have fought for union recognition and first-ever contracts. Indianapolis International Airport food-service workers won union recognition and have negotiated contracts with three companies staffing airport restaurants and stores. The Service Employees International Union (SEIU) has been organizing local security guards and janitors for several years and has recently begun working to organize Indiana home care workers. An energetic campaign for citizenship for undocumented immigrants, funded by the local Roman Catholic archdiocese and fueled in large part by the activism of local Latino Catholics, is integrated into the low-wage workers' campaigns.

It has been a struggle. UNITE HERE's seven-year community-wide campaign to organize the city's hotel workers like Keisha Johnson has not yet broken through. Some union activists have lost their hotel jobs in the process, and Indianapolis remains one of the country's largest cities without a unionized hotel. The SEIU campaigns have had mixed results. Most Indianapolis-area home care workers, security guards, and janitors are not unionized, and even most of those who are unionized still have low wages and limited benefits. Some union supporters in the community retain hard feelings for SEIU, believing the union largely abandoned Indianapolis's janitors in 2007 after recruiting significant community involvement in winning the union and a contract for the janitors. The wage increases and benefit access negotiated by UNITE HERE for the airport and IUPUI workers are better than what they had before they organized, but some of those workers still struggle to afford health care and make ends meet.

However, there are bright spots. It appears that local hotels' practice of relying on low-paid contract labor has been reduced. The change is likely due in part to union-supported legislative campaigns that focused a spotlight on the workers' plight. The campaigns were followed by successful wage and hour litigation against one contractor accused of forcing hotel housekeepers to work off the clock. UNITE HERE's long siege against the local hotels has not yet achieved direct success, but it became the incubator for the union's more fruitful organizing of local food-service and university workers. The local Community Faith and Labor Coalition launched a program that has helped nonunionized workers who are victimized by wage theft. It also then pulled unions and other community partners into an effort to create Indianapolis's first-ever worker center.

The national Fight for 15 campaign to raise the wages of fast-food and retail workers has included a lively presence in Indianapolis, where community supporters, union activists, and low-wage workers have engaged in high-profile demonstrations. The first contracts earned by Indianapolis-area service-sector workers have not included remarkable increases in wages, but they do significantly increase access to benefits and enshrine seniority rights and grievance procedures that boost job security. Plus, the union members hope that the first contracts reflect a historic pattern in labor organizing, a pattern that suggests the contracts are likely to be significantly improved in subsequent negotiations.[7] That improvement comes about when new leaders are identified among the workforce, then recruited and trained to a point where they provide the impetus once supplied by outside organizers. Leadership development is the stuff of all successful social movements. In Indianapolis, new worker leaders are being developed among the community's custodians, food-service workers, and security guards.

Many economists, academics, and labor professionals believe that service-sector workers like Keisha Johnson will dictate the future of the U.S. labor movement.[8] After all, cleaning bathrooms and washing dishes are jobs that cannot be outsourced to a Bangladeshi sweatshop or to a call center overseas. And many of the employers of service-sector workers—including multinational hotel chains and food-service or building cleaning companies—are earning healthy profits and can afford to pay better wages and provide better benefits. Many historians and economists insist that there is no reason why service-sector jobs cannot evolve into middle-class employment. They point to the early to mid-twentieth-century union activism that transformed manufacturing jobs from backbreaking, low-wage work into careers that allowed workers to buy homes and send their kids to college.[9] Can janitors, fry cooks, and health care aides blaze the same path now? And can they do so in a community, like Indianapolis, that is not a stronghold for organized labor?

I hope that the answer is yes. I am far from a disinterested observer of the struggles chronicled in this book. I work as a teacher and director of a law school clinic in Indianapolis, my hometown. In our clinic, my students and I devote most of our efforts to advocating for low-income workers in our community. We tend to get called on only when things have gone horribly wrong for these workers—usually when they have been victimized by wage theft or have been fired without just cause. Through our clients, we get a front-row view of the struggles to make ends meet on a low-wage job.

So I certainly noticed when our state legislature voted to adopt a right-to-work law. And I was intrigued when food-service workers on my own campus voted for union representation for the first time. I knew about the local hotel workers trying to fight their way to middle-class incomes, and I heard that security guards and custodians were struggling to organize, too.

Soon after the IUPUI food-service workers formed their union, I began to write this book.

For a period of about a year and a half, I accompanied workers on their jobs and on the picket lines, notebook in hand. During that same time, dozens of local workers allowed me to sit in on their conversations with each other. Many of them were kind enough to also talk to me at length during one-on-one interviews. On a few occasions, they asked that some matters be kept private. But such requests were rare. Much more often, these workers were remarkably open and generous with their observations and their time. I am a long-time contributor to Indianapolis's daily and weekly newspapers, so some of their stories you will read here were shared with local readers along the way.

I soon found that the workers had some intriguing allies, so this book also tells the story of the union organizers with whom the workers have made common cause. Because of the community's demographics, Indianapolis's service-sector workers are a rainbow coalition of whites, African Americans, and Latinos. The union organizers are mostly white, college-educated, and younger, as is so often the case with social movement leadership. As with the workers, it turned out the organizers had intriguing backstories, too.

Sometimes, the organizing efforts in Indianapolis were focused on immigrant workers. Sometimes, the outreach and advocacy were focused on the needs of nonunionized low-wage workers, even when there was not a clear path to creating a unionized workplace. Sometimes, the workers involved in the efforts lost their jobs because they stood up for their rights. In all these respects, Indianapolis reflects the changes to the workforce, the economy, and the labor movement that are occurring across the country in the early twenty-first century.

This book chronicles these Indianapolis workers' and organizers' setbacks and victories, and their internal bonds and conflicts, all while placing their journey in the broader context of the global economy and labor history.[10] As one local union organizer says of the battles in Indianapolis, "If we can win here, we can win anywhere."

1

A Campus Union

James Holder and Eric Gomez are the first pair to perform their role-play. Holder, a tall, angular African American man in his late fifties, with graying hair and goatee, has been a custodian at Marian University for twenty years. In the late evening and early morning hours, he cleans the floors and bathrooms at the university library, empties the trash cans, and then performs the same tasks at the campus center. "I am voting 'yes' because I am trying to make things better," Holder says to Gomez. "I am tired of seeing my friends getting fired. Why are you voting yes?" Gomez, slighter and shorter than Holder, is a Latino in his twenties, a former hotel worker turned UNITE HERE organizer. Portraying a Marian worker, he gives a noncommittal answer. Holder steps forward. An old foot injury has left Holder with a pronounced limp, but his voice rises in volume as he walks toward Gomez. "If you mark 'yes' on that ballot, you'll see a change in your life for the better!"

It is December 2012. In three days, a National Labor Relations Board-supervised election will determine whether Marian cafeteria, maintenance, and grounds workers will be represented by a union for the first time. Today is the workers' final prep meeting before the election. Outside, it is a cold, raw Monday afternoon, and the room at the one-story AFL-CIO headquarters has been overheated to compensate. Nine Marian workers gather around mismatched tables under a large sheet of Post-it paper stuck to the wall. The Post-it is labeled "RAP," and starts out, "Why I'm voting yes . . . Why are you voting yes?" Item two is an admonishment for all to wear their new union buttons at work this week. "What time are you voting? (Push for early—offer ride)" comes next. Of the nine workers here, five are white men, three are African American men, and one is a white woman everyone calls "Panda." Gomez, who leads the meeting, is one of four UNITE HERE organizers in the room. Each is younger than any of the Marian workers here.

The lead UNITE HERE organizer for Indianapolis, Mike Biskar, stands up and delivers a pep talk to the Marian workers: "You all have done a great job, and you should feel good. There are seventy-plus people who can vote Thursday, and fifty of them have done something publicly in support of the union—they have worn a button, been in a group photo, come to a rally, something. So our job now is not to convince people, it's just getting people out to vote."

Gomez follows with a review of the logistics for the election—a sample ballot, the times that voting will be allowed, the limitations on campaigning near the voting place. UNITE HERE does not want to share the details publicly, but it has a partial agreement with the contractor, Aramark, a multinational company that operates Marian's maintenance, grounds, and food services. The company has promised to stay neutral in the election. But, as the election day approaches, that neutrality has not quite held firm among the company's on-site managers. Gomez tells the workers not to worry about it. "Don't forget: Every time we do this, the managers get nervous and there is a little 'Hail Mary' pass against the union. But this is way beyond one manager talking to a worker or two now, and we need to give them [the workers] that confidence. Between now and the vote, we just want to talk to all of our people and make sure we know when they are voting."

Herb Latigne sits in a folding chair to the side of the tables, both a part of the meeting and self-consciously separate. Latigne is sixty-six years old, with curly white hair, a bushy white beard, and large glasses that retain some of their dark tint even indoors. Think of a cross between Santa Claus and Hank Williams Jr. He worked twenty-two years at Marian as a woodworker. ("Not a carpenter, a woodworker," he corrects someone. "A carpenter builds houses and walls and stuff. I create things with wood.") Latigne projects a gruff exterior, but over the years dozens of Marian students have been welcomed to his home workshop to learn the basics of woodworking. The first Latigne-supervised project is always the same: the student makes a mallet. Latigne himself is particularly proud of a garden bridge he built on campus, a Japanese-style span that was commissioned by the Japan-American Society of Indiana. "I've got a lot invested in that place," he says of Marian.

But he no longer works there. A couple of years ago, Latigne suffered a stroke. He had to miss several months of work, but he spent that time pushing himself through therapy to regain his strength and reclaim his job. One Thursday, Latigne came back to Marian and proudly presented his physician release allowing him to return to work the following Monday. The next day, he received a call at home from a human resources staffer from Aramark. Don't bother coming in, Latigne was told. You have already been replaced. "If we had a union, I still would have a job," Latigne says. The organizers and workers hope that a future union contract will include his reinstatement.

The formal agenda for the meeting is mostly completed, and the workers start talking to one another across the tables. "Has anyone talked to Bob?" someone asks, "because he is on vacation this week." Stacy Shirar nods. "He'll be there. I talked to him." Shirar is a thickset white man, bald, with a heavily tattooed right forearm. He has not said much during the meeting, but the organizers describe him admiringly as "solid" for the union and as a natural leader among the Marian maintenance workers. Shirar needed no convincing about the value of a union. Before coming to Marian, he had worked for fifteen years in a union shop at an automobile brake and clutch manufacturer. When those jobs were outsourced, he had to find other work. "I made more in the 1990s than I do today," Shirar says. "My dad was in the union, too. And I know that without union wages, there is no way he could have raised us four children. Not only does the union provide better health insurance and benefits, it provides a sense of security. For me, that is key. Wages are not my main concern. Retirement is not my main concern. Being a part of a union gives me the sense that I won't be looking for a job the next day, that favoritism will not come into play anymore."

The meeting starts to break up, but a few of the workers relaunch a discussion about managers interfering with the election. James Holder raises his voice to be heard over the chatter. "Do you ever go fishing?" he asks. 'What I tell people when they talk about management running their mouths against the union is this: When the fish is on the hook, it still keeps squirming and struggling. And that's OK. Because the end of the story is this: it ends up skinned and in hot grease!"

Three days later, the mood is more somber. The same workers and organizers are here, their group now swollen to three times the size with the addition of more workers, along with Marian students and staff who support the union. They gather in a hallway outside a small classroom in one of Marian's main buildings, making nervous small talk. It is shortly after 4:00 p.m., and the second and final shift of voting has officially concluded. Finally, two NLRB officials announce that the group can come inside the classroom to witness the counting of the ballots. A solitary Aramark manager appears and sits down at a table. Most of the workers stand. As one of the NLRB officials opens the cardboard box containing the ballots, no one speaks.

The official pulls out each pink ballot one at a time and uses both hands to hold it up and show it to the group. The ballots read, "Do you wish to be represented for purposes of collective bargaining by UNITE HERE, Local 23, AFL-CIO? Mark an 'X' in the square of your choice." Two large boxes are labeled "Yes" and "No." One NLRB official reads the ballot out loud so the other can mark her tally.

The first ballot is "Yes." So is the next one, and the next, and the next. The NLRB official keeps holding up pink ballots, keeps saying "Yes." The workers exchange raised-eyebrow glances and nervous half-smiles. Mike Biskar has his eyes on a pad of paper in front of him. He is keeping his own tally.

Another ballot. "Yes." Another. "Yes." Another. "Yes."

Finally, the NLRB official stops and asks her colleague to announce the tally: fifty-four to one for the union. The room erupts in cheers. The workers hug and exchange high fives as the Aramark manager, head down, walks quickly out the door.

Stacy Shirar is not much of a hugger, but he allows himself a satisfied smile. "This is no surprise," he says. "I knew people were fed up with being walked over. We just want to be heard and have a say in what is going on here."

Herb Latigne was not allowed to vote, but he is here for the counting. He nods his head in approval. "The next ten years here are going to be exciting," he says.

The workers, organizers, and supporters linger in the hallway outside the classroom, telling stories and making plans for the next step—negotiating a first contract with Aramark. One of the organizers prompts James Holder to share his story with the group. The Marian campaign was slow to begin, with some workers having little faith that a union could ever be a reality at the university. It turns out that even Holder, the most eloquent of Marian's workers, was initially a union opponent. "I thought union people were greedy, and everyone should just stand up for their own selves," he says. "But I also really believed in the Franciscan values the Sisters of St. Francis put forth as the mission of Marian. For a long time, I always felt privileged to work at Marian. But sometime after the subcontractor took over, I looked at one of those plaques on campus that list the values. The first one is 'Dignity of the Individual.' And I realized those values no longer applied to me. The way we were talked to—we were called everything but our name. People who had been here decades were let go. I did not know what to do about it, and I was getting ready to quit.

"Then Sister Monica and Eric and another union fellow came out to visit me at my home. At first, I said I was against the union. But then I realized that right here is a way to tell my story, to be a part of getting respect back. It is a long road, and we ain't at the end of it yet. But when we started, I couldn't imagine us getting this far."

Holder takes a deep breath, struggling to control his emotions. "When things started going bad here, I felt so alone. But look at what happened today. Fifty-four to one. I'm sure not alone now!"

The Marian workers' union victory harkens back to a different era in Indiana history. At the national level, and particularly in Indiana, the manufacturing industry formed the heart of the twentieth-century labor movement. That has changed now, due to a combination of factors. The most impactful have been the globalization and technology advances that have made it easier for corporations to send jobs to countries that allow lower wages and fewer worker protections than the United States requires.

The Bureau of Labor Statistics shows that the percentage of all nonfarm workers employed in manufacturing declined from 24 percent of the U.S. workforce in 1973 to just 10 percent of the workforce in March 2007. The percentage of workers in the service sector grew during the same period from 70 percent to 83 percent.[1] The drop in manufacturing jobs was accompanied by a plummeting in the number of unionized workers. As of January 2013 the U.S. Bureau of Labor Statistics reported that only 6.6 percent of American workers in the private sector belong to unions. Even when adding in more heavily unionized public sector jobs, the overall U.S. union membership of 11.3 percent is at its lowest level since 1916.

Indiana mirrors the national trend. The state's overall union membership of 9.1 percent, reported in 2012, was a big drop from the previous year, and it was the lowest level ever recorded in the state. Thirty years ago, in 1983, 22 percent of Hoosier workers belonged to unions. Many of them worked in manufacturing jobs like the one Marian worker Stacy Shirar used to hold. In the 1980s, Shadeland Avenue on the east side of Indianapolis was a four-lane concrete corridor between massive plants for RCA, Chrysler, and multiple parts manufacturers. On this one street alone, over ten thousand union jobs were housed. Just north and east of Indianapolis off Interstate 69, the cities of Anderson and Muncie were once union strongholds filled with workers making products such as Delco batteries, GM headlights, and Goodyear tires. In the 1970s, one of every three people in Anderson worked for GM.[2] "When I graduated from Muncie Central High School [in the 1950s], you could go just about anyplace and get a job—a decent job," says Muncie mayor Dennis Tyler. "You could go to Borg Warner, and if you didn't like Borg Warner you could leave and go to Chevrolet; if you didn't like Chevrolet you could go to Delco; if you didn't like Delco you could leave and go to Acme-Lee, or dozens and dozens of other little places that were spinning off mom-and-pop tool-and-die shops."[3]

But in the 1980s and 1990s, Borg Warner, Chevrolet, and Delco Remy left Muncie, and GM vacated Anderson. In Indianapolis, over twenty-eight thousand manufacturing jobs were lost in the 1980s.[4] The Shadeland Avenue manufacturing corridor is nearly empty now. The children of the manufacturing workers who once made $23 per hour with generous health and retirement benefits are now likely to be employed at fast-food restaurants, in retail shops, or as security guards or janitors. Sometimes, like Stacy Shirar, the former manufacturing workers themselves have had to make the transition to the service sector.

These service-sector workers are almost never in unions, usually work without benefits, and often struggle to get full-time hours. Even as these jobs replaced the middle-wage jobs of manufacturing, the jobs remained low paying.[5] The National Employment Law Project recently reported that the service-sector growth meant that the majority of jobs created since the end of the recession in 2009 pay less than $14 per hour, well below the estimate for a living wage in Indianapolis.[6] Despite steady gains in U.S. worker productivity over the past decades, overall wages have not increased when adjusted for inflation. Across the nation, and in Indiana, income inequality has reached limits not seen since before the Great Depression.[7] In a recent study of upward mobility in the country's fifty biggest cities, Indianapolis ranked third from last.[8]

So far, organized labor has been powerless to reverse or even slow this decline. Its apparent helplessness has led some to say that the concept of unionization has outlived its time. Peter List, a former Communication Workers of America shop steward who now advises companies opposing union drives, wrote an op-ed column citing some of these same dismal figures. The title of the column was unsubtle: "The Labor Movement Is Brain Dead (And It's Time to Pull the Plug)."[9] Even a labor supporter like historian Nelson Lichtenstein, who directs the Center for the Study of Work, Labor, and Democracy at the University of California, Santa Barbara, says, "Because the payoff is so little and the amount of energy and risk are so great, collective bargaining per se, whether public- or private-sector, is pretty much a dead end."[10]

Justin Wilson, managing director of the Center for Union Facts, a not-for-profit organization affiliated with the business lobbying and public relations firm Berman and Company, says that twenty-first-century U.S. workers no longer need unions. "Unions were too successful for their own good," Wilson says. "Issues that were once part of bargaining are now addressed by federal statutes and agencies pushed for by labor, including safety issues by OSHA [Occupational Safety and Health Administration] and discrimination by the EEOC [Equal Employment Opportunity Commission], and now that is starting to be the case for health care, too. What is left is wages, and I don't think there is an enormous amount of trust by workers that unions are going to bring in substantial increases in wages."

Yet, while the news is mostly bad for the labor movement, there are some bright spots. Spurred in part by enthusiastic union participation among Latinos, California's union membership defied the national trend in 2012 by increasing to 18.5 percent of all workers. High-profile union drives in recent years successfully organized car wash workers in Los Angeles, janitors in Houston, and hospitality workers in Las Vegas. Labor activists and their supporters argue that the real message of the dismal income and wealth gap numbers is that the labor movement is needed now more than ever.

There is some historical basis for this argument. The departed manufacturing jobs in Indiana and elsewhere were not always high-wage, good-benefits paths to the middle class. In fact, when the nation in the early twentieth century undertook a jarring transition from a rural, agricultural economy to an urban, industrial one, the process initially created manufacturing jobs that were low-paying, dangerous, and provided little security or long-term benefits. After long and hard struggle, the labor movement transformed these jobs for the better. Now, a similar challenge is posed by the equally jarring early twenty-first-century transition from a manufacturing-based economy to a service-based one.

Today's service-sector jobs can be improved by unions, too. Studies by the Center for Economic and Policy Research show that unionization raises service-sector worker wages by over 10 percent—about $2 per hour—compared to the wages of similar nonunion workers. Unionized service-sector workers are also far more likely to have employer-provided health insurance and pension plans.[11] The history of service-sector unionization success is still a limited one. But the work of washing dishes in U.S. restaurants and cleaning U.S. hotel rooms is not going to follow automobile manufacturing jobs overseas. And most low-wage workers are employed by large corporations that can adjust their economic models to pay better wages. Of the fifty largest low-wage employers, almost two-thirds are earning higher profits now than before the recession of 2007–09. The top three low-wage employers are the thriving corporations Wal-Mart, Yum! Brands (Taco Bell, KFC, Pizza Hut), and McDonald's. McDonald's profits grew 130 percent from 2009 to 2011, and it pays its executives as much as $4.1 million per year. Yum! Brands has seen its profits increase by 45 percent over the same period, and it pays its CEO over $20 million annually.[12] "The fundamental issue is how we are going to divide the outcome of what is produced," says John Schmitt, the Center on Economic and Policy Research economist who authored the studies on unionization's effect on service-sector jobs. "U.S. workers are very highly productive, and unionization helps workers increase their percentage of the value produced. And that leads to higher living standards."

That is the goal of unions like the Service Employees International Union (SEIU) and UNITE HERE. At the national level, SEIU has led the successful "Justice for Janitors" campaign and supported high-profile 2012–14 short-term strikes by fast-food workers in major cities including New York, Chicago, Seattle, and Detroit. The unprecedented fast-food actions were often convened under the banner of "Fight for 15," framing the struggle to be paid the $15 per hour that approaches a living wage in those communities. (Chapters 4 and 5 include an account of the Indianapolis version of these strikes.) UNITE HERE organizes hospitality workers in the hotel industry and food-service workers in institutions such as airports and universities. In Indianapolis, SEIU has organized janitors working for contractors at downtown office buildings and is trying to do the same among security guards at the same buildings. UNITE HERE has achieved the most local success, with the Marian workers joining some four hundred other Indianapolis workers represented by unions who are employed by contractors providing services at Butler University, the Indianapolis International Airport, and Indiana University–Purdue University at Indianapolis, known as IUPUI.

While the former manufacturing centers of central Indiana lie quiet, things are bustling at the IUPUI food court. It is shortly before noon, and hundreds of people crowd into both the dining and counter areas. Students and faculty members, including students and staff from the Indiana University Schools of Medicine and Nursing, distinctive in their light-blue scrubs, line up under brightly lit signs for restaurants like Chick-fil-A, Papa John's, Wild Greens, and Spotz. Men and women fill orders from behind the counters, take payment at the cash registers, wipe down tables, and prepare the food in the back. They do not work for the name-brand restaurants. Nor do they work for the state university, despite the lettering "IUPUI Food Service" on their black polo shirts and white chef jackets. They are employees of Chartwells, a division of the British corporation Compass Group, the world's largest food-service management company.

James Meyers came to work here in August 2009. A broad-shouldered, stocky African American man with a goatee, Meyers grew up on Indianapolis's east side, the youngest of seven children and a product of Public School 103 and John Marshall High School. When his plans to join the military out of high school fell through, Meyers drove tractor trailers and dump trucks before switching to food service. He managed a kitchen at a nursing home for a while and was a shift manager at Popeye's and KFC fast-food restaurants. In his late forties by the time he came to IUPUI, Meyers was hired as a prep cook, preparing vegetables for the various restaurants at the food court and also for the catering jobs and a day care center that Chartwells serves from this location.

Before long, Meyers began noticing problems in the workplace. Some of his fellow cooks were making barely above minimum wage, and the health insurance offered by Chartwells was so costly that he knew of no workers who were actually enrolled in the plan. Meyers and his colleagues were promised two breaks each shift, plus a thirty-minute lunch off the clock. But the kitchen was chronically understaffed, and the breaks rarely occurred. When his colleague in vegetable prep fell ill and had to leave work for several months, management refused to get Meyers replacement help. He learned that other colleagues were also working multiple roles without any increase in pay. Two Chartwells workers, whose duties put them in the Caribou Coffee shop in the same campus center building as the food court, were forced to work for three hours in a foot of standing water after the back of the store flooded. When the workers complained about problems like these, management told them to deal with it or look for another job.

Then, just as Meyers's prep cook duties began to stabilize, he was pulled aside by a Chartwells manager. Meyers was ordered to switch jobs, moving to the front of the food court with more responsibilities but no increase in pay. Meyers said he would prefer to stay in his cook role. The response was succinct. "Move or we fire you," he was told.

"I had trouble keeping my peace with that," Meyers says now. But by then he had discovered a possible outlet for his frustration. Meyers and a handful of other Chartwells IUPUI workers had begun meeting with an organizer for UNITE HERE. The union's Local 23 had already organized food-service workers at the Indianapolis International Airport and had negotiated contracts with Chartwells at other locations around the country. Meyers was plenty angry at the company for its treatment of him and his coworkers at IUPUI, but he had no previous experience with unions. He had never even had a family member who had belonged to a union. He had his doubts. "I'd heard all kinds of things about unions, that they just want to take your [dues] money, and that unions are for lazy people," he says. "So I was pretty reluctant." Finally, after multiple conversations with his coworkers and some soul-searching, Meyers decided he was in: "I just wanted my job to change. I found that I was tired of going from job to job, and that I wanted to stay here and make this job better."

By contrast, Meyers's colleague Delbert Tardy was all in from the first time he heard the word "union." A large man with a shaved head, wire-rim glasses, and wide forearms spilling out of his massive white apron, the fifty-two-year-old Tardy cuts an imposing figure. His words are no less powerful. "I have no problem speaking my mind, here or anywhere else," says Tardy, who has worked at IUPUI since 2006. Meyers and Tardy were among a half dozen workers who formed a committee to reach out to their

Figure 1.1. James Meyers helped lead a successful campaign to organize the food-service workers at the Indianapolis campus of Indiana and Purdue Universities. "I felt like I had won a million dollars," Meyers says of the day the campaign went public. "I got to tell the manager, 'You are the boss, I understand that. But I am a man, too, and we can respect each other.'"
Photo by Mark A. Lee.

colleagues, quietly and one at a time. They asked the workers about what Meyers calls their "agitations" and sounded out their interest in joining a union. Tardy, whose coworkers call him "Doc," encouraged his colleagues to follow his outspoken example. "A lot of them were scared to be part of a union, but I said you have to be strong and you have to believe," Tardy says. "It gives you more pride and self-respect when you come to work and you know that you are not going to be harassed or disrespected."

After a few months of conversations like these, nearly three-quarters of the Chartwells IUPUI workers had signed cards indicating their desire to join the union. In September 2011 the union effort went public when a delegation of workers, joined by supportive IUPUI students and faculty, paid a visit to Chartwells management. On that day, the group of nearly thirty people gathered in the food court. Led by Meyers, they walked to the manager's office and knocked on the door. The manager—the same man who had told Meyers to accept his transfer and extra duties or look for another job—opened the door, and his eyes widened. "He was very surprised, and he said to me, 'Why do you have all these people here?',", Meyers recalls. "I said, 'Because we want to have a union and all these people support what we are doing.'" Meyers smiles at the memory. "We finally got a chance to talk to him without him brushing us off. He *had* to listen this time."

After that show of solidarity, Chartwells quickly agreed to recognize the union. Negotiations began over a contract, but things did not go well at first. The company's initial offer proposed no raises at all for the first year of the contract and then just a ten cents an hour raise in year two. Insulted, the workers rejected the offer and began wearing buttons to work that read "RESPECT." The company came back to the table. Eventually, Chartwells agreed to a contract that included annual pay raises, paid sick and vacation days, a 401(k) retirement plan, and recognition of seniority in transfers and overtime work. As part of the agreement, health insurance costs were cut and are guaranteed to decrease each year. Now, half the staff has signed up for the coverage. Meyers and Tardy became union shop stewards and began meeting with management regularly to discuss workplace issues.

Sometimes, they brought a few friends to those discussions. A couple of months after the contract was ratified, a Chartwells worker was moved into a higher classification job. The contract called for a pay increase of

$1.50 per hour for work in that new role. But the manager, thinking the worker was not aware of the contract terms, took her aside and proposed to give her just an extra fifty cents per hour. When Meyers was told about the situation, he made plans to meet with the manager. A half dozen fellow workers agreed to accompany him, but when Meyers reached the office door, three times that number were behind him. Meyers confronted the manager and demanded that the worker receive the full raise. The manager said he would look into it. The workers were not satisfied with that response. They decided to leave, but not before marching around the office area for a bit, chanting "We'll be back! We'll be back!" They did not have to return. The next day, the manager gave the transferred worker her full raise.

Several months after the contract was approved, Meyers took a leave of absence from Chartwells to help UNITE HERE organize workers at Marian and Butler. He helps make the house visits to workers, telling the story of the IUPUI workers' journey from doubting the power of solidarity to securing a workplace where employees' rights are guaranteed. Meyers enjoys the role. "I know firsthand how workers are mistreated, so I want to see all workers being treated with dignity and respect," he says.

If asked, Meyers will also share with the workers the story of his longer and more personal journey. Beginning in high school, he started heavy use of alcohol and marijuana. By twenty-two, he was addicted to both and had expanded to regular use of cocaine. For twenty years, his alcoholism caused him to lose jobs and antagonize loved ones. "I carried this cloud over me for a good while," he says. Then, one Thursday he got paid and did not come back home until Sunday, having spent his entire paycheck on alcohol and drugs. It was not the first time Meyers had done this. But this time he returned to the home he shared with his girlfriend Debbie to find that she had changed all the locks on the doors. "She told me to just go back to wherever it was that I was coming from," Meyers says. "It was an eye-opener for me."

Meyers checked himself into a rehab facility, sobered up, and eventually married Debbie. He has now been clean for over nine years. Meyers sees a link between the struggle for workplace respect and the struggle for sobriety: "The connection for me is that we can all make our lives better. Once I got clean, I realized I had been putting a limit on my life by stunting my growth. I was able to get help, so now I want to help somebody else, whether it is to better their personal life or their job."

2

"We Can Win Here"

When union organizers are assigned to Indianapolis, they are routinely instructed to read a 2005 book by Richard Pierce, a former Indiana University graduate student who is now a history professor at Notre Dame. The book is called *Polite Protest*, and its thesis is that the African American community of Indianapolis was largely nonconfrontational in its twentieth-century efforts to secure equality and opportunity.[1] Compared to other Northern cities, Pierce writes, Indianapolis had a large and relatively prosperous African American population for several generations before the Civil Rights and Black Power eras. In part for that reason, African Americans had already made some gains that propelled them to favor negotiations with white city leaders over dramatic boycotts, sit-ins, and demonstrations.

Polite Protest is assigned for the purpose of giving organizers some insight into the basis for Indianapolis' reputation for taking a peaceful, and sometimes even passive, approach to issues of injustice. The city's nickname, "Naptown," referred not just to limited nightlife but an absence of high-profile race and class conflict. In African American history, Indianapolis is known for its entrepreneurs like Madame C. J. Walker, the nation's first self-made woman millionaire, jazz legends like Wes Montgomery and Jimmy Coe, and athletes like basketball great Oscar Robertson. There is no comparable Indianapolis figure of African American protest and activism.

IUPUI professor Tom Marvin, who directs a program for students interested in labor and community organizing, says that Pierce's conclusion extends beyond race-oriented advocacy. "Indianapolis is not only politically conservative, it also has a dominant culture that values avoiding confrontation," Marvin wrote in a 2013 paper. "Hoosiers are reluctant to make demands on government or corporate elites and prefer to deal with social problems through volunteerism and faith-based charities."[2] When UNITE HERE lead organizer Mike Biskar was sent to Indianapolis, a more senior organizer who had spent some time in the city summed up its twentieth-century legacy for Biskar: Indianapolis was too far north for the great battles of the civil rights movement, and too far south for the great battles of the labor movement.

There is plenty of truth in these conclusions. To this day, white and African American city leaders alike commemorate the events of April 4, 1968, the night after Martin Luther King Jr. was killed, precisely because no major demonstrations or riots occurred. Then-presidential candidate Robert F. Kennedy, in Indianapolis for a previously scheduled campaign event in an African American neighborhood, stood on the back of a flatbed truck and delivered a stirring plea for nonviolence. "What we need in the United States is not division; what we need in the United States is not hatred; what we need in the United States is not violence or lawlessness, but love and wisdom, and compassion toward one another, and a feeling of justice towards those who still suffer within our country, whether they be white or whether they be black," Kennedy said.[3] Riots broke out in over one hundred U.S. cities that night, but not in Indianapolis. A memorial with sculptures of both King and Kennedy has been erected in the park where Kennedy spoke.

But it would be a mistake to label Indianapolis's racial history as uniformly peaceful. As recently as 1995, following reports of an African American youth being beaten in police custody, two days of sometimes violent demonstrations occurred in a near-northside neighborhood just a few blocks from the site of Kennedy's famous speech. During the civil rights era, there were plenty of marches, vigils, and demonstrations in Indianapolis, including a multiday outbreak of violence in 1969 along Indiana Avenue, onetime site of Madame Walker's hair care and cosmetics company and the city's iconic jazz clubs.[4]

No companion book to *Polite Protest* is assigned to organizers to brief them on Indianapolis' labor history. But there is actually some significant precedent for modern-day activists to draw from. In the late nineteenth and early twentieth century, Indianapolis was considered to be the labor capital of the United States. Multiple national union headquarters were housed in the city known as the "Crossroads of America" for its central location and direct rail access to the rest of the country. The United Mine Workers, the Teamsters, the Iron Workers, the Carpenters, and even the American Federation of Labor were once based in Indianapolis. Labor legends like John L. Lewis and Samuel Gompers once led their organizations from offices in the city's downtown.

In 1891, Indianapolis building trades workers became among the first in the nation to earn the eight-hour day. Two years later, Indiana became a trailblazer in banning the "yellow dog contract," which required an employee to be nonunion as a condition of employment.[5] Indianapolis was the site of a massive and violent strike by streetcar operators in 1913. Earlier in that decade, Iron Workers Union secretary-treasurer John J. McNamara and fifty-one others, most of them also connected to the union, were arrested in Indianapolis for their alleged roles in the 1910 dynamiting of the building of the fiercely antiunion *Los Angeles Times*. McNamara and his younger brother James, also a union official, were extradited to California, where they were convicted in proceedings that led to their famed attorney, Clarence Darrow, being charged with jury tampering. Thirty-eight others, including the union's president, were convicted in Indianapolis.

One of the most visible labor and political leaders of the era was Terre Haute, Indiana's Eugene V. Debs, a former railroad car painter and Democratic member of the Indiana General Assembly. Debs founded the American Railway Union, led the Pullman Strike of 1894, and was thrown in jail for defying court injunctions against the strike. While imprisoned, Debs read the writings of Karl Marx and emerged to become the nation's leading socialist. He would go on to help found the radical Industrial Workers of the World (known as the "Wobblies"), created with the mission to organize all workers into one large union. Debs also was the Socialist Party's nominee for president four times. His last campaign was conducted from a Georgia prison cell in 1920, where he was serving a sentence for sedition based on a speech against World War I and the military draft. Debs's statement at his sentencing hearing—"While there is a lower class, I am in it, and while there is a criminal element, I am of it, and while there is a soul in prison, I am not free"—is widely cited, and formed the basis for Tom Joad's famous declaration in John Steinbeck's novel *The Grapes of Wrath*. During his career, Debs was called "an enemy of the human race" by the *New York Times* and a "traitor to his country" by President Woodrow Wilson. But he endures as a figure beloved by U.S. labor supporters and left-wing activists, and his home in Terre Haute has been restored as a museum dedicated to preserving his legacy. Souvenirs for sale include reproductions of campaign buttons with Debs's photo in prison uniform, over a caption that reads, "For President, Convict 9653."

In 1917, Indianapolis was the site of a notable experiment in industrial democracy. William Hapgood turned over to workers the operation and ownership of Columbia Conserve, a canning plant on the southwest side of town. The governing council of workers, who averaged less than a fourth-grade education, adopted a series of progressive workplace policies. Work hours were dropped to fifty hours per week, and health and pension plans were created. Salaries were adjusted to reflect workers' needs, with additional wages given to workers for each minor child in their household. The cooperative model at Columbia Conserve survived for over twenty years. After the company was battered by the Great Depression and a back-wages dispute, the cooperative was dissolved by court order in 1942.[6]

William's son, Powers Hapgood, took his Harvard degree to the labor movement, working as a miner and an organizer for the United Mine Workers and the progressive Congress of Industrial Organizations (CIO). The younger Hapgood was immortalized by his fellow Indianapolis native Kurt Vonnegut in Vonnegut's novel *Jailbird* and in multiple speeches and interviews. As Vonnegut tells the story, Powers Hapgood was called in to an Indianapolis court to testify about a picket line conflict involving CIO members. The judge interrupted the hearing to direct a question to Hapgood. "Why would a man with your advantages, from a wealthy, respected family, a Harvard graduate, lead such a life?" Hapgood replied, "Why, the Sermon on the Mount, sir."[7]

By the mid twentieth-century, labor unions had moved their headquarters out of Indianapolis to Washington, D.C. The union reputation of the town and the state became intertwined with the rise—and then the precipitous fall—of well-paying union jobs in the manufacturing industry, especially the automobile parts industry. By 2012, Indiana unions and their supporters were unable to block the passage of the state's "right to work" law, just as they were powerless in 2011 to prevent the state's leaders from passing a law preventing local living wage ordinances. When new automobile manufacturing came to the state, as it did in the form of a forty-five hundred worker Toyota plant in 1996, the workforce was nonunion. Despite union opposition, a 2012 policy that blocks laid-off school-year cafeteria workers and bus drivers from receiving unemployment benefits sailed through the Indiana legislature.[8] In Indianapolis and across the state, shifts in the economic and political climate left unions looking like dinosaurs doomed to extinction.

UNITE HERE and its lead local organizer, Mike Biskar, aim to reverse Indiana's dispiriting trend. An example of their aggressive approach is provided in a Saturday morning meeting in the spring of 2013, where Marian and Butler workers gather at the local AFL-CIO headquarters again, sipping coffee and orange juice from paper cups. The purpose of the meeting is to train the workers as union shop stewards at their workplaces. But there is a catch: there is not yet any agreement with their employers to run grievances and other issues through stewards. The union has placed the cart firmly in front of the horse. "We are going to start acting like we have a contract before we do," Biskar cheerfully admits to the group.

Most of the workers nod. But there is a small amount of push-back. James Holder says, "I hear you. But shouldn't we wait for the contract? It's like pulling a gun without any bullets in it." Biskar replies that the contract is still priority #1, and they would also discuss today ways to ratchet up the pressure on Aramark to secure the contract. But he also outlines the ways an unofficial worker leader can still advocate for her colleagues without a contract in place. As the group discusses the possibilities, it turns out some of the leaders here have already begun taking up the causes of their Marian and Butler colleagues. Holder is satisfied by this exchange, and the training goes forward.

Biskar has jet-black hair and dark eyebrows, and today he is wearing a dress shirt with his sleeves rolled up to his elbows. He is the only one in the room wearing a tie, which only partially obscures the fact that, at twenty-nine years old, he is also one of the youngest in the room. Biskar did not start out his organizing career dressing this way. Initially, he felt it was important to wear jeans, to "dress like the workers," he recalls. But a senior UNITE HERE organizer, after three days of accompanying Biskar around to meetings and house visits in Indianapolis during his early tenure, turned to Biskar and asked, "Mike, when are you going to get out of the sandbox?" The message was clear. It would be hard enough for Biskar to lead workers at a young age; at least if he dressed more formally, he would look like someone who deserves respect.[9] In some UNITE HERE locals, there is a rule that organizers have to wear a tie when visiting workers at their homes.

Yet, despite his youth, Biskar has been organizing workers in Indianapolis for nearly seven years now. So he has the group's attention as he sharply summarizes the union's track record during that period. Hotel workers have been organizing here since 2007 and have yet to achieve union recognition. But Biskar quickly points out that they have achieved notable success in raising the average wages for hotel workers. This has been accomplished in part by suing in federal court to stop wage theft by temp agencies, and in part by pushing local legislative efforts to raise hotel worker pay and stop the blacklisting of temp agency workers. Red-shirted UNITE HERE members and community allies have flocked by the hundreds to noisy demonstrations at City-County Council meetings and on-the-street protests during the 2012 Super Bowl festivities in Indianapolis. In 2010, dozens of supporters were arrested for civil disobedience in support of downtown Hyatt workers.

Although the city's hotel workers are still struggling for union recognition, the university and airport workers have broken through. Since 2010, UNITE HERE's membership in Indianapolis has swelled from zero to five hundred workers. "You should feel amazing," Biskar says. "The places where you work have never had a union. Workers like you have traditionally had no power here." Illustrating his point, a City-County Council member nods over Biskar's shoulder. The legislator, who at the time was openly mulling a run for mayor, is just the latest local politician to drop by such meetings. For Indianapolis's Democratic leaders, it has become part of the routine to pay respects to the dishwashers, cooks, and janitors gathered together under the union banner.

This can be just the beginning, Biskar promises the soon-to-be stewards. There are an estimated sixty thousand hospitality workers in downtown Indianapolis alone, he says. "You are the exception. These thousands of workers like you are not in a union and they are getting paid the smallest amount their bosses can pay and still have them show up at the job." The two dozen people in this room will be the ones to decide if that is going to change, Biskar says. "Big union victories in the past did not come about because thousands of people suddenly took action. It was because a handful of people took a stand and others decided to follow."

Most of the workers in this room were born and raised in central Indiana. Few showed any political or class consciousness before getting involved in the union. Both geographically and philosophically, Biskar grew up thousands of miles away from them. Biskar's parents, Dan and Margaret, raised him in Southern California to be, as he calls it, "super leftist." Biskar's father is a Marxist who encouraged his son to read pro-communist authors like Michael Parenti.[10] Biskar's mother was active in a militant renters' rights movement in Santa Monica where the family lived. Biskar was a precocious student, skipping a grade and enrolling in Georgetown University's School of Foreign Service at age seventeen. In one of Biskar's Georgetown classes, Radicalism in American History, the professor invited labor rights and racial justice activist Bill Fletcher Jr. to be a guest speaker. Fletcher told the students if they wanted to work in the labor movement, they should start by getting a job in a nonunion workplace and try to organize a union there. The idea appealed to Biskar. When he mentioned the suggestion to his father, the elder Biskar replied, "Well, that's just what your grandfather did."

It was the first time Mike Biskar had been told about the family legacy of labor and political activism. His grandfather, Marvin Biskar, had been an organizer for trade unions and the Communist Party USA. In fact, Marvin met his future wife, Ida Gelpert, at a protest gone wrong. In the late 1940s, a group of Communist Party members were supposed to join African American youth in an effort to integrate a segregated swimming pool in Washington, D.C. Marvin and Ida were the only white people to show up, and when the group stormed the pool, police grabbed Marvin and delivered a beating. Ida, who had been raised in an Orthodox Jewish family, was grabbed too. She was subjected to taunts by police and onlookers, who called her a "nigger lover." *The Washington Post* printed a photograph of her being led away in handcuffs, identifying her by name and address, triggering a backlash that forced her to leave her boarding house and move to an African American part of the city.

Marvin and Ida became a couple, and soon married. Marvin continued to work as an organizer at factories and other workplaces, and was eventually called to testify in 1958 before the notorious U.S. House Committee on Un-American Activities. The hearing transcript shows that Marvin Biskar would not name names or respond to explicit requests for information about his wife and brother. Moreover, he refused to even confirm his address or where he had attended school, even though the Committee knew that information. Challenged on his refusal to answer even seemingly innocuous questions, Marvin Biskar stood his ground. "I don't feel the Committee is honestly seeking legislative information, but [instead] has a certain malicious intent," he said.[11]

Like others who refused to disclose names or renounce Communism, Marvin Biskar was blacklisted. FBI agents routinely made unwelcome visits to the family home, and they followed Marvin when he looked for work. One year, Marvin had nine different jobs, losing each one after the FBI told the employers they were courting trouble if they did not get rid of the known Communist. Eventually, Marvin Biskar gave up trying to be hired and became a self-employed auto parts salesman. He and Ida remained opposed to private property, and refused to ever buy a home.

Mike Biskar was enthralled with this revelation of radical family lore, and determined to follow in his grandfather's footsteps. To his surprise, his father resisted. Dan Biskar had inherited Marvin's political viewpoint and was proud of his parents' sacrifices. (By contrast, Dan's siblings never told their children of their grandparents' blacklisted past.) But Dan, an engineer, had chosen a safer and more traditional career path for himself, and he encouraged Mike to do the same. Dan Biskar saw first-hand in his childhood the costs his parents paid for a life of organizing. "For most parents [whose children want to become organizers], it's like, 'Oh, come on, do something more important with your life,'" Mike Biskar says. "My dad, though, saw this as incredibly important work, but also incredibly threatening work, and was scared for that reason."

Mike Biskar was not deterred. While still at Georgetown, he got a part-time job doing political canvassing in wealthy Maryland neighborhoods, knocking on doors, requesting donations, and honing a critical organizing skill: making an ask. It was a difficult and often demoralizing job, but it forced Biskar to get past the fear of going to strangers' houses and making conversation and a request. "I couldn't articulate it at the time, but I think if you are going to build a movement, you have got to talk to people who are not in the movement," he says. "Talking to people you don't know is an incredibly important skill in union organizing."

Biskar made contact with a UNITE HERE recruiter, who urged him to attend a meeting while he was home in Los Angeles on his school Christmas break. UNITE HERE was in the midst of a campaign to unionize multiple hotels along Century Boulevard in Los Angeles. Every Wednesday morning, two dozen college students working at the hotels would hold a meeting. The students had volunteered to be "salts," applying for jobs and becoming actual working employees of companies, while also trying to organize their fellow workers from within. (For more on salting, see chapter 16.)

The meeting was held at 9 a.m., and Biskar was struck by how many students there had just come from a graveyard shift or were sacrificing their day off to attend. Many had worked at the hotels—and advocated for the union—for several years. Biskar looked around the room, absorbing the day's discussion about learning Spanish and studying up on workplace sexual harassment laws. He was blown away. "I had worked at non-profits, and worked with other union organizations and in political advocacy, too. I had gone to Georgetown because I wanted to use my language skills to help the people in Latin America. (Biskar studied in Argentina, Mexico, and Brazil, and is fluent in Spanish and Portuguese.) All the while, I was looking for the real deal, the real movement. I remember feeling when I walked into that meeting: 'This is it.'" Many of the students in that room were eventually fired for their union advocacy, but that only inspired Biskar more. Some of them became career leaders of the union, and Biskar maintains friendships with several of them to this day.

Biskar returned to D.C. and got a job working as a front desk clerk at the Doubletree Crystal City hotel in Arlington, Virginia. He continued to take a full course load, cramming all his classes into two days each week and working at the hotel the other five. (UNITE HERE's current president, Donald "D." Taylor, followed a similar path in the 1970s, working his way through Georgetown's School of Foreign Service while waiting tables.) When Biskar finally cleared his schedule for his graduation ceremonies, he realized he had not had a day off for eight months.

The hotel's workers had a union campaign going when Biskar arrived, but it was limping along. At first, Biskar's efforts were not much help. He remembers identifying potential union leaders among his coworkers, only to discover that they wanted nothing to do with confronting management. It is a lesson many union organizers describe having to learn by trial-and-error: the most vocal workers or the ones most sensitized to class and labor issues are not necessarily the ones who are the best leaders of their colleagues. So Biskar kept at it. "It was scary, putting myself out there to my coworkers," he says. "But I wanted to be a union organizer, and I felt like I had to do it myself before I could pretend I knew how to teach others to do it." Eventually, Biskar found his footing, and the union effort succeeded. Biskar was elated, particularly when he realized it was the first social justice cause he had worked on that actually won. He recalled helping oppose the U.S. trade embargo of Cuba, working through an organization that lost repeatedly but each year celebrated fighting the good fight. With the hotel effort, by contrast, he had helped make tangible changes to his coworkers' lives.

Figure 2.1. Mike Biskar was the lead organizer for UNITE HERE in Indianapolis. "In every city, you have working people getting taken advantage of, and that provides an opportunity for organizing," he said. Photo by author.

Biskar's colleague Tracy Lingo is a UNITE HERE organizer in Baltimore. She says that it was clear early on that Biskar would be effective in the role. "The thing with Mike is that he does not just have the commitment to building more economic equality, he actually loves his coworkers," she says. "As an organizer, you see workers get scared and mad during the struggle. Sometimes you can't talk to people at their workplace, and then they get mad at you when you visit them at home. All that is natural, and you have to get past it. If you really love your coworkers, you take that as part of the process and just move forward. Mike is great at doing that."

Biskar is nearly evangelical in discussing the importance of grassroots union organizing. (Transcripts of Biskar interviews can sometimes yield full single-space pages of an answer to just one question on the topic.) He says he feels sorry for union activists who are tasked, by choice or by assignment, with lobbying state legislators or Congress. With union membership at record lows, there is little incentive for elected officials to follow a labor-oriented agenda, and the recent antilabor legislation at the Indiana and federal level reflect that numerical reality. "You are fighting an avalanche of one bad law after another," he says. "The whole labor movement is doing it. You might win one little victory here and there, but you are going to be in a worse place a year from now if you just do that. Instead, we have to go back to our base of workers and build political power by organizing." When Indiana labor unions were protesting in vain against the General Assembly's advancement of the state's right-to-work law in 2011 and early 2012, UNITE HERE instead spent its time organizing food-service workers. "This is part of a historical path," Biskar says. "The New Deal and the Wagner Act [that protects the rights of workers to form unions] happened because workers were already organizing, not the other way around."

Biskar's philosophy reflects that of his union. Compared to other unions, UNITE HERE does not devote much time or treasure to national political elections, and the union proudly points to a record of successful organizing even in right-to-work states. (Chapter 7 includes a discussion of UNITE HERE's strategy and track record.) "I wouldn't say we [at UNITE HERE] have it all figured out," Biskar says. "But at least we are picking fights instead of just worrying about problems. That's the thing that drives me crazy about other unions—[they ought to] just pick some fights. You're going to lose some of them, but at least you are going to learn in the process how to organize."

As an object lesson, Biskar points to UNITE HERE's struggle to unionize the downtown Indianapolis hotels, which he says laid the groundwork for the subsequent successes at universities and the airport. The latter institutions have certainly not welcomed the union with open arms, but the local hotel industry has fought much more fiercely to keep the union out. Eric Gomez, who led the union campaign at Marian University, had first worked inside the Hyatt. "Eric had to deal with so much pressure there, including standing up in meetings and have coworkers shouting at him to sit down," Biskar says. "After that, Aramark [at Marian] was nothing. Going through the fight with the Hyatt has been good for our team's confidence."

But winning helps, too, especially when the goal is to reverse the mindset that unions cannot prevail in Indiana. After Biskar's success in the Virginia hotel organizing, he was asked by UNITE HERE on a Friday to move to Indianapolis on the following Monday. He was just twenty-three years old, and had never been to the Midwest, much less Indiana.

His UNITE HERE supervisors were not concerned that Biskar would refuse the assignment. "I always say to young people who want to work for us, 'Do you think this is what you want to do with the rest of your life?'" says UNITE HERE director of organizing Jo Marie Agriesti. "A lot of organizing directors say it is too early to ask a question like that, but I just want to know what they will say. And Mike is one of those who said, 'Yep, this is what I want to do for the rest of my life.' We've had the most success with people who say, 'I'll go anywhere the union asks me to go,' and Mike is definitely one of those people."

When a senior organizer brought him to Indianapolis for the first time, Biskar felt a little like a freshman being dropped off at college. He soon heard an earful about the dismal local labor picture. But as he immersed himself in the community and the process, Biskar found himself questioning the conventional wisdom that Indianapolis was not a good union town. "All that stuff can add up to being just one big distraction," he says. "In every city, you have working people getting taken advantage of, and that provides an opportunity for organizing." In Indianapolis, he found workers hungry for change in their workplace and a community of students, clergy, and labor supporters eager to show their solidarity with those workers.

"We can win here," he says. "And if we can win here, we can win anywhere."

3

Dreaming of One Good Job

Abdelhakim Ejjair has been on his feet for nearly all of the past seven hours, but he is still moving quickly. It is just past 2 p.m., and he speed-walks out of the Downtown Indianapolis Hyatt Regency, headed for his van after a shift as a server assistant at the One South restaurant in the hotel. He has been up since 6 a.m., but Ejjair's haste is inspired not by the fact that he is leaving one job, but by the fact that he is already on his way to another. If he can rush home, he should have time to grab lunch and maybe even nap for a few minutes. Then, he will leave for his second job as a lot attendant at the Hertz rental car facility at the Indianapolis International Airport. Today, he is allowing me to accompany him on the transition.

Ejjair has been working at the Hyatt a full fourteen years but still makes only $9 per hour, not counting the occasions when a server shares tips with him. He is paid slightly more at Hertz, but neither job provides much in the way of benefits. Ejjair cannot afford the premiums for family health insurance coverage through the Hyatt, so his two children are covered by Medicaid. His wife goes without health coverage.

Ejjair and I climb into his van, which has an odometer creeping up on two hundred thousand miles, a mysterious knock coming from the engine, and a laminated verse from the Koran hanging from the dashboard. We head northwest out of downtown on Interstate 65. In accented English revealing the Arabic and French he grew up speaking in his home country of Morocco, Ejjair patiently answers my questions while he drives. Yes, he would prefer to work just one job: "If they pay me good, I would not have to work two jobs." He would like to buy a home one day, if he could save the money. Yes, he is tired. Ejjair is short and slight, with his black hair yielding only a few flecks of gray, and he looks younger than his forty-seven years. But he has dark circles under his eyes, and admits that he sleeps only about five hours on the nights between his double-shift days.

Ejjair arrived in the United States from Morocco on April 22, 1998, a date he recites from memory. He had worked as a draftsman in his home country, and his skills earned him a visa to move to the United States. He hoped to become an engineer, but he learned that he would need extra training even to be a draftsman in the United States, and he could not afford the classes. So he got a job as a dishwasher at the Hyatt and taught himself English, first by watching TV and writing down the words. Once he could afford a computer, he switched to language lesson CDs. Ejjair was embarrassed when people laughed at his early attempts to speak English, and he remains frustrated by his limitations with the language. "I am still picking words," he says.

But Ejjair has become an advocate for the UNITE HERE drive to unionize the Hyatt. "Many other people want the union, too, but they are scared," he says. Any hesitation Ejjair once had evaporated when his counterparts at unionized Hyatt hotels in other cities showed him their paychecks. "It is the same corporation, and they do the same job as me, but it is not the same paycheck," he says. "They get paid good money, and they pay very little for health coverage. My paycheck is too low."

So Ejjair works 60–70 hour weeks, including shifts at the Hyatt where he is on his feet busing tables for every minute except for his half hour break. Many days, he leaves home for his first job before his children are awake, and he comes home from his second job after they have already gone to bed. I ask him if he is concerned about how long he can keep up this pace. He shrugs: "I don't promise myself. It is hard to tell."

Figure 3.1. Abdelhakim Ejjair has worked as a dishwasher and busboy at the Hyatt Regency in downtown Indianapolis for fourteen years, but his salary is so low he has to take on a second job to support his family. He supports a union because he learned that workers at unionized hotels in other cities make far higher wages and are able to afford health insurance. "It is the same corporation, and they do the same job as me, but it is not the same paycheck," he says. Photo by Mark A. Lee.

In addition to talking to Ejjair while he transitioned between jobs, I decided it would also be good to get a sense of Ejjair at work. On a breakfast visit to the One South restaurant in the downtown Hyatt, I saw him across the room, carrying off dirty dishes to the kitchen. He wore a chocolate brown uniform shirt, a "Hakim" silver nametag, and a long black apron that hung far below his knees. The restaurant setting was comfortable and pristine, and the server was charming and attentive. The chicken and egg white breakfast sandwich, including bacon and a side of fried potatoes, was delicious.

Countless times, I have been fortunate enough to enjoy similar meals in similar settings. But it had never been so clear that my pleasure was directly connected to someone else's labor. Like most American consumers, I rarely think that the price for my shoes or cell phone is directly connected to the subpoverty wages of those who manufactured them. But in this case, I could not ignore the link between my affordable meal and the toil of a trilingual trained draftsman making nine bucks an hour.

Some labor advocates insist that consumers should not feel this kind of guilt about the cost of goods and services. They point out that the corporations that own hotels and restaurants and shoe companies make plenty of profit to allow them to pay better wages and still keep prices low. Ejjair's employer, Hyatt Hotels, for example, reported gross earnings of almost $4 billion in 2012, with $88 million in profit—despite a global boycott led by UNITE HERE. But, sitting in the restaurant, I could not help thinking back to my visit to Ejjair's home, where I met his shyly smiling wife and watched his curly haired preschool-age children play with toy cars on the carpet. We had discussed Moroccan home design and Muslim concerns over the defamation of the prophet Muhammad. Ejjair shared his plans for his children's schooling.

Suddenly, I did not feel so good about my Hyatt meal anymore. I paid my bill and got up to leave. As I walked out the restaurant door, I looked back to see if I could catch a last glimpse of Ejjair at work. I did.

He was cleaning up after me.

According to the U.S. Department of Labor, Abdelhakim Ejjair is one of twenty-five million foreign-born persons working in the United States, a total that comprises 16 percent of the workforce.[1] In Indianapolis, most of the immigrant workers are Latino, with 2010 census data showing over sixty-six thousand additional Latinos coming to Indianapolis from 2000 to 2010. Almost 10 percent of the city's population is now Latino.

From the Chinese who built the country's railroads to the eastern Europeans who toiled in garment shops, the United States has long relied on immigrants to do the most demanding and thankless work in our economy. The story is the same today, with immigrants making up a disproportionate share of U.S. workers in low-wage, physically taxing roles like housekeepers, roofers, and farmworkers.[2]

The conventional wisdom in U.S. organized labor once considered the current wave of immigrant workers to be unorganizable at best, and enemies of U.S.-born workers at worst.[3] About one in three current immigrant workers is undocumented, a key difference from prior generations of immigrants who faced limited barriers to entering the United States.[4] Many labor advocates assumed that these workers would be unwilling to engage in workplace advocacy, given the understandable fear of retaliation, especially deportation. Even if immigrant workers would be interested in collective action, many would be unprotected by the National Labor Relations Act, which specifically excludes agricultural and domestic workers. The federal law also does not cover workers classified as self-employed independent contractors, a common designation for immigrants in the construction industry or for those working for temporary agencies.[5] Immigrants are willing to work for so little pay and in such bad conditions, the argument went, they would only undermine the efforts of native-born workers who seek improved wages and benefits. "They're dragging down the pay. It's pure economics," one African American slaughterhouse worker told the *New York Times* in 2000 after the company hired an influx of Mexican immigrants to work in the North Carolina plant. "They say Americans don't want the job. That ain't exactly true. We don't want to do it for eight dollars [an hour]. Pay fifteen dollars and we'll do it."[6]

There is an undeniable logic behind these arguments. Threats of immigration-related retaliation are certainly a part of the reality for foreign-born workers who advocate for workplace rights. And many immigrant workers are willing to toil for extremely low wages, at least for a while. But it turns out that the U.S. immigrant workforce has been highly receptive to joining in actions to improve wages and conditions. One of the iconic labor struggles of the last century, the late 1960s fight of the Cesar Chavez-led United Farm Workers, was a product of courageous stands made by Mexican and Filipino grape and lettuce pickers. These workers built a full-scale social movement, complete with boycotts, rallies, and hunger strikes. In the process, they earned better deals with growers and the passage of California state laws that provided farmworkers the labor rights that federal law denied them.[7]

Beginning in the 1980s, SEIU self-consciously emulated the spirit and narrative of the farmworkers movement while it successfully organized in the heavily immigrant janitorial industry. Soon after, the AFL-CIO abandoned its opposition to liberalized immigration policies and became an active supporter of immigrant rights. Now, unions like UNITE HERE have joined SEIU's efforts to organize immigrant workers. As of 2011, the percentage of immigrant workers who were unionized in the private sector was equal to that of U.S.-born workers.[8]

Defying the downward trend among U.S.-born workers, immigrant union membership in the United States seems poised to grow even more. In 2012, union membership among non-Hispanic whites dropped by 547,000 nationally but increased by over 150,000 among Latinos.[9] For sheer logistical reasons, the service-sector jobs that immigrants disproportionately hold, including construction and hospitality work, are the ones least likely to be outsourced. And immigrants often readily embrace the prospects of collective action. Compared to U.S.-born workers, immigrants have been found to have deeper social networks and to think of their individual fate as more intertwined with the conditions endured by other community members. It is a mind-set that has contributed to daring collective worker action by U.S. immigrants like the South Asian limousine drivers, Mexican greengrocers, and West African deliverymen portrayed in Immanuel Ness's *Immigrants, Unions, and the New U.S. Labor Market*.[10] On May 1, 2006, many in the United States were introduced to this phenomenon on a grand scale when millions of immigrants and their supporters refused to go to work and instead flooded the streets of major U.S. cities. "A Day Without Immigrants" was conducted in part to protest U.S. immigration policies and in part to demonstrate the economic power of the U.S. immigrant population.

Some researchers argue that immigrants are by definition a self-selected group of economically motivated individuals.[11] After all, for most immigrants the pursuit of financial security is what inspired them to leave the familiar environs of home. For many, they risked arrest and deportation to do so. Those aspirations and sacrifices may be why many union organizers believe, and at least one survey shows, that immigrants are actually more receptive to union membership than are native-born workers.[12] As UNITE HERE's Mike Biskar says, "In Los Angeles and a lot of other places in California, you can go to a Latino household and say you are with the union, and they immediately say, 'OK, that is for me.' There is just a confidence that unions will help them improve their lives. That is where we want to get in Indianapolis."

With a few exceptions, unauthorized immigrants in the United States enjoy a similar level of workplace protections as other workers in the same industries—at least on paper.[13] Yet immigrant workers are disproportionately victimized by the most fundamental employer abuse of all: not being paid the wages they are owed.[14] Wage theft can take many forms: flat-out refusal to pay the worker what she is owed, being forced to work off the clock, being paid below the minimum wage, and being misclassified as an independent contractor (cheating both the worker and the government out of employer contributions to payroll taxes, Social Security, and so forth).

At a mid-2013 forum sponsored by the central Indiana chapter of the SEIU-affiliated Jobs with Justice, local immigrant workers stood up one by one and described variations of wage theft going on in the Indianapolis community. Paulino Pedrosa told how he worked for many years in the local construction industry, doing jobs varying from carpentry to electrical work to plumbing. Pedrosa's employers called him an independent contractor, even though the bosses controlled his hours and working conditions to such an extent that he clearly should have been treated as an employee. Pedrosa was paid in cash, with the amount sometimes dropping below minimum wage and never including overtime pay. When Pedrosa complained, the employer threatened him with deportation—even though, as a resident alien, both Pedrosa's presence and work activity were fully legal.

After Pedrosa spoke, Silvia Garcia told how she had worked as a server in a restaurant where she and her coworkers went several months without a paycheck. Flouting the most basic foundations of federal and state labor law, Garcia's employer refused to pay any wage to supplement the server's tip income. Worse, he forced them to stay after hours to clean the restaurant—for no pay. Garcia first disclosed her name at the public hearing, and then afterward asked if she could be anonymous. She feared retaliation by the business owner. Only after Garcia and two colleagues filed suit against the employer in federal court did she agree to have her name be public.

Eva Sanchez told her wage theft story at the forum, too. Sanchez, like the majority of housekeepers in downtown Indianapolis hotels, was never a direct employee of those hotels. Instead, most are immigrants working for temporary staffing agencies, usually for pay barely above minimum wage and without benefits. Until 2012, the dominant agency in the field was Georgia-based Hospitality Staffing Solutions, known as HSS. An industry magazine ad placed by HSS portrayed rows of hotel workers—housekeepers, chefs, servers—lined up in a vending machine like bags of chips, ready for purchase. The ad touted the lower hourly wages of its employees and the avoidance of overtime costs. "As the leader in hospitality staffing, we're experts at saving clients money," the ad read.[15]

From Eva Sanchez's perspective, HSS saved its clients money in part by mistreating and shortchanging its workers. Sanchez moved to Indianapolis from Mexico City in 2002, and she worked for HSS for nearly ten years, usually making about $8 per hour and never receiving any sick days, vacation time, or benefits. While on the job for HSS at the Indianapolis Westin Hotel in 2006 setting up for a banquet, Sanchez was struck in the groin by one of the chairs. She was bleeding and in pain. Sanchez says the manager told her, "This kind of thing happens to you every month down there, so just put a towel on it and get back to work." A coworker took Sanchez to the hospital, where she received stitches and a bill for $1,400. HSS refused to pay it. Sanchez also says she often saw banquet prep coworkers get cut and burned on the job. In 2012, the Indiana Department of Labor fined HSS and the downtown Hyatt Regency Hotel together more than $50,000 for violations of the Indiana Occupational Safety and Health Act. The violations included failure to train HSS-hired housekeepers on handling chemical hazards, blood, and needles they may encounter in their cleaning duties, and failure to provide the agency with worker injury records.[16]

Sanchez says her HSS paychecks would routinely omit an hour or two that she worked, and eventually grew to undercount her wages by multiple hours and even full days. Coworkers had the same problem. At first, their manager apologized and said the next check would make up the difference. When it didn't, Sanchez and her coworkers went to the manager again. This time, he reacted angrily, telling them if they did not like working for the company, the door was open and they should leave. Sanchez didn't. As she tells the story, tears well in her eyes. "I got very frustrated and very angry," she says. "But what was I going to do? I was a single mom, and I had to support my daughter."

Although UNITE HERE was not trying to organize a union at the temporary agencies, it felt an obligation to advocate for these workers— and saw an opportunity to publicize unfair practices within the hotels. "We need to be involved with issues like wage theft and with the big-picture issue of immigration reform," Biskar says. In pushing for passage of a law that would allow a path to citizenship for the eleven million undocumented persons in the United States, UNITE HERE and SEIU are part of a central Indiana coalition that includes the local Roman Catholic Archdiocese, the Chamber of Commerce, and large Indianapolis-based corporations like Eli Lilly and Company. (The Indiana citizenship campaign is described in chapters 11 and 12.) "So many of our members are immigrants that this kind of advocacy is obviously the right thing to do," Biskar says. "And it also helps show local Latino workers who are not our members yet that the union is on their side."

The union helped Eva Sanchez and fifteen other HSS workers find a lawyer. In January 2012 they filed a lawsuit against HSS in U.S. District Court, alleging a sweeping pattern of wage theft and labor law violations. The plaintiffs had worked as housekeepers, cooks, and banquet servers in nearly all of the major Indianapolis hotels. In a twenty-two-page complaint, they alleged they were routinely forced to work off the clock with full knowledge of the hotel management, were regularly paid for less than the full number of hours they worked, and were not given overtime pay as required by law. One of the plaintiffs, Anastasia Amantecatl, claimed that she regularly worked two hours before clocking in at the Marriott Downtown because this was the only way she could clean the required number of daily rooms. Another plaintiff, Elizabeth Guzman, said the same thing happened to her at the Hyatt Regency; Leyla Fairfield had a similar experience at the Canterbury. According to the complaint, this practice was common for dozens of HSS workers and was endorsed by hotel management. HSS denied the allegations, but the lawsuit was settled in late 2012. The terms were not disclosed, but the workers held a press conference celebrating the outcome. The workers and UNITE HERE also reported that multiple area hotels severed ties with HSS after the lawsuit was filed.

Sanchez said she was very pleased with the terms of the agreement and the precedent established by the litigation. "We have set the example for people in the Latino community that they should not be treated like slaves," she said. Sanchez has since left hotel work to be an organizer for UNITE HERE, focusing on immigrant and women workers. "I believe in my union and it is needed," she says. "My coworkers were working in the shadow and being abused. I think everyone working hard in these hotels should have an equal opportunity to find a better future."

Like Abdelhakim Ejjair, Enriqueta Sanchez can be hard to catch at home. I have been told that I will get a chance to talk to Sanchez (no relation to Eva Sanchez) beginning at 4:20 p.m. Sure enough, Sanchez pulls up at 4:19 to the modest house in the Fountain Square neighborhood that she rents for herself along with her three children and four grandchildren. Sanchez's two-year-old granddaughter- Tiffany- rushes out to greet her. Tiffany has limited time with her *abuela* and is not happy that visitors are here to ask some questions. But Sanchez invites us in.

Sanchez has just finished a day of work cleaning downtown hotel rooms, and now she is home for a quick dinner and visit with Tiffany and other family. In an hour, she will head out the door again, drive back downtown, and report for her second job. This time, Sanchez will clean offices at the 300 North Meridian building, one of the city's tallest buildings and home to some of the community's most prestigious law and accounting firms. There, Sanchez will pick up garbage, mop floors, and vacuum carpets until midnight. I ask her if she is tired. It seems like a dumb question to pose to someone in the midst of a seventy-hour workweek. Enriqueta's daughter is sitting in the next room, and she yells out, "*Si!*" Sanchez laughs. "*Poco*," she says. A little.

But she has no choice, she explains. It takes two jobs to pay the bills. She lists the water bill, the gas bill, rent, electricity, food. "The cost of everything keeps going up," she says. But after six years of working for the company GSF-USA, Sanchez makes just $8.90 per hour. According to GSF-USA's website, its parent company, Group Services France, employs over twenty-five thousand people worldwide. The company's most recent reported revenue, for 2008, was over $700 million. GSF did not return my calls asking for an interview.

Figure 3.2. Enriqueta Sanchez visits with her granddaughter during her daily break between two janitorial jobs in downtown Indianapolis. Sanchez works seventy hours a week but cannot afford health insurance. Photo by author.

Sanchez is one of seven hundred Indianapolis janitors who believe that companies like GSF can afford to pay them a better wage and provide access to affordable health care. The janitors are members of SEIU Local 1, and they clean the majority of downtown Indianapolis's office space, including the offices of Eli Lilly and Company, Simon Property Group, and WellPoint, one of the largest health insurance companies in the United States. Like Sanchez, most of the janitors are paid around $9 per hour and are usually given less than thirty hours a week of work. They have no retirement plan. Most are immigrants.

At the national level, the most high-profile recent example of successful organizing of immigrant workers has been SEIU's "Justice for Janitors" campaign. In the early 1980s, office-cleaning companies in Los Angeles switched from native-born janitors to immigrants making far lower wages. But, within a few years, those immigrant janitors came together under the SEIU banner to demand fair wages and treatment. The union coordinated demonstrations that sometimes included civil disobedience and usually highlighted the janitors' community supporters, including a heavy clergy presence. SEIU secured contracts for janitors in dozens of major cities, including Los Angeles, Houston, and Washington, D.C. The campaign was even the inspiration for a 2000 feature film, *Bread and Roses*. From 2005 to 2007, Indianapolis janitors followed this same script, complete with lively purple-shirted tub-thumping downtown pickets. They drew momentum from widespread community support expressed by elected officials and other labor unions. In May 2007, a half-dozen clergy were arrested for engaging in a civil disobedience action of blocking the entrance to an office tower where the janitors worked. The Indianapolis contractors finally agreed to the janitors' union representation and a contract, but the contract did not provide dramatic improvements for workers and was poorly enforced by the union.[17] Sanchez and others are seeking much better contract terms this time.

Author Campbell works at one of the Eli Lilly buildings in Indianapolis, and is a union steward for SEIU Local 1. Campbell, in his sixties, is a tall, thin African American man with large glasses. When he talks about learning that janitors in other cities are making several dollars more each hour than are workers like Sanchez, he shakes his head in disappointment. "We want janitors here to be able to support a family with their work," Campbell says. "Most of all, it is about self-dignity." Union members also argue that Indiana taxpayers are helping subsidize the cleaning companies' business model. Enrequita Sanchez's grandchildren are on Medicaid, and Sanchez is among many janitors who use the local public Wishard-Eskenazi Health clinics or hospital emergency room because they cannot afford the employer's offered health insurance. As for Sanchez, she feels she has held up her end of the bargain with her employer. "They want things clean, and I am providing that service," she says, still bouncing Tiffany on her knee. In return, she is asking that her employer pay a wage that would allow her to support herself and her family—with just one job.

ALT-LABOR HITS INDIANAPOLIS

Steve Rufo walks up to the counter of the Nestle Toll House Café in Circle Centre Mall in downtown Indianapolis. Instead of ordering a slice of cookie cake or a brownie, he strikes up a conversation with the worker in the brown and gold uniform. "Have you heard of the Fight for 15?" he asks. "We are a group of fast-food and retail workers who are fighting for better wages and better treatment."

The worker nods. She has heard the name, but doesn't know much beyond that. She glances over at her manager, who is out of earshot across the store. She says that she is open to hearing more. Rufo types her number into his iPhone and promises to call. The entire conversation lasts less than two minutes. "You always get the number," Rufo says, walking away. "It is impossible to have a real conversation in that setting, so this way we can talk in more detail later."

Beginning in April 2012, workers at fast-food restaurants and some big-chain retail companies began staging one-day strikes in U.S. cities. Most have done so under the banner of an SEIU-supported campaign, Fight for 15, asking for a wage of $15 per hour, an amount they characterize as a living wage. (Living wage calculations actually vary by location and by size of the worker's family. The Indianapolis estimated living wage is nearly $18 per hour for a family of two.[1]) The strikes have gained national media attention, shut down a handful of stores, and sometimes earned wage, hour, and conditions concessions. One of the campaign fliers explains "Why We Fight": "Our work generates BILLIONS OF DOLLARS for the fast-food and retail industry each year, but we can't afford to take care of our family's basic needs for food and housing."

It is a Wednesday afternoon in July 2013, and Indianapolis is not one of the Fight for 15 cities yet. But Rufo is working on it. His main mission today is to walk around the mall and reconnect with Indianapolis workers who have said they are interested in striking. There is a worker meeting tonight, and he is pushing for a good turnout. After leaving the Nestle store, Rufo has quick conversations with a Subway worker and then a Taco Bell worker. He has spoken to both before, and both give him vague answers about whether they will show up this evening. An A& W All American Food worker says she had hoped to come, but her shift won't end in time.

Rufo's phone rings. Another worker is calling to say she has class tonight and can't make the meeting. By now, Rufo has circled the food court a few times, so he walks out of the mall to a nearby Arby's. He does not recognize any of the workers inside, so he heads to the parking lot and walks toward the dumpster. "I talk to people here a lot while they are out sneaking a smoke," he laughs.

For union organizers, connecting with fast-food workers is a challenge. The workers' shifts are so unpredictable that home visits are hard to arrange, as are group meetings. Talking to workers on the job is precarious. One Fight for 15 organizer who SEIU sent to help Rufo in Indianapolis was too obvious, carrying a clipboard and holding conversations at high volume. Mall security kicked him out. "I heard you talking about a union," the guard said. "We don't allow that here." Rufo, a small, olive-skinned man in his thirties with a goatee, full sideburns, and elaborate tattoos, picks his spots more carefully, trying to approach workers while they are on break or when no customers or managers are around. Compared to connecting with fast-food workers, Rufo says that talking to retail employees is a bit easier, especially for young women organizers. They walk into a store, browse among the merchandise, and workers come right up to them. The organizer remarks that the worker must be getting paid real well to sell this nice stuff. Not really, the worker replies. The conversation goes from there.

Rufo decides to walk back to the mall and position himself at the entrance. On the sidewalk, workers can speak more freely when they are not on the clock and under a manager's gaze. A Latina woman in her twenties passes by, wearing a chocolate brown Cinnabon T-shirt and matching visor. "Excuse me, do you work at the mall?" Rufo asks. She says yes, looking a little nervous. Rufo introduces himself and the Fight for 15. It turns out two of her Cinnabon colleagues have already shown an interest, and she agrees to attend a future meeting. Rufo asks her to put down her contact info and signature on a large "Fight for 15" card. It reads in part, "It's wrong that so much of the money made every day ends up in the hands of a few rich individuals and corporations, while those of us who work in retail stores and restaurants are struggling to make ends meet." She signs, and then goes into the mall to begin her shift. Rufo is pleased. "We are trying to focus on the stores where we already have two or three signed up," he says.

A thin young African American man walks out of the mall, pulling off his royal blue Auntie Anne's Pretzels visor as he walks. Rufo says, "Hey, bro, you work at the mall?" They begin to talk. The young man has heard of the Fight for 15, so Rufo transitions to a series of open-ended questions: "How are things going at your job?" "How long have you worked there?" The young man needs to hustle to catch his bus home, so Rufo walks with him the two blocks to the bus stop.

The conversation is fairly standard union organizing "rap": open-ended questions about job conditions leading up to a discussion of fairness of treatment. Rufo and other organizers say that fast-food workers are so consistently and thoroughly exploited that the conversation practically drives itself. It turns out the young man has worked for the company for seven months and still makes the very bottom minimum wage of $7.25 per hour. Rufo asks him how much he thinks the store profits while he is on shift and whether he knows what the company CEO's salary is. "Do you think you deserve more than what you are getting?" Rufo asks. The young man signs up, and Rufo heads back to the mall entrance.

The foot traffic leading into the mall from Washington Street is dominated by two distinct populations. The first group is the suburban dwellers or hotel guests heading to stores like Abercrombie and Fitch and Carson Pirie Scott, often stopping for a quick meal or coffee during their visit. The vast majority of these people are white. The second group is mostly young people of color heading to work and wearing uniform T-shirts or polos with matching ball caps or visors. The white shoppers park SUVs in the attached garage; many of the workers hustle over from the bus stop. Fight for 15 organizers from out of town call Circle Centre "The Tale of Two Cities." The mall complex cost Indiana taxpayers over $300 million, with debts still being paid for its construction.

The shoppers see outwardly cheerful workers serving a Diet Coke or waffle fries, but Rufo has learned that there are usually struggles hidden by the smiles. The Steak-n-Shake workers are bone tired from overnight shifts at their twenty-four-hour restaurant adjacent to the mall. Taco Bell workers are punished for taking sick days, even with a doctor's note. A retail worker is frustrated that she is never granted her request for Sunday mornings off to attend church. Almost every employee is at his or her wits' end trying to get more hours to pay the bills, or at least predictable hours so it will be possible to get another job. The "turn and burn" model in these industries demands continual hiring of new workers and suppression of hours for existing employees, in part to avoid paying benefits and in part to ensure an eager on-call workforce.[2]

After the Fight for 15 succeeded in other large cities, SEIU created an online survey asking Indianapolis fast-food and retail workers about workplace issues. One of the workers to respond was a young woman named Julia Osborne who worked at a McDonald's on the south side of town. Rufo followed up by phone with some of the online respondents. "They are working us around the clock; they are working us like dogs," Osborne told him. Complaints by Osborne and others about hours, wages, and treatment were so numerous that the union concluded that Indianapolis was sufficiently "heated" to justify exploration as a new Fight for 15 city. After the first wave of spring 2013 strikes in other cities, Rufo and a half dozen other organizers came to Indianapolis to spend a few days at the mall, asking workers if they would be interested in joining the campaign. When ninety workers signed commitment cards, the union decided to send Rufo and a colleague down from their home in Chicago—a three-hour drive from Indianapolis—a couple days a week. Rufo is a veteran of the successful April 2013 Fight for 15 strikes in Chicago, where five hundred workers staged a rolling series of demonstrations across multiple worksites.

Very quickly, Rufo had a lot of promising one-on-one meetings with Indianapolis workers. Subway restaurant workers are a tight-knit group that is ready to take action. Osborne was ready to strike McDonald's during her first conversation with Rufo, where she immediately started texting coworkers to encourage them to join her. The first meeting of the Indianapolis workers attracted seven attendees, which Rufo insists was a good number. "Chicago started as a baby campaign, too," he says. "We had five people at our first meeting there. Now we have 130 or 140 committee members who are not just willing to strike but to lead others." Rufo estimates that the Chicago core of activist workers was derived from a group of over two thousand who signed commitment cards. Given that ratio of planting to harvest, there is much more work to be done in Indianapolis. Rufo is hoping that SEIU will soon assign other organizers to join him. A good turnout at the second meeting will help his argument.

The December 2012 National Labor Relations Board-sanctioned election at Marian University described in chapter 1 is an anomaly in the twenty-first century. In the current economic climate, a variety of factors make it extremely difficult to create a new labor bargaining unit. Large corporations are increasingly turning to temporary workers to perform tasks once handled by permanent employees.[3] The fast-food and low-wage retail industries in particular feature decentralized employees who struggle to build the solidarity necessary to form a union; they seem to have little chance to get a majority of highly transient workers in place long enough to win a traditional union election. In other industries, an increasing number of workers are labeled as independent contractors, putting them outside the protection of U.S. labor law. Domestic workers and agricultural workers are not covered by federal labor law, either.

These jobs make up some of the fastest growing sectors of the U.S. economy, and they are increasingly being filled by older and better educated workers whose families are dependent on the income earned.[4] Yet they are also jobs that are highly resistant to traditional union organizing models. Even when old-school labor organizing efforts are possible, they are plagued by employer intimidation and retaliation that is barely discouraged under existing U.S. labor law. (See chapter 6 for a discussion of the problems with current labor regulations and enforcement.) In an environment so toxic for labor organizing, it is no surprise that U.S. union membership has dropped to historically low levels.

The major powers of U.S. labor readily acknowledge the problem. "Working people and labor unions have been vulnerable for years," AFL-CIO president Richard Trumka said in early 2013. "No amount of bluster or head-in-the-sand insistence that everything is fine will change that reality."[5] As a result, the AFL-CIO has been openly looking for alternatives to the traditional majority election, dues-paying model of unionism. The effort is in part a response to the most unnoticed but promising data point in the entire U.S. labor discussion: workers still want to join unions. More than half of all U.S. workers, nearly 60 million in all, have responded to polling by saying they would join a union if they had the opportunity. That number has increased even as union membership has dropped.[6] The millions of union-friendly workers who are toiling as independent contractors or in hard-to-organize industries could trigger the labor movement's revival, if only they could be brought into the fold. "We'll try a whole bunch of new forms of representation," Trumka told labor journalist Harold Myerson in early 2013. "Some will work; some won't, but we'll be opening up the labor movement."[7]

As the summer 2013 scene in Indianapolis's Circle Centre Mall attests, that process has already begun. For several decades now, nonunion groups often referred to as "alt-labor" have been trying to fill in the gaps left by the failure of traditional labor unions and organizing models. Rutgers University labor studies professor Janice Fine studies alt-labor organizations commonly called "worker centers," and she says that there are now over two hundred such organizations advocating for workers outside of the traditional elected union structure. In late 2013, Indianapolis opened the Worker Justice Center in a building that formerly housed a Carpenters' Union local.

One of the most high-profile worker centers is the New York City–based Restaurant Opportunities Center, which has used a combination of wage-and-hour lawsuits, street protests, and know-your-rights trainings to win sick pay, back wages, and legislative reforms for restaurant workers. These victories have been achieved in an industry where workers are victimized by low pay and high turnover—exactly the type of workforce that desperately needs a union but would struggle to organize under current rules. In the late 1990s and 2000s, New York taxi drivers also overcame seemingly insurmountable challenges posed by their work status. Although the drivers were independent contractors and many were undocumented immigrants, they came together as the New York Taxi Alliance and conducted strikes that led to fare increases and the creation of a health care and disability fund.[8] The Austin, Texas-based Workers Defense Project has two thousand largely immigrant members and a focus on combatting wage theft and increasing worker safety in Texas's construction industry.[9] Domestic Workers United has successfully pushed for a bill of rights for housekeepers and nannies in New York.[10]

In the early and mid-2000s, Immokalee, Florida, farmworkers actually took strategic advantage of the nonunion status of their Coalition of Immokalee Workers. The National Labor Relations Act (NLRA) prohibits unions from engaging in what is known as a secondary boycott, trying to influence the company employing the workers by directing pressure toward a second company. For example, a union trying to organize workers at a hammer manufacturer is prohibited from applying the economic pressure of a picket or strike directed at a hardware store that purchases the company's hammers for retail sales. But the nonunion Coalition of Immokalee Workers had no such legal bar against organizing a nationwide boycott of Yum Brands' Taco Bell, a major buyer of the tomatoes produced by the growers that were shortchanging the farmworkers.[11] The boycott included a Student Farmworker Alliance-led Ban the Bell campaign that forced twenty-two Taco Bell restaurants off high school and college campuses. In 2005, the image-conscious Taco Bell agreed to buy tomatoes only from growers that paid higher wages, a concession that earned the farmworkers a 75 percent raise.[12]

The Coalition of Immokalee Workers campaign approach is not completely foreign to the traditional labor movement, which in recent decades has increasingly embraced "corporate campaigns" directed at a company's customers. UNITE HERE, for example, pursued a global boycott of Hyatt Hotels under the banner "Hyatt Hurts." But alt-labor campaigns also derive tactics and language from the legacies of social justice causes like the feminist movement, the peace movement, and the civil rights movement. Journalist and labor activist Vanessa Tait, in her 2005 book *Poor People's Unions*, describes 1970s campaigns advocating for U.S. welfare rights, unemployed workers, and youth employment movements. Tait also points out that nonunion worker advocacy is not limited to the United States, identifying large nonunion organizations for street laborers in India, farmers in South America, and the Workers' Party in Brazil.[13] Labor historians note that the nineteenth-century Knights of Labor shared the modern worker center and Fight for 15 mission to organize and mobilize a wide swath of workers regardless of their employers.[14]

The alt-labor movement faces challenges, though. Worker centers are usually funded more by external foundation grants or union donations than by membership dues, a model that is less stable than the traditional dues-supported union. A staff-run worker center may be a less effective long-term structure than a member-governance union: research has shown that the more democratic a union is, the stronger it is.[15] Worker centers struggle to balance the demand to respond to the grievances of individual workers with the desire to effect big-picture change. And worker centers and alt-labor campaigns appear to be better suited for the task of exposing and prosecuting illegal practices like wage theft than for the long-term agenda of negotiating and enforcing agreements across industries.

Some of the alt-labor movements' most notable successes have been achieved in campaigns to change laws to the benefit of large categories of low-wage workers. Compared to individual workplace campaigns, these kinds of legislative reform efforts have the advantage of helping low-wage workers who work in industries where it is exceedingly difficult to engage in collective bargaining to achieve higher wages and benefits. Legislative campaigns also have the benefit of impacting workers, such as agricultural laborers or home care workers, who are excluded from the workplace organizing protections of the National Labor Relations Act. Most of these legislative campaigns have occurred at the state and local level, helping spark a trend of workplace conditions being mandated locally as a supplement to the historic concentration of such regulation at the federal level. Since the 1990s, coalitions led by workers' rights groups have pushed 140 municipalities to adopt "living wage" requirements that raise the floor for some or all workers in the community. In 2012, the not-for-profit group Los Angeles Alliance for a New Economy, UNITE HERE, and local coalitions led successful ballot initiative campaigns in Long Beach and San Jose, California. A full 63 percent of Long Beach voters approved a $13 per hour minimum wage for hotel workers, and San Jose passed a $10 minimum wage that applies to all workers in the city. (The federal minimum wage is $7.25 per hour.) Similar hotel worker wage hikes were approved in Los Angeles and Emeryville, California. AFL-CIO's Working America program ran a door-to-door canvassing campaign that spurred an increase in the minimum wage in Albuquerque, New Mexico.

These legislative efforts have been most successful in states that allow voters to directly place initiatives on the ballot, as polls consistently show widespread popular support for raising the minimum wage.[16] But in most states, including Indiana, changes to the law have to be initiated by legislators. The Indiana General Assembly in 2011 passed a law that blocks even local city councils from adopting a minimum wage that exceeds the state level.[17] Partly as a result, Indiana alt-labor groups, including the SEIU-supported Jobs with Justice and the local Indianapolis Community Faith and Labor Coalition, have struggled to respond to the needs of local workers like Miryah Lazaropolis.

Lazaropolis works at a southside Indianapolis Walmart, where she straightens and stocks racks of clothes. But she is paid only $7.40 per hour, and her paycheck does not come close to meeting even the bare-bones needs of her family. When she fell behind on the rent on her home, she and her twin three-year-old boys were evicted. Fortunately, Lazaropolis's parents allowed her and the kids to stay with them for awhile. But she owes money from the eviction and overdue utility bills, and the still-unpaid hospital fees for the twins' birth add up to nearly $20,000.

Lazaropolis tries to push the worry about the unpaid debts behind her. But some money problems are more immediate. On the day I spoke with her, Lazaropolis had no gas in her car and no way to buy some much-needed baby wipes. She is unlikely to be able to join a union anytime soon. Multiple efforts to organize Walmart workers nationally have been unsuccessful, even though recent years have seen spirited Black Friday protests around the country, including in Indianapolis, during the post-Thanksgiving shopping day. An increase in the minimum wage would help Lazaropolis, but previous efforts to adopt a local living wage ordinance in Indianapolis were not successful. Now, local minimum wage increases are banned by the new state law.

So Indianapolis alt-labor advocates, and many local union members, have joined the effort to increase the federal minimum wage. They hold press conferences, write op-ed articles, and visit the offices of Indiana's congressional delegation, all in support of the Fair Minimum Wage Act.

Figure 4.1. Indianapolis Walmart worker Miryah Lazarapolis could not afford rent or food for her two children on part-time work at $7.40 per hour. Photo by Mark A. Lee.

The bill is designed to raise the federal minimum to $10.10 per hour, index the wage amount to inflation, and raise the tipped employee minimum from $2.13 per hour to 70 percent of the full minimum wage. As of the autumn of 2014, only two of Indiana's nine representatives to the U.S. House of Representatives had cosponsored the bill. The state's senators were split on the issue, with Senator Joe Donnelly supporting a minimum wage increase and Senator Dan Coats opposing it.

Some business owners have complained that efforts like minimum wage increase campaigns reflect unions simply trying to accomplish at the ballot box and in legislatures what they cannot achieve through collective bargaining. The antiunion Center for Union Facts launched a 2013 ad campaign claiming that worker centers push "the union agenda." Clearly, that is often an accurate depiction of alt-labor, especially when it refers to the recent successful UNITE HERE–supported ballot initiatives for hospitality worker wage increases. And many living wage ordinances contain exceptions for companies that have union contracts, thus creating a significant prolabor bargaining chip. But UNITE HERE, for one, is not apologizing. In fact, it is exploring similar tactics in Indianapolis.

Several years into the Indianapolis hotel worker campaign, UNITE HERE organizers recognized that the effort to sign up hotel employees for the union was not impacting the lives of many who toiled in the hotels every day. Those workers were employees of subcontracting firms, not the hotel, and thus not likely members of any unionized bargaining unit. "The subcontracting here is unlike anything that our unionized cities have ever seen," Mike Biskar says. "The majority of workers who clean rooms downtown are not direct employees. In the end, I don't think those are ever going to be good jobs until they are union jobs. But we knew we were still a while way from winning the union, and we wanted to respond to these workers' problems."

This posed a strategic and philosophical problem for the union, whose leaders have a skeptical view of stand-alone legislative or referendum efforts to raise the minimum wage, institute mandatory sick days, or otherwise impose favorable work conditions across the board. "Legislation drawing attention to these issues is a good thing because it helps public opinion, but in the end I think it has to lead to unionization in order to have lasting value," says UNITE HERE director of organizing Jo Marie Agriesti. "I just believe you have to organize the majority of workers in a workplace to fight. Otherwise, you can get a higher minimum wage or a few sick days, but they can still fire you for looking at them wrong. Then you have permanent sick days!" UNITE HERE director of research Antony Dugdale says that minimum wage increases in communities across the country are the result of successful union organizing, not a substitute for it. He says favorable across-the-board legislation usually passes because unionized workers there acted to make sure their contracts and employers are not being undercut by businesses paying substandard wages. "The workers [in those communities] were empowered to codify basic standards to make sure their competition was on a level playing field with them," Dugdale says.

But, in 2011, UNITE HERE faced a series of problems. The subcontracted workers in Indianapolis hotel were nowhere close to being unionized, nor did the community's union density or political climate support a minimum wage increase by legislation. Many of the subcontracted workers were undocumented immigrants, and thus were understandably reluctant to become the public faces of a campaign. So UNITE HERE decided on an approach that was far more modest than a living wage effort, but one the union felt would raise awareness of the poor wages and working conditions. The union persuaded friendly Democratic City-County Council members to propose what was called "Hotel Worker Tax Relief" legislation. The bill would have given a $200 local tax rebate for hotel workers earning less than $25,000 per year. Dugdale says the proposal was crafted to reflect the conservative politics of the region. "We were thinking about how we could build support in a red state with Republican-dominated politics. Something like a living wage for workers may work in a blue state, but it seemed that a tax break would connect better with working-class Republicans in Indiana," he says. "The wage tax is something concrete the city-county council could do. In Indianapolis's system [which limits council power], opportunities for them to make an impact like that are few and far between."

But for the hotel worker tax relief legislation to have any chance, the union would need to mobilize the community in support of the workers. By this time, UNITE HERE organizer Becky Smith had been working on that task for several years.

Smith grew up in Lafayette, Indiana, in a working-class family. Her father was a locksmith, and her mother worked in a bank. Before Smith, no one in the family had graduated from college. Smith earned an education and political science degree from her hometown Purdue University, obtaining a teaching license in the process. She began teaching fourth grade in a school located in Perry Township on the south side of Indianapolis. The teachers' union was engaged in a struggle against statewide cuts in public education spending, and Smith became active in the cause. She found that she enjoyed organizing rallies and events, but it did not seem like anything that would divert her from her career path in education.

Then, one Sunday night, Smith got a call at home. Word had leaked out that some members of the township school board planned to vote to fire the school superintendent at a meeting to be held the following night. Smith admired the superintendent, who worked well with the teachers but had clashed with some board members. Smith was asked if she could pull some people together to appear at the meeting in support of the superintendent. "I started making calls, and when it was too late to call people any more, I went to 24-hour store to get materials to make buttons and signs," she recalls. "I don't think I slept that night at all." A large crowd showed up to the meeting and local media filled the room. A school board member announced that teachers would not be allowed to give any statements. Smith argued that, as a local taxpayer, she had the right to be heard. She was thrown out of the meeting, and a majority of the board members voted to put the superintendent on involuntary leave. The protesters formed an organization to challenge the school board's actions. Within the year, Smith would be thrown out of two more school board meetings.

"The whole experience clearly fanned the flames of a fire that was, I think, already inside me," she says now. Smith describes her parents as "typical Hoosiers—they considered themselves lucky to have the jobs they did, and they had no interest in challenging the system." But, from an early age, the red-haired Smith looked at the world differently. She remembers traveling on family trips as a child to visit relatives in western Pennsylvania who had been working as coal miners for generations. During one of those visits, Smith's family went to see an exhibit about the Johnstown Flood. Smith was struck by the story of the 1889 disaster when the South Fork Dam, shoddily modified to provide a vacation home reservoir lake for wealthy families, collapsed. The resulting deluge killed over two thousand mostly working-class people who lived downstream. Smith was only in third grade, but an uncle responded to her obvious interest by giving her an adult-level book about the great flood. "I read that book three times over, and then I started reading other books about how working-class people get pushed around," she says. While still in elementary school, Smith began raising issues of class conflict around the family dinner table. Her developing sensitivity to injustice puzzled her more laid-back family members. Smith's brothers took to introducing her to their friends as "my sister Rebecca, the hippie."

Although the fight with the Perry Township school board continued, the superintendent was eventually fired. Smith began to grow restless in the classroom. She found herself increasingly disturbed by parent-teacher meetings where she learned that parents were working two or three jobs to make ends meet, leaving them with too little time and energy to help their kids with schoolwork. Smith volunteered to help with the state legislature campaign of the lawyer who represented the fired school superintendent. One day, Smith was going door-to-door passing out leaflets. The campaign manager realized that Smith's school was on spring break and asked her why she was not off on a beach somewhere. Smith had to think about that question for a minute. "I don't know," she finally replied. "I just like this kind of stuff." The campaign manager connected Smith with the UNITE HERE team, and Smith joined the union's staff shortly afterward.

Smith's original union assignment was to conduct research, but she was soon moved to community mobilization. There was plenty of work to be done. "At first, I would call up people and say I was with UNITE HERE and the response, even from people in the labor movement, would be, 'UNITE who?'" Lettie Oliver, a well-respected leader of the American Federation of State, County and Municipal Employees (AFSCME) and president of the Central Indiana Labor Council, took Smith under her wing and introduced her to local leaders and organizations. (Oliver died suddenly after an asthma attack in March 2010. She was fifty-eight.) Smith forged ties between UNITE HERE and local labor unions, along with some sympathetic religious leaders and community activists. Such alliances would add up to a vibrant network in a city like Chicago, Smith says, but the group was simply not large enough in Indianapolis: "My ability to get people out to demonstrations and events was pretty much capped at seventy-five people. Indianapolis is not a very politically active city, but in a metropolitan area of over a million people, I knew there had to be more potential supporters out there."

Smith faced an additional challenge. SEIU had conducted a vigorous community mobilization effort on behalf of Indianapolis janitors a few years before Smith began working for UNITE HERE. But SEIU abruptly pulled its organizers out of town after winning the union. Indianapolis community leaders were left to field the frantic calls from aggrieved janitors who could not reach their union representatives when there were contract violations and workplace disputes. When Smith came to see these community leaders, they were reluctant to again link arms with a service-sector union. In an unfortunate coincidence for Smith, the most visible departed SEIU organizer was also named Becky. "I remember my first meeting with Concerned Clergy [an African American social justice group] where I introduced myself to everyone," she recalled. "They said, 'Oh, yes, we remember you. You asked for our help, and then you left all the workers hanging.' I spent a long time just convincing people I was a different Becky!"

To build support for the hotel worker tax relief bill, Smith and the local UNITE HERE team decided to build a campaign around the theme of "Adopt-a-Worker." Since so many at-risk hotel workers were undocumented immigrants, and thus too vulnerable to make public statements for themselves, community supporters would each be asked to stand in—and speak out—for a worker. Now with a clear "ask" on her agenda, Smith began conducting one-on-one trainings with her handful of community allies. She sat down with ministers and professors and nonprofit staffers, coaching them on how to recruit among their own networks. They began to add to the coalition. Like many labor organizers, Smith started out with a reluctance to aggressively encourage others to take action. But now Smith was growing increasingly comfortable pushing supporters to step up their efforts, and she reached out beyond the usual labor supporters to make connections with small neighborhood groups.

Soon, red and black yard designs with silhouettes of workers and the slogan "They Deserve a Break, Too" began popping up across the city. Letters to the editor of the local *Indianapolis Star* were penned by residents who said why they were standing up for hotel workers. "I 'adopted' Maria and pledged to represent her at the [City-County Council] meeting because if she were to attend, she'd be fired from her Downtown hotel job which she has held for more than 10 years," community supporter Erin Polley wrote, in a letter published in the *Star* in August 2011. "At $9 an hour with no benefits, the job barely sustains her and she has to get food from a local shelter most weeks. Still, Maria needs the job and lives under constant threat of losing it."[18] In the summer of 2011, the City-County Council formally reviewed the tax relief proposal and put it to a vote. At these hearings, over three hundred community members, all wearing cardinal red UNITE HERE T-shirts, filled the Council assembly room and spilled out into the adjacent hallway. Their efforts earned a great deal of local media attention and the full support of all the Council's Democratic members. In October 2011, the tax relief plan was voted down on party lines, sixteen to thirteen.

Yet the legislative campaign was not over. Emboldened by the community support, hotel workers employed by temporary agencies were reporting that they were being turned away when they applied for permanent jobs in the hotels. Hotel officials and the temporary staffing agencies denied it, but multiple workers said they were told by hotel management that the hotels had promised not to hire the temporary agencies' employees.

At UNITE HERE's urging, Democratic Council members responded by proposing another ordinance, this one aimed at the alleged blacklisting.

They called it the Freedom to Work bill. They held more hearings that allowed workers to tell their stories and gave UNITE HERE an opportunity to again mobilize the community. In February 2012, the allegations of blacklisting formed a rallying cry at a four-hundred-person protest held outside the Hyatt Regency on the day before Indianapolis hosted the Super Bowl. "There have been decades of efforts by city government to build our local hotel industry, including direct and indirect subsidies to the hotels," City-County Councilor Brian Mahern scolded hotel representatives at one of the legislative hearings. "The community's goal was to create good paying jobs, so this is a real concern for us." Democrats, now holding a Council majority, passed the blacklisting ordinance, but the Republican mayor vetoed it. The union moved on to wage theft lawsuits against the temporary staffing agencies, and is considering an antitrust suit against the hotels and temporary agencies. If the party makeup of local government shifts, they say, they will pursue legislative action again.

5

THE FIGHT FOR 15

Like the Indianapolis legislative campaigns, the Fight for 15 was born out of frustration with the limits of traditional union organizing models in increasingly important industries. The same fast-food and low-wage retail companies that are so difficult to unionize are also the source of millions of jobs that U.S. workers rely on. Since the recession ended in 2009, the majority of jobs being created in the U.S. economy are low-wage positions.[1] One out of every four U.S. worker in the private sector makes less than $10 per hour, and many struggle to get full-time hours.[2] "I've talked to thousands of fast-food and retail workers in the recent months," Fight for Fifteen's Jerry Hellman said in 2013. "And the concerns always come back to wages and hours. And hours even more than wages. They are always on call with short notice, and you just can't make it on $8.25 an hour and thirty hours a week. But if you think, 'They should get a union,' the next thought is, 'Can they get a majority?' And that is a barrier."

In a traditional election or card-check (sign-up) union campaign, the union is established after a formally certified process establishes that a majority of workers choose to unionize. Compared to that process, Hellman says, the tactical freedom of the Fight for 15 has been liberating. "We don't need to count votes or cards to come up with a majority. We only need two or three people for a meaningful work action," he says.

Hellman is referencing Section 7 of the National Labor Relations Act, which protects workers' rights to engage in "concerted activities" for the purposes of not just collective bargaining but "other mutual aid or protection." U.S. labor law is usually invoked in the context of majority fights for union representation or collective bargaining over contracts. But the law also protects workers' rights to come together in much smaller groups to simply raise their voices and call for change. Workers are informed by Fight for 15 organizers of these rights before they strike, a reassurance that helps recruit commitments. But one of the other powerful forces behind the actions derives from many workers seeing their job conditions as so miserable that there is little to lose by striking. "I'm making minimum wage, plus 50 cents," KFC worker Shenita Simon told the *New York Times* in July 2013. "I can definitely find another job."[3]

Once a fast-food worker has decided to strike, the Fight for 15 template has been to collect and catalog workplace grievances and then file prestrike formal NLRB complaints about unfair labor practices. Often, these complaints include allegations of retaliation for collective action. Federal law protects a worker's ability to strike to protest unfair labor practices and still retain the right to return to work. By contrast, striking only to protest wages exposes the workers to permanent replacement. In the Fight for 15 model, community supporters are recruited in part to help support the picket line and in part to assist with the strikers' return to work. In New York City, after a Wendy's worker was barred from returning to her job site after a strike, local religious and government leaders occupied and picketed the store until the worker was reinstated.

Workers and organizers have discovered that a properly framed strike not only triggers legal protections, it creates conflict and drama that shines a spotlight on miserable work conditions. Retired Roosevelt University professor Jack Metzgar compared the fast-food strikes to the process of "witness," calling for attention to injustice in the spirit of draft card burning in the Vietnam War era. "In this case, it means taking the risk that they may be fired or otherwise disciplined for leaving work and going in the streets to proclaim, 'We are worth more,'" Metzgar wrote. "Witnessing is meant to make us think about justice as the witnesses simultaneously inspire and shame us with the courage of their individual actions."[4] At least one Fight for 15 action created instant inspiration. In May 2013, when managers at a Detroit McDonald's called on replacement workers to take the spots of strikers, the replacement workers saw the demonstration, listened to the message, and decided to join the strike themselves.[5]

The long-term goals of the Fight for 15 campaign are not clear. The preoccupation with public displays in the campaign has triggered some criticism. One labor activist said of the Fight for 15, "Instead of a 'march on the boss' directed towards the corporations robbing workers daily, rather this is a 'march on the media' where the strikes serve as the visuals in a narrative of worker protest crafted by professional media consultants."[6] Others speculate that the strikes will fuel legislative campaigns to raise the minimum wage or mandated polices on sick leave. "People ask me what I think this fast-food organizing is," says the antiunion Center for Union Facts' Justin Wilson. "I say that I think it is a play to have a conversation started about the minimum wage." Some lawyers, arguing that the original intent of the National Labor Relations Act was to allow workers to organize and bargain without needing to first demonstrate majority status, say that workers like the Fight for 15 activists should be allowed to form a minority or "pre-majority" union that employers would be compelled to bargain with in good faith.[7] More broadly, noisy and embarrassing exposure of worker exploitation could inspire large corporations to seek "labor peace" outside the formal union process, as was the case when Taco Bell changed its practices after facing the Coalition of Immokalee Workers' boycott.

The evening of Steve Rufo's July 24, 2013, mall organizing efforts, the second meeting of Indianapolis workers for the Fight for 15 is ready to begin. Rufo sits in a cramped back room of a nondescript, worn-down office building just north of downtown. In front of him are two pizzas, liters of Mountain Dew and Sprite, and a meeting agenda listed on white paper stuck on the office wall. Jerry Hellman paces by the front door of the building, waiting to direct workers to the meeting location.

The meeting is set to start at 8 p.m., but 8:10 has come already, and things are not looking good. There are only two workers here. One is a young man named Johnny, who works at the Sweet Factory in Circle Centre Mall. Johnny is friendly, but somewhat soft-spoken and reserved.

He came to last week's meeting, but he has already said he doubted that he could persuade any of his coworkers to strike. When union organizers are in the field, they sometimes refer to workers by way of a shorthand number system that indicates the workers' potential role in an organizing effort. The scale ranges from "one," a potential leader among other workers, to "five," an antiunion leader. Johnny appears to be a classic "two:" sympathetic to the union, but someone who will need a leader to follow.

The other attendee is a woman young enough that her mother brought her to the meeting. As Rufo tries to buy time for others to arrive, he receives a call from a Taco Bell worker whom he was counting on. Her ride has fallen through. The pizza and soft drinks sit untouched.

Rufo decides to plunge ahead. The meeting agenda begins with a recitation of workplace problems. Johnny makes only $7.75 an hour after a year and a half on the job. He has received a promotion but not an accompanying raise. The young woman works in a retail clothing store, where she has an abusive manager and wildly unpredictable hours.

Rufo uses a black marker to write the issues on the sheet of paper, and then tries to show a video commemorating the success of the Chicago Fight for 15 actions. The video starts with the legendary quote from Dr. Martin Luther King Jr.: "What good does it do to be able to eat at a lunch counter if you can't buy a hamburger?" But the Internet connection in the building is sketchy. The video halts and won't reload.

The meeting transitions to Hellman discussing what is listed on the agenda as "Plan of Action." With his 6' 4" frame folded into a small chair, Hellman peers over his glasses and delivers an animated explanation of how the process works. "Step one is talking to your coworkers," he says. "Find out who is as fed up and as brave as you are." He explains that the key number for workplace action is anything two or above—going on strike with coworkers is protected by the law in a way individual protests aren't. "You learned about the constitution in the eighth grade, but they never taught you the rights you can actually use—if you set up a strike correctly, you are protected from retaliation," he says. In the Chicago Fight for 15 action, he says, none of the hundreds of workers who struck lost their job.

For Indianapolis, the hope is for a critical mass of workers to strike on or near Labor Day, in conjunction with workers in as many as twenty other cities. The workers will go from job site to job site, holding brief demonstrations at each. In many respects, as the critics have said, these one-day actions do resemble public relations events more than traditional strikes. Hellman makes no apology for that, saying the goal is to attract as much outside attention as possible. "There are other ways to raise concerns, but nothing substitutes for the impact of a strike," he says. "The public takes notice when they see workers taking a risk."

Despite the sparse meeting attendance, the evening may not be a total loss. The young retail store clerk has been hanging on every word, and says she can get several coworkers to join in a strike. She asks a little more about the message. "Our first argument is pretty straightforward," Hellman says. "Stop friggin' hiring until the people already here are getting enough hours. That is a hard message for the companies to answer in public, because the truthful answer is they like to have people on call for fifty hours and only pay them for twenty-five."

The meeting wraps up so Hellman can drive an hour and a half north of Indianapolis to see another group of workers. This meeting is scheduled for midnight in Kokomo, Indiana, a city of forty-five thousand hit hard by the downturn in U.S. manufacturing. Kokomo is a fraction of the size of other cities that have been the site of Fight for 15 strikes, but organizers have been asked to advise a fired-up group of young workers at a KFC restaurant. The scenario is an example of "hot shop" organizing: the workers themselves are angry enough to reach out for help in forming a union. The KFC is one of dozens of fast-food establishments along Highway U.S. 31, which runs north-south through town on the way between Indianapolis and South Bend.

Hellman weaves between the orange barrels marking major construction along the highway, then turns east off the lighted thoroughfare onto a pitch-black country road. He parks in a driveway under a basketball goal as multiple dogs bark to herald his arrival. He is welcomed into the home and ushered into the darkened kitchen. Five young men and one woman are gathered around a table barely illuminated by a single, low-hanging overhead light. Some have come directly from the late shift at the KFC restaurant, one of fifty-two franchises owned by a Grand Rapids, Michigan–based company.

Unlike the earlier Indianapolis meeting, there is no need for introductory comments here. The workers are already committed and led by an intense young man who has done extensive research on the employer. He rattles off the grievances—hours, wages ("there is no such thing as a raise there"), safety issues. A grease-gun hose has a hole in it that causes workers to be sprayed with hot grease every shift. The air conditioner has broken down during the hottest weeks of the summer, and the kitchen floor is uneven and cracked, putting the workers at risk of falls. The young man asks about the state law on these conditions and inquires about the possibility of filing a complaint. Hellman gently diverts him from this path. "You don't want to wait for a government response," he says. "That process goes so slow you won't even believe it. What you do want to do is go directly to the public and demand that fair and safe conditions be part of the workplace. Think of the impact if a local clergy member goes to the manager and says, 'I know you want to have a safe workplace. So when are you going to get that hose fixed?'"

The Kokomo strike is also planned for near Labor Day. The KFC workers know other disgruntled fast-food employees, so they are ready to start recruiting fellow strikers. SEIU will reach out to UAW contacts in town—there is still some manufacturing activity here—and enlist community allies and clergy to accompany the strikers on their action and when they return to work.

This group needs no convincing, so Hellman focuses on the messages they will want to share with their KFC colleagues and other fast-food workers: if you work full-time, you should not be in poverty. Companies can pay $15 per hour if they raise their prices by just 2 percent, and the public would accept that. The job may be a nightmare, but you can change it.

Around the table, heads nod in agreement. It is now one in the morning, and Hellman stands up to leave. "The long-term goal is for you to be able to form unions across all the KFC's in the country, but that's a long way away," he says. "In the short term, let's get you some more money and more hours."

It is a hot Thursday afternoon three weeks later, and I am hanging out by the dumpster next to McDonald's. To be completely accurate, I am not standing next to the dumpster the entire afternoon. Fight for 15 organizer Marwan Mawiri and I sometimes sit in his car parked at the edge of the parking lot. Sometimes we walk down the alley just east of the intersection of 16th and North Meridian streets on the near-north side of Indianapolis. But it is by the dumpster where Mawiri ends up having most of his conversations with McDonald's workers headed home after their shift.

A worker leaves the restaurant, and starts walking in our direction. We are in Mawiri's car at the time, but when he spots someone in the distinctive all-black McDonald's uniform walking across the parking lot, Mawiri pops out and begins striding parallel with the worker. "You work at this McDonald's?" he asks. "Is it a good job?" The first answer to that question is a reflexive, "It's all right." But when Mawiri asks him a few more open-ended questions, the worker's frustration begins to bubble to the surface. The pay is too low—he makes only eight dollars an hour—and the managers seem to yank workers like him from cashier to making fries to the drive-through window without any clear plan. Neither Indiana nor federal law requires adult workers to be provided any breaks during a work shift, and this McDonald's management team takes full advantage. The worker routinely works eight hours straight without a minute of break time.

The McDonald's worker has never heard of the Fight for 15, but he pays close attention while Mawiri explains the concept. The two make for unlikely dumpster-side conversation partners: the worker is a young African American man still in his work uniform, Mawiri is older, a Yemeni American from Detroit who is fluent in Arabic and wears a long dark beard. Despite his appearance, Mawiri seems to have a knack for attracting minimum attention from companies wary of labor organizers. Before the most recent Chicago retail workers strike, several Fight for 15 organizers were kicked out of a downtown Sears store. But when they were replaced by Mawiri, he seemed to cause no suspicion. Mawiri has been sent along with a young woman organizer to help Rufo prepare for an August 29 Indianapolis strike, set to be coordinated among dozens of U.S. cities. Mawiri would spend the better part of two weeks in this McDonald's parking lot without being bothered.

It turns out the worker's girlfriend works at another nearby McDonald's, run by the same franchise holder as this one, and they have a young daughter. He says he does not really know what a union is, but he is intrigued when Mawiri turns the conversation toward the profits generated by the fast-food business. This is a bustling twenty-four-hour restaurant located at a major intersection headed into Indianapolis's downtown. It makes a lot of money, the worker says. Who is making the money, Mawiri asks. "We are making it, but Reggie [the owner] is keeping it!" the worker replies with gusto. Mawiri asks what power he and his coworkers have. The worker struggles with this question a bit. At first, he says they have no power. But he eventually concludes that they possess the power of their labor: Reggie does not make his money if the worker and his colleagues do not make the Big Macs. The worker carefully reads the strike agreement Mawiri gives him, and signs his name. Another McDonald's worker, also a young man, has already agreed to go on strike. When we see him a bit later by the dumpster, Mawiri tells him that a colleague has signed on to join him. The young man smiles. "That is good damn news," he says.

It is 5:45 a.m. on strike day, the Thursday before Labor Day, and Mawiri and I are again outside this same McDonald's. But this time, we are on the sidewalk next to Meridian Street, and dozens of other people are here with us, carrying signs and banging on drums made out of flipped-over plastic food tubs. Some of the chants are standard picket line fare: "We are the union / The mighty, mighty union," "Tell me what democracy looks like / This is what democracy looks like." Some are more tailored for the occasion: "Indy workers can't survive / making seven twenty-five," "Hold the burgers, hold the fries / Make our wages super size." It is still dark, but the high beams of TV cameras provide more than enough light. All four local television stations are here to chronicle the strike, most of them via live shots direct to the living rooms of early risers checking out the traffic and weather. The strike story is already featured in the morning's *Indianapolis Star*, and there is an explosion of online comments on the topic at the newspaper and TV stations. Throughout the day, local UNITE HERE and SEIU organizers and workers come to walk the picket lines. "It is clear these fast-food workers are affecting the national debate about wage inequality," Mike Biskar says.

My own role in this process has shifted. For weeks, I have been only an observer of the organizing efforts, albeit a persistent and sympathetic one. I took notes and asked the occasional interview question. But the fast-food strikes are nothing if not a public relations event, and as strike day approached the Indianapolis workers and organizers needed someone to fill the role of community spokesperson. I was asked to put on my law professor hat and help make the case that the workers were justified in their strike and deserved better treatment. So, as strike day dawns, I put my own reporter's notebook in my back pocket. I become the interviewee for multiple print, television, and radio reporters.

Today's strike is going on simultaneously in fifty-eight cities, and the national attention seems to fuel the local interest as well. The Indianapolis version of the strike covers three different locations, including a raucous lunchtime lap through Circle Centre Mall. TV cameras show up at each

spot. There are man-in-the-street interviews and graphics showing a prepared statement from McDonald's, asserting that they offer "competitive"
wages and that McDonald's often was a first job for workers who went on to
success elsewhere. In addition to interviews with the local journalists, I field
phone calls from reporters from the *Toronto Star* and the BBC. The latter
conversation goes well, but the host expresses surprise that there is any public
support for the workers. "You Americans do like your inexpensive fast food,
wouldn't you say?" he asks. I would also participate in the next day's "walk-
backs," lawyer-heavy escorts that accompanied the strikers back to the job.
All the striking Indianapolis workers returned to work without incident.

The strike provides an object lesson in the low-yield nature of organizing such a tenuous and unprotected workforce. Neither of the young
McDonald's workers who Mawiri and I talked to by the dumpster end
up striking, both apparently talked out of it by fearful family members.
The Kokomo KFC workers are not striking, either. One got into some
trouble with the law and one had a relative up for a management position
in another store. But several workers do strike, and they make a compel-
ling case for themselves and their colleagues. Tall, husky Dwight Murray,
wearing the iconic golden arches on his visor and uniform shirt, tells the
media what it is like to be twenty-seven years old, a father, and still making $8 an hour after three years at McDonald's. "I struggle with providing
child care and putting groceries on the table—it is very hard to do," he
says. "McDonald's is a six billion dollar company.[8] We are not asking to
be millionaires, but they can afford to pay us $15 an hour." Later, Murray
would admit that his girlfriend and his cousin had urged him to avoid the
strike, saying he risked losing his job. "I just thought this was a way to
get my voice heard without anyone resorting to violence or anything like
that," he said. In the days after the strike, several of Murray's coworkers
told him they wished they had walked out, too.

During the demonstration, Amber Hortoe tells a TV reporter she is
striking in support of her Taco Bell colleagues, even though many are
scared to walk off the job that day. "We bust our butts, me for just $7.50,
and that's just not enough," she says. Nick Williams, short and loquacious,
discovers that he enjoys access to a strike megaphone and TV cameras. The
front page of the next day's *Indianapolis Star* would feature a large photo of
Williams strutting in front of the picket line, wearing his McDonald's uniform and banging on a food-container drum. The outspoken retail worker

from the early Fight for 15 meeting does not strike, but quiet Johnny from the Sweet Factory is in the picket line all day. He says he might even want to talk on camera next time.

Julia Osborne, who answered the original online poll about worker treatment in Indianapolis, is on the picket line all day, too. "From the first time I talked to Steve, I was on board," she says. "I was excited; I was ready for something to happen." The small, thin Osborne, with her black hair pulled back and her McDonald's uniform on, is usually in the front line of the demonstration, often holding the main banner that reads, "Indy On Strike! #Fight for 15." A few times, I notice her looking around wide-eyed, taking in the unlikely specter of all the demonstrators and the noise and the TV cameras. Later, she would admit to being surprised that so many people would care about the problems of fast-food workers.

The last stop of the day is the McDonald's restaurant where Oswald works, located at a busy intersection on the south side of town off of U.S. 31. By now, the afternoon has turned scorching hot, and the demonstration breaks off for a few minutes so that people can get some water and shade. But, twelve hours after the strike day began, Osborne seems not to be tired at all. Several supporters and strikers crowd into a narrow strip of shade provided by a parked van, and Osborne takes advantage of the chance to hold court about the situation inside the restaurant. "There is one worker there who has been there six years and still makes only eight dollars an hour," she says. "They are treating us like a joke, but we are not a joke."

Osborne has recruited several of her coworkers to join the strike. ("She has real leadership potential," one organizer told me.) Turns out she is still not done organizing. When she spies one of her coworkers looking out wistfully at the demonstration from the restaurant's open drive-through window, Osborne calls out to the worker by name. "Come on, Bree," she yells. "I know you want to come out!" Then Osborne pulls together her striking colleagues to form an impromptu, pleading chant: "Come on out! We got your back! / Come on out! We got your back!"

Bree did not come out. But she later told Osborne that she was sorely tempted to do so, and that she would join her colleagues in the next strike. Several of Osborne's coworkers said the same, and a few managers even quietly expressed support for the demonstrations. "I feel we accomplished a lot, and we got our point across," Osborne said. "But there is still a lot to be done."

6

LEGAL PROBLEMS

When Indianapolis hotel workers and their supporters sought to pass the antiblacklisting ordinance through the City-County Council in the summer of 2012, one of the witnesses at the July 10 Council hearing was Elvia Bahena. Through an interpreter, Bahena told the Council that she had been employed at the temporary worker agency Hospitality Staffing Solutions, also known as HSS, for ten years. Her wages were very low, she had never received any health or retirement benefits from the company, and she complained of wage theft. (Bahena would eventually be one of the plaintiffs in the successful lawsuit against HSS.) When the new J. W. Marriott hotel opened in downtown Indianapolis in early 2011, Bahena applied for a permanent job with the hotel.

"They [J. W. Marriott personnel] asked me, 'Where do you work now?' I said, 'I currently work at HSS.' And they said that we can't hire you directly for the hotel because you work for the agency. They said I would have to quit my work at the agency for at least one year and then I could apply directly at the hotel," Bahena testified. "There is no way I could be without a job for one year. I have three children to take care of." Bahena decided instead to take a job at United Services Companies, another agency that provides temporary staffing for hotels.

Bahena's Council testimony was delivered in front of hotel industry representatives and broadcast on local cable access television. Two weeks after testifying, she was fired from United Services. After union advocates and local Council leaders alleged that Bahena was fired in retaliation for her testimony, United Services issued a statement that Bahena was merely "unassigned," citing unspecified performance issues.

Several months after her un-assignment, Bahena finally found work in an Indianapolis tomato processing plant, making the minimum wage of $7.25 per hour. Around the same time, her friends and union advocates held a small fund-raiser to help her and her family. At the entrance to a church hall on the near-east side of town, a glass jar was set up on a table at the entrance and people stuffed bills into it as they walked in. A pitch-in buffet table was laid out, and three young men climbed up on a small stage and began to play electric guitars. Bahena does not speak much English, so she was led around to greet guests by her former colleague-turned-UNITE HERE organizer Eva Sanchez. Bahena, less than five feet tall and with her dark hair pulled back into a ponytail, went up and down the buffet line with Sanchez, thanking each person there. As she did so, the band played a Lucinda Williams song: "It's over, I know it. But I can't let go."

Bahena was not the first Indianapolis hotel worker to learn that speaking out can be risky business. Longtime hotel bellman William Selm, a past Westin Hotel employee of the year and winner of the prestigious ROSE Award for hospitality workers, had always been a favorite of the hotel's customers and management. As recently as 2005, Selm had been asked to speak at an Indiana Statehouse rally in support of $275 million in government funding for an expansion of the Indiana Convention Center, a development with clear benefits to the local hotel industry. "They would often trot me out for causes like that, and I was fully in favor," Selm recalls. "I loved my job." But he also thought the job could be improved. So, in late 2007, he joined the union effort. "Things began to unravel pretty quickly after that," he says. A few months after receiving a petition asking that the union recognition process be started for its employees, the Westin terminated more than a dozen bellman positions, including Selm's. The Westin allowed the fired workers to reapply for their jobs with a subcontractor, but the offered pay was less. Six months later, the Westin subcontracted another thirty-plus positions of workers in the hotel's Shula Steakhouse.

Moving jobs from workers who are direct employees of the hotel to subcontracting agencies is an increasingly common phenomenon in the hospitality industry.[1] Hotels publicly state that the goal of subcontracting is to reduce administrative costs, but unions and workers say the real savings comes in sharply reduced wages paid to workers, including many undocumented workers hired by subcontractors. Union activists also say separating the jobs into different companies helps hotels avoid dealing with a coherent bargaining unit as defined under labor law. They also say the outsourcing reinforces the common racial division of labor between the largely white workers in the "front of the house" and the predominately nonwhite "back of the house" positions.[2]

Selm decided to take a job with a parking subcontractor, Towne Park. He continued his Westin bellman duties even though he was now compelled to surrender 40 percent of his tips to the new company. Then, in early 2009, Selm was told that the Westin wanted him removed from working at the hotel because Selm had complained to a coworker about the Westin's subcontracting trend. Westin general manager Dale McCarty acknowledged to the *Indianapolis Star* that he had told the subcontractor to transfer Selm, but he would not disclose his reasons for the move.[3] When I called the Westin to ask them about Selm's situation, a spokesman declined comment.

"What happened to Bill scared a lot of workers, there is no doubt about that," Mike Biskar said. The subcontracting practices were just one part of the local hotels' response to the Indianapolis organizing drive, a response that included both carrots and sticks. Soon after UNITE HERE's campaign was made public, the Westin and Sheraton held filet mignon and lobster dinners for their employees and gave them small raises. The Hyatt lifted a cap on long-time employees' salaries and allowed workers to keep a higher percentage of gratuities from room service meals. But the Westin also took disciplinary action against workers who joined a delegation seeking a meeting with the general manager, alleging the delegation was blocking guests' passage. After the union filed unfair labor practices complaints with the National Labor Relations Board, the disciplinary "write-ups" were eventually withdrawn. But Bahena, Selm, and other union advocates never got their old jobs back.

Unfortunately for Bahena and Selm, and for many U.S. workers who advocate for union representation, U.S. labor laws provide little meaningful protection for workers who are punished for speaking out. The core of U.S. labor law is found in the National Labor Relations Act (NLRA), known as the Wagner Act when it was adopted in 1935. Part of President Franklin Delano Roosevelt's "New Deal" package of reforms designed to address the devastating effects of the Great Depression, the Wagner Act formalized workers' rights to form unions, prohibited employers from discriminating against workers because of their union activity, and created the National Labor Relations Board (NLRB) to administer the law. But, in 1947, a Republican-controlled Congress amended U.S. labor law by passing the employer-friendly Taft-Hartley Act over President Harry Truman's veto. Taft-Hartley outlaws mass picketing and secondary strikes or boycotts and allows employers the option to block the practice of "card checks" that enabled unions to be recognized when a majority of workers signed cards saying they want to join. Taft-Hartley also neutralizes unions' ability to make an in-the-streets protest over unfair labor practices.

Even the union-friendly Wagner Act does not contain sufficient teeth to protect workers from employer retaliation. For example, the NLRA allows employers who fire workers for union activity to risk only the prospect of eventually having to pay back wages, minus any pay the workers may have earned in the interim. The law thus provides no disincentive for employers to crush a union through targeted firings. "It is just like if I were to break into your house and take your TV, and the worst thing that could happen to me is that I may have to put it back—after I use it for awhile," says Gordon Lafer, an associate professor at the University of Oregon's Labor Education and Research Center. Unsurprisingly, National Labor Relations Board data shows that one in every five union advocates can expect to be fired for their union activity.[4] Labor lawyer Thomas Geoghegan assessed the state of the current law this way: "Union busting now is almost a science. And the science is a pretty simple one: you go out and fire people. And keep firing until the organizing stops. . . . An employer who didn't break the law would have to be what economists call an 'irrational firm.'"[5]

The antiworker state of current U.S. law is part of a hostile political and legal environment for organized labor. In some ways, the current era was heralded in 1981 when President Ronald Reagan summarily fired eleven thousand unionized air traffic controllers and imposed a lifetime ban on their rehire, sending a clear signal to employers across the country that they were free to deal harshly with union activity.[6] Under current law and practice at the NLRB, there has been virtually no penalty for employers who refuse to bargain in good faith with unions representing their workers. Predictably, barely half of workers are able to secure a contract with their employer even after their union has been recognized by the National Labor Relations Board.[7] For workers who go out on strike for economic reasons, as opposed to striking in protest of unfair labor practices, the law provides no protection against them being permanently replaced by the employer.

Since the passage of the antiunion Taft-Hartley Act, there have been several efforts to remake U.S. law to better defend workers' rights. In 1978, during President Jimmy Carter's term, a bill was proposed in Congress to allow for immediate reinstatement of workers fired for union organizing and to increase penalties for employers who engaged in union-busting. Similar proposals were floated during President Bill Clinton's first term in 1993 and 1994. But no changes were ever passed. When another Democrat, Barack Obama, was elected president in 2008, prolabor members of Congress promoted the Employee Free Choice Act. EFCA would allow card check recognition and increase employer penalties for violation of the NLRA. It would also bypass drawn-out first contract negotiations by allowing binding arbitration of the terms when negotiations reached an impasse. Card-check procedures and first-contract arbitration are allowed under Canadian labor law, and EFCA advocates say the Canadian system effectively blocks employers from bullying workers through an antiunion election campaign and from stalling the contract negotiations through bad-faith negotiations.

At this writing, EFCA appears to have little chance of passage into law. After EFCA's introduction, employers launched an opposition lobbying campaign that has successfully labeled the card-check provisions as antidemocratic. An employer group aired anti-EFCA ads showing the actor who played mobster Johnny Sack in "The Sopranos" forcing a worker to sign a union card. Center for Union Facts' Justin Wilson says that EFCA is the labor movement's attempt to distract from the real reason for its struggles. "The real problem is that unions are having an increasingly difficult time finding workplaces where the workers are so frustrated that they are willing to go to a [union] meeting," Wilson says. "Unions have an enormous number of opportunities to do things to make sure employees know they are there and trying to organize. If employees truly want the union, they would have no problem getting each others' contact information." Even some worker advocates are not enthusiastic about EFCA, saying its first-contract arbitration process takes workers out of the process, and that the other provisions would not resolve many of the most notorious problems with current U.S. labor law.

To some union advocates, the preferred remedy is to scrap the NLRA altogether. "I say abolish the Act," AFL-CIO president Richard Trumka declared back in 1987. "Abolish the affirmative protections of labor that it promises but does not deliver as well as the secondary boycott provisions that hamstring labor at every turn."[8] Geoghegan and others say that labor unions were better off in the deregulated days before the Wagner Act. At that time, the 1932 Norris-LaGuardia Act provided no affirmative right to organize but stripped federal courts of jurisdiction to enjoin strikes or to enforce "yellow dog" contracts that employers used to block union membership. Workers had the legal right to conduct sit-down strikes, mass pickets, and secondary strikes. Law professor James Gray Pope and union leaders Peter Kellman and Ed Bruno say that Norris-LaGuardia was the strongest workers' rights statute ever enacted in the United States. Labor advocates pushed for Norris-LaGuardia by invoking the Thirteenth Amendment's ban on involuntary servitude, Pope, Kellman, and Bruno point out. They argue that a new labor rights movement should be similarly grounded in the Thirteenth Amendment and the significant international human rights law protections for workers' freedom to organize.[9]

University of Texas law professor Julius Getman, one of the country's leading experts on labor law, agrees that the NLRA is deeply flawed. But Getman says the Act is worth saving, albeit with significant changes. Getman argues that the law should grant unions and employers equal access to employees at the workplace, counteracting the "captive audience" effect when employers enjoy exclusive rights to use the workplace forum to argue against the union. He also believes that the NLRA should not allow employers to permanently replace workers who are exercising their right to strike, and that it should provide for faster and more severe penalties for employers' unfair labor practices. In an interview for this book, Getman takes the position that Taft-Hartley's prohibition of secondary boycotts and organizational picketing violates the First Amendment and should be struck down by the courts, if not by Congress.[10] "It seems impossible to me that the First Amendment protects Westboro Baptist Church members' right to picket military funerals [as allowed in the 2011 U.S. Supreme Court decision[11]] and corporations can spend unlimited amounts of funds to affect political campaigns [as allowed in the 2010 U.S. Supreme Court decision in *Citizens United v. Federal Election Commission*[12]], but unions can't use their best weapon, which is the appeal to other unions."[13]

The sorry state of U.S. labor law clearly has a negative impact on union organizing. "You take away [the prohibition on] secondary boycotts, I'll organize 30,000 hotel workers in a year," one high-level UNITE HERE organizer told Getman.[14] But many unions take pride in their ability to organize workers even in hostile legal environments. UNITE HERE, for example, often points to successful union drives it has led in right-to-work states. Strong labor laws are important, organizers like Mike Biskar say, but they cannot distract unions from the core mission of organizing workers. "It seems like the labor movement is in this transition period where for many years we were taking on fights and losing, so now we've stopped taking on fights," Biskar says. "Now the labor movement overall is in a phase where everything is in the legal realm, and we've supposedly got to fight things just in the legal realm." Jane McAlevey, a former top SEIU organizer, makes a similar point more colorfully: "Screw labor law, and definitely screw the Democratic Party as we know it. We know how to do the work."[15]

To some union advocates, the hue and cry over right-to-work legislation is a symptom of this disease. In Indiana, as in other states, the individual rights and freedom-to-choose language used to support right-to-work laws resonates more strongly with the public than the counterarguments couched in terms like "right to shirk [paying union dues]" or "right to work for less." The concept of workers getting to choose whether to contribute to a union is a good match for the individualistic culture of the United States. Labor historians like Nelson Lichtenstein say that the right-to-work argument, where businesses have appropriated the rhetoric of the civil rights and women's rights movements, is just one example of a larger problem for labor: the notion of individual rights has been elevated over collective solidarity in both U.S. law and the culture.[16]

Many labor advocates expect that a federal right-to-work law may be in place in the near future. Even in public, some union supporters express frustration over the labor movement mobilizing chiefly around issues like right-to-work that appear to the public to be more about preserving union finances than about workers' rights to fair wages and treatment. Opposing "right-to-work is essentially a way to maintain union membership, not expand it," worker advocate Shawn Gude wrote after Michigan passed right-to-work legislation in December 2012. "It's the instrument of unions who rest on their laurels . . . [and] corralling antipathetic workers and collecting their dues was never a sustainable model."[17]

Mike Biskar and other UNITE HERE organizers do not dismiss the value of legislative advocacy or litigation. UNITE HERE has done both in Indianapolis, in the form of the proposed ordinances giving hotel worker tax relief and outlawing blacklisting. Legislative strategies like living wage ordinances have been critical for its efforts on behalf of hospitality workers in many communities. But Biskar says strong labor laws are the product of good organizing, not the platform for it. "When will labor laws improve and when will politicians stand up for workers?" he asks. "When workers are organized."

7

UNITE HERE

Angel Castillo stands in front of the large room in UNITE HERE Local 1's downtown Chicago office, the home base for the training of Indianapolis organizers and workers. He claps his hands vigorously to quiet down the chatter of the four dozen people seated before him. His audience is a group of hotel, university, and casino workers from the Chicago area who are identified by the union as rank-and-file leaders. That means these cooks, cashiers, bellmen, and housekeepers have led delegations to the bosses, gone on home visits to recruit new union members, and lead worker committees of as many as one hundred people or more. The majority of today's attendees are women, and most are either African American or Latino. Earlier during 2013 the versions of these monthly Saturday meetings focused on winning a union contract at the Hyatt. The workers in this room pulled out five hundred of their colleagues in Chicago for demonstrations that helped seal the local contract and a nationwide agreement. Both were finalized just a few weeks before this gathering.

But the workers are not here this morning to celebrate the recent victory. Once the crowd quiets, Castillo starts the meeting with a near shout, "Today is about new organizing!" he says. He lets that sink in for a moment, and then begins again. "Let me tell you some history: Unions used to be real strong here, and then they got real weak. Who here worked in the hotels in 1999?" A few hands go up. "Were the unions strong then?" Castillo asks. "No!" comes the answer from the veterans.

"Do you know where our union is most strong now?" Castillo asks. "Vegas! If you want to run a hotel or casino in Vegas, you have to work with the union. That is where we need to get in Chicago, too." Castillo cues up a short film about UNITE HERE's success in Las Vegas. It is a town where hospitality workers enjoy a standard of living that is unmatched in any other U.S. city, and the film features cocktail servers and cooks talking about earning pay, benefits, and job security they never thought possible in their line of work. Then the film transitions to a review of the struggles that won the union this strength, including multiple citywide strikes in the 1970s and early 1980s, and a strike against the Frontier Hotel and Casino that lasted a full six years. The Frontier strike was one of the longest in labor history and the eventual worker victory in 1997 inspired a documentary film of its own, *One Day Longer*, and earned the union a reputation for tenacity. In Las Vegas, the union insisted on contracts that would guarantee that workers in new casinos and hotels would be able to earn union representation whenever a majority of workers sign a statement, or card, that they want to join the union. The agreements also typically call for the hotels to refrain from opposing the union campaign, a promise known as "card check neutrality." Today, all but one hotel on the iconic Las Vegas Strip is unionized.

While the film plays, the stories of union success produce several cheers and an occasional excited "Yes!" from the Chicago workers. After the film ends, Castillo sticks a large sheet of blank white paper on a board at the front of the room and asks the workers to identify the crucial elements of the Las Vegas union success. The paper quickly fills up with their observations—citywide solidarity, the workers became the movement, card check neutrality, organizing the new hotels. Then Castillo makes his transition. "Now, let's talk about Chicago! What have been the turning points for our accomplishments here?" Another white sheet is produced, and workers call out items to be listed there. The people in this room have conducted multiple short strikes at the Hyatt, won a strike of the cafeteria at Chicago State University, and marched down the city's "Magnificent Mile" on Michigan Avenue. They won a bitter three-year struggle with the Blackstone Hotel, earning back pay and a return to work for fired union leader workers.

"And how did we get here?" Castillo asks.

"A lot of house visits!" a woman shouts. Heads nod in agreement, remembering weekend and evening treks to coworkers' homes to persuade them of the value of joining the union. "A lot of door knocking," she concludes. "The turning points were when we organized the [workplace] committees."

Castillo's fellow UNITE HERE organizer Lou Weeks, tasked with writing the notes on the paper tacked to the front wall, quickly scribbles down this observation. Weeks and other union staffers and members say that this training of worker leaders captures the essence of UNITE HERE's approach to growing the labor movement. When the training pauses for a quick lunch, Weeks talks to me about the mission behind these sessions. "There has never been a movement that truly changed things that was led by paid people," he says. "That includes the successful labor movements— they were all led by rank-and-file membership." He points toward two women, one Asian American and one Latina, sitting together and talking over their sandwiches. An African American woman, paper plate in hand, walks over to join them. These are housekeeper leaders of the Hyatt union, Weeks explains. 'There is nothing more scary to the boss than seeing something like that," he says, referring to the women's different ethnicities. "It completely undermines the strategy of divide and conquer."

Castillo does not allow the group to linger over lunch very long, much less bask in the glow of their accomplishments. He returns to the list of Chicago hotels and cafeterias and casinos where the union has contracts. "Now that we have won in these places, we need to build our union," he says. He tacks up another white sheet of paper and draws an enormous circle. "Here is the pie of the hospitality industry here," he says, then shades in about half of the circle. The union represents only 48 percent of hospitality workers in the community, and Castillo points out that the nonunion piece of the pie grows with every new hotel opening without a union contract. Union "density" is the key to high contract standards and stability, as a large number of nonunion shops depresses wages and saps the bargaining power of union workers. In Las Vegas, UNITE HERE claims about 90 percent density in major hotels, and Chicago has a long way to go to catch up. So Castillo tells the workers they will spend the rest of the day preparing for a "blitz" campaign of home visits to nonunion Chicago workers. Before dividing the workers into small groups for preparation and role-playing exercises, he points one last time to the list of Chicago accomplishments. "If we want to have more moments like these, we have to do new organizing!"

Castillo's call for new organizing is later echoed by Karen Kent, the newly elected president of UNITE HERE's Local 1, based in Chicago. Kent is the first woman to ever hold that post. The daughter of a Boston stockbroker father and a mother who was a substitute teacher, Kent got her union baptism while working as a banquet server at the Holiday Inn Palo Alto. Her coworkers began organizing a union under the Teamsters, and Kent decided to join in. She was content to be a follower of her more experienced—and 100 percent male—colleagues, at least until the day the owner of the hotel called a mandatory staff meeting to rail against the union. Kent kept waiting for one of her colleagues to stand up and respond. "I remember thinking, 'OK, guys, it is time to speak up here. The meeting is going to end soon.' But no one was saying anything," she says. "Finally I just got up and did it. I was terrified, but I could not have lived with myself if I didn't say something." The owner responded to Kent's statement by shutting down the meeting, but Kent had won a battlefield promotion. Her coworkers looked to her for leadership now, and the union won the election by a 2–1 margin.

Kent says she can empathize with workers who are reluctant to make uninvited visits to their coworkers' homes and to speak up against the boss. "When people tell me how hard it is, I completely get it," she says. "But I just say, 'I know you're scared, but you have to do it anyways. We all do.'" Kent and other UNITE HERE leaders feel so strongly about the need for new organizing that they agreed to longer-than-usual five-year contracts in 2013 so that the staff and membership could dedicate their energies to growing the union's membership in Chicago. "Our members see how important this is," she says. "When we had a higher union density here, we won contracts faster and more easily. With the growth spurt in hotel development in downtown Chicago, we have no choice but to get out there and organize, organize, organize."

Every modern-day union voices a commitment to new organizing and worker empowerment, but UNITE HERE may be the most dedicated to making good on those pledges. The monthly rank-and-file leader trainings in Chicago are unique to UNITE HERE, and the iconic Vegas success story begins and ends with strong worker leadership. The union's most dedicated and skillful workplace leaders—like James Meyers in Indianapolis and several of the people in the Chicago training—routinely take union-paid leaves of absence from their regular jobs in order to organize new workers or help with contract campaigns.

Julius Getman devoted a significant portion of his 2010 book, *Restoring the Power of Unions: It Takes a Movement*, to describing the modern-day UNITE HERE as a model that the broader labor movement needs to emulate.[1] In a 2013 interview for this book, Getman repeated his belief that UNITE HERE sets the standard for worker empowerment. "They are committed to constantly training and constantly searching for organizers among the workers," Getman said. "Even SEIU, who also does a lot of new organizing, does not have the same commitment to worker training and involvement in continual organizing that UNITE HERE has."

The modern-day version of the union represents the combination of the former Hotel Employees and Restaurant Employees International Union (HERE) and the Union of Needletrades, Industrial, and Textile Employees (UNITE). UNITE was itself a successor union to the storied Industrial Ladies Garment Workers' Union and the Amalgamated Clothing and Textile Workers Union, whose battle with the J.P. Stevens Company was immortalized in the movie *Norma Rae*. The seemingly odd-bedfellows pairing of the two unions in 2004 made sense, according to former UNITE HERE president John Wilhelm, who originated with HERE. "We had an industry that can't move overseas, and no money, and they [UNITE] had an industry that was rapidly disappearing [in the United States] and piles of money," he said.[2]

A high-profile complement to HERE's Las Vegas success was the union's successful organizing of Yale University workers in the late 1980s and 1990s. Led in part by veterans of the Yale fights, the union is known for its skillful use of comprehensive campaigns, sometimes known as corporate campaigns. Those efforts weaken the targets of organizing by leveraging the union's community alliances, government contacts, and public relations outreach. The legendary Frontier Hotel strike was concluded in part because the union uncovered illegal activities that jeopardized the union-resistant owners' casino license. Similarly, the 2013 agreement with the Hyatt, which covered the Chicago hotels along with several others, was triggered in part by a corporate campaign. First, UNITE HERE led an international boycott of Hyatt hotels, characterized by multimedia "Hyatt Hurts" PR outreach. Then it cited the hotel's clash with the union when protesting President Obama's nomination of Hyatt Hotels heir Penny Prisker to be the U.S. secretary of commerce.

UNITE HERE is known for preferring to build its union through community-based campaigns instead of the formal NLRB election process. The union's leaders say such campaigns more reliably lead to contracts and naturally create community support that can be mobilized to prevent or respond to retaliation against workers, which the NLRA does not effectively address. UNITE HERE also believes that the employee activism required for a strong comprehensive campaign ensures a committed workforce, and that in turn helps inspire dues contributions in right-to-work states.[3]

UNITE HERE has not escaped criticism. Previous generations of HERE leadership were alleged to be corrupt and connected to organized crime, and the current organizing model has been the subject of former organizers' complaints. They alleged that the union used information shared as part of its "personal story" organizing model to intimidate and suppress dissent within the organization. The process known as "pink sheeting" was expressly forbidden by the union in early 2009.[4] Other organizers have registered a complaint, an age-old concern among labor activists, that the union engages in a hierarchical system of organizing that elevates staff decision making over workers' priorities.[5]

But, like Getman, the UNITE HERE staffers and members I spoke with focused on the union's dedication to empowering and training worker leaders. "We see building the [internal workplace] committee as the core of our work," says Baltimore lead organizer Tracy Lingo. "To do that, we have to commit to a deep focus on leadership development. Working-class people who can lead and inspire others are the ones who really create social change." Some union staffers say it is impossible to conclusively identify strong workplace leaders in their early contacts. "Some of the folks who you think are going to be great break your heart, and some keep learning and growing and amaze you," Lou Weeks says. "The capacity to learn is much more important than giving a good speech."

In a separate conversation, Mike Biskar says the same phenomenon has occurred in the Indianapolis organizing. "Obviously, passion and charisma count in determining who is a good leader. But I think most of the stuff people can learn if they really want to," he says. "It's not enough to be excited the weekend we sign everyone up, because everyone is excited that weekend. You got to have the hunger to learn and grow." Workers who are set in their ways don't tend to assume leadership roles, he says. But the workers who do—even those who are middle-aged and beyond—evidence a remarkable commitment to lifelong learning and personal growth. In Indianapolis, both James Meyers at IUPUI and James Holder at Marian University identify the process of learning new skills as a core attraction for being involved in the union. Sixty-one-year-old Cathy Youngblood, a West Hollywood, California, Hyatt housekeeper who was put forward by the union as a candidate to be the first-ever worker on the Hyatt board of directors, proudly told me, "There is not a day that goes by that I don't learn something that makes me better."

Back at the Chicago rank-and-file training, the worker leaders are now in small groups. The first task in the group sessions is for everyone present to identify the moment when they decided they would "fight for change" in the workplace. Will Spain is a veteran Hyatt bellman who today wears an off-hours uniform of navy blue Chicago Bears cap and matching polo shirt. He says his moment came when managers falsely alleged that he had charged a guest five dollars to carry a bag. Spain was suspended for eight days, but his coworkers put up signs at the hotel saying "Bring Will Back!" A server named Dante got motivated when a coworker was unjustly fired. Meno, a cook, reached his tipping point when he realized that people of color were never being allowed to work in the front of his restaurant.

Misti Crull shared her moment, too. After graduating with a chemistry degree from Loyola University, Crull had worked in financial investigation positions with credit card agencies and the City of Chicago. When she turned forty, Crull decided to pursue a long-held dream and enroll in culinary school. During her very first semester of training, she was hired to cook at the Fairmount Hotel. Educated and savvy about workplace dynamics, Crull was blessed with a high level of self-confidence. She certainly did not think of herself as someone who needed union protection.

But, one evening after work, Crull and another woman cook went out for drinks with a couple of male cooks who the more experienced women had recently trained on the job. "We thought, 'This is great, they [the management] are trusting us to train these guys.' We felt pretty good about ourselves," she says. Then one of the men proposed a toast to their recent promotions. Crull and the other woman had no idea what they were talking about. Neither the male or female cooks knew it, but it turned out that the women had been training the men to be promoted above them.

At the time, Crull did not even know who her union shop steward was. But she quickly found him, and he connected her with a UNITE HERE staffer. The women filed grievances, and the union staffer won them backdated promotions and several thousand dollars each in back pay. The union staffer was Angel Castillo. "What I learned was that it should be impossible to have gender discrimination in a union shop," Crull says. "That's the beauty of a collective bargaining agreement. When it comes to gender, age, race, sexual orientation, you name it: if we are doing the same job, we get the same pay." Soon, Castillo circled back to Crull and told her it was time to pay it forward with other workers she could help.

Unions have a saying: nothing organizes like winning. Worker activists are often people like Crull who have seen the power of a union successfully exercised. But Crull was not fully on board at first. Her midcareer switch to the kitchen had worked beautifully for her, and she liked her job at the Fairmount. She was hesitant to risk her position by angering management with aggressive advocacy for her fellow workers. That changed when a new chef was hired and announced plans to reduce the hours of an Asian American cook who had been with the hotel for over fifteen years. The chef said the veteran cook could not do the job because she spoke little English. Crull was furious, and she pushed the matter to a meeting with the hotel human resources director. There, she told the chef that the cook was doing a damn good job without speaking English before the chef arrived and she would still be doing a damn good job when he was long gone. "And that turned out to be the case," Crull says, laughing. "Seriously, once I started looking around at the problems and unfairness happening to my colleagues all around me, I woke up. And once you are awake, you cannot go back to sleep."

Crull now works directly for the union two or three days each week, advocating for workers when the union feels that management is breaking the law or not honoring its agreement. The role is a good fit for her, as Crull is not the least bit shy about going toe-to-toe with corporate bosses or their lawyers. Once I saw her introduced to a union cook at a different hotel, and she said matter-of-factly, "Oh yeah, I was just at your hotel the other day. I had to cut the balls off the lead chef there because he was violating your contract." One of the UNITE HERE organizers admits to being more than a little afraid of Crull: "Whenever I pass by her in the office, she is on the phone screaming at a HR director or somebody. Every time I see her, I think, "Thank God you're on our team.'"

Crull has had multiple offers of a full-time union assignment, but turns them down each time. She still wants to cook at her hotel several days a week. At a picket line a few years ago, a veteran union leader told Crull there is no more important position in a union than a shop steward, and she took that to heart. She loves the fact that union fights are usually about the rights of others, not just members' individual self-interests, and she sees UNITE HERE as unusually focused on the needs of the working poor: "When people talk about the gap between the rich and the poor, that is not make-believe. So we are putting our focus on the folks who make minimum wage, and we are saying that you can do better. These are people who want to support their families and not rely on public benefits, so a livable wage and contract terms like sick leave and guaranteed hours can really change lives."

I soon learned that Misti Crull is a Hoosier. She grew up on her grandparents' two-hundred-acre corn and soybean farm in Blackford County, near the town of Hartford City about an hour's drive northeast of Indianapolis. She remembers adults in the area working in just three types of jobs: farming, minimum wage jobs, and union jobs, the latter mostly in auto manufacturing. Minimum wage workers' families struggled and union workers' families were financially stable. But Crull's grandparents never talked about politics or the economy, and the only political activism Crull remembers growing up was a Ku Klux Klan march in a nearby town. Crull enrolled at Indiana University, and her grandparents drove down to visit once a month with their pickup truck filled with canned goods and groceries. "Other kids would have ramen noodles, and I was the kid who had a ham," she says. "It was fantastic." After a few years of having what she describes as a bit too much fun in the college town of Bloomington, Crull moved to Chicago. She reenrolled in college, and began to work. But she still returns monthly to visit her family in Indiana.

Her grandparents left her the farm after they passed away, and she intends to move back there for good one day.

So Crull is closely following UNITE HERE's work in Indianapolis. "Indiana is a self-reliant state, and most people have real pride in their own sustainability," she says. "But there is also such a clear divide between the rich and the poor. You look around and see all this wealth right in our faces. You see people paying $40,000 per year for a kid to go to school and then the university workers get minimum wage. You see the universities building these multimillion dollar facilities. You are happy for them and the students, but the workers there have no health insurance? Really? Whether it is food service or the airport or the hotels in Indianapolis, I am proud that we are working with people that no one else is targeting."

At the UNITE HERE training, in Misti Crull's and multiple other small groups, the workers frankly discuss the fear they once had of filing grievances, standing up for coworkers, and putting their jobs at the mercy of angry bosses. "Sharing stories is important because the message from the companies is, by and large, that the workers are stupid and deserve their circumstance. The message is that it is their fault they are cleaning toilets," Weeks says. "Stories inspire folks because they hear from role models who face the same challenges they do. If you are an African American in Chicago, you can see yourself as poor and as someone with family members in prison, and you can think you don't deserve any different. Or you can see yourself as someone who has persevered through real challenges."

Several worker leaders admit they knew almost nothing about the union before fellow workers knocked on their door. Their stories and disclosures in the group scenes are followed by role-play exercises where the workers rehearse making these same home visits to nonunion members in the city. At this stage of the day's meeting, the concept of new organizing makes the transition from an abstract idea to a concrete agenda. Fresh off its Hyatt contract success, UNITE HERE is organizing a Chicago casino-hotel with 450 employees, and the workers here will soon be the stars of the outreach to potential new union members. The name of the hotel is not disclosed at the meeting—its union-supporting workers are still "underground"—but the goal is no secret. UNITE HERE wants to get 70 percent of the hotel's workers signed up to support the union before the effort goes public. "It is demoralizing for the boss when they see the ratio is two to one," Castillo says. "When we get to 70 percent, we feel powerful."

The small groups wrap up the role-play, and the workers reconvene in the larger room to sign up for home visits and a likely mass demonstration at the targeted hotel. Before they adjourn, Castillo introduces the gathering to Mike, a bartender at the nonunion hotel being targeted. Workers there are on constant video surveillance, Mike says, and he has been placed on "final warning" status because he allegedly undercharged a customer in the amount of two dollars. As he explains the situation, Mike shoves his hands in his pockets and nervously shifts his weight from one foot to the other. Castillo opens the floor for questions. Will Spain asks him if he is scared about what might happen. Mike admits that he is worried that he will be fired for supporting a union.

Misti Crull raises her hand. "Mike, I just want to let you know that everyone here has been where you are at," she says. Heads nod across the room. "They always target the leader, but we have your back. If you get fired, we'll fight them about that. You are not alone."

Mike smiles in appreciation. But Crull is not done.

"Oh, and by the way," she says. "You *will* get the union."

The room erupts in cheers.

8

STRUGGLING FOR CONTRACTS

Rebecca Bradley is our host at her home just a few miles west of Butler University's campus, but it is clear that she would lead the conversation wherever we were meeting. She laughs freely, her deep voice always the first to weigh in on the questions about the working conditions in Butler's food service. Tanya Gray is more reserved. She speaks less, and only after giving the subject some thought.

The women grew up near each other on Indianapolis's west side. Both attended Crispus Attucks High School, long the home of African American students in Indianapolis's then-segregated school system. They are both grandmothers now, and they share the distinction of long tenures serving food to the students, faculty, and staff at Butler, a private school on the north side of Indianapolis. The university has a small enrollment of just forty-five hundred students, but its sprawling, leafy campus with Gothic buildings is situated on 295 acres running next to the White River. Butler also has a big price tag: a student's tuition plus room and board runs almost $50,000 per year. Bradley is a grill cook at the Atherton Union, the main campus dining hall. Gray preps the salad bar at a residential hall cafeteria. Bradley has been at Butler for twenty-seven years, Gray for twenty-two.

The first thing Bradley and Gray want me to know is that they like their jobs. "We love the students," Bradley says. "They come and go and then they come back and see us, and they say, 'Oh, I remember you from 1987!' Even when you are having a bad day, the kids can make you smile."

Gray nods. "The kids are what have kept us there. We enjoy our job— how many people can say that?"

But all is not well in the world of Butler food service. Several years ago, the university contracted the work out to private companies, first Marriott, Inc., and now Aramark, a multinational food service and facilities management company. Most of the company's workers at Butler make little more than $8 per hour. The company does not contribute anything to their retirement accounts, something both Bradley and Gray say they learned only after they had paid into the accounts for several years.

When management decides what hours to assign, their seniority seems to carry no weight. "I've never had a weekend off, period," says Bradley, who works each Sunday. Workers must pay 80 percent of the employer-provided health insurance, with Aramark kicking in only 20 percent. Only five or six of the one hundred Butler Aramark workers choose to enroll in the plan. Gray, who is in her fifties, is one of the exceptions. "It is not that I can afford it," she says. "It is just that I can't be without it."

The burden of maintaining the insurance and paying other bills gets much heavier in the summer months, when most of the Butler workers are laid off. "Last summer, I got a letter in the mail that said if I wanted to keep the insurance, I would have to pay about $400 per month. I thought, OK, I have no job, I don't have income, so how am I supposed to keep my insurance?" Gray says. Some Butler workers who lose their insurance in the summer have had their checks garnished to collect on health care bills. Both Bradley and Gray have spoken to food-service workers at IUPUI and at campuses outside Indianapolis. They found that their counterparts had more predictable hours, more affordable health care, and that their employers contributed toward their retirement.

Those workers have a union contract, and Bradley, Gray, and the Butler workers are now pushing for the same status. In 2012, the workers began meeting quietly to talk about the possibility of joining UNITE HERE, which had already organized food-service workers at the Indianapolis

International Airport as well as at IUPUI. About a dozen Butler workers formed an organizing committee and spent fifteen months "underground," not sharing their plans with the company or even all of their coworkers. Then they circulated a document called a "Petition for a Fair Process," asking Aramark to recognize the union if a majority of workers signed statements supporting the union. The committee went public, published a flier with their photos and names, wore union buttons to work, and asked their coworkers to sign up.

Bradley and Gray had long known what impact a union could have. Both of their fathers were union members. Gray's eighty-seven-year-old father still attends his union meeting the first Tuesday of each month. "When we found out about a union, baby, we were ready!" Bradley says. After a strong majority of workers signed a statement of support for the union, Aramark agreed to talks that could lead to the Butler workers' first contract. As the negotiations begin, Bradley and Gray have tangible goals for both pay and security. "I want to pay some bills and get that stress off me," Bradley says. Gray is a little more future-oriented. "I have been working a long time, and I want to get some kind of retirement benefit," she says.

The union buttons they wore on the job had just one word: "Respect." And although both women do talk about pay and benefits, they reliably circle back to that theme. "We are talked down to [by managers]," Bradley says. "They can be sarcastic." Gray says her managers are better, but even a well-meaning manager does not have the power to make the real changes a union contract would bring: "Plain and simple, we are looking for a better environment to work in. That does not just benefit us. It benefits the campus as a whole. You want the employees happy in a place where you are asking people to come eat."

Both Bradley and Gray are nervous about risking their years on the job by demanding a union contract for all the workers. Gray had to push herself beyond her comfort zone to talk to coworkers about the union. Bradley was scared when she was asked to speak at a rally on campus. "I'm still nervous," Gray says. "But it is truly time for a change, and I'm not getting any younger."

Bradley brings up the student support for the workers, pointing out that students have worn buttons saying "We Love Our Campus Workers" and spoken up at rallies. "I love it. It makes me feel good that the students

Figure 8.1. From left, Tanya Gray of Butler University, James Holder of Marian University, and Rebecca Bradley of Butler University were leaders of campaigns to unionize Aramark workers on their Indianapolis campuses. Photo by author.

are standing there with us. We are there for them, after all—we'd just like a better work place," she says. "When we knew we are all together, it made me feel much stronger."

Gray nods again. "There is no turning back now, we have to finish the fight." She pauses, then decides some explanation may be necessary. "I like what I do. Sometimes people make it seem like it is a 'beneath' job. I don't feel that way. But sometimes when we talk raises, they [Aramark] make it seem that way."

Then, after over an hour of the two women taking turns speaking, Bradley's and Gray's words come together, and they say the same thing at the same time: "I just feel we are worth more than what they are doing now."

During this conversation at Rebecca Bradley's house, UNITE HERE organizer Liam Roche sits quietly in a living room chair, occasionally nodding and smiling. Bradley and Gray come largely from the same world. By comparison, Roche is an alien creature. Thirty years the women's junior, Roche is a white man who grew up in the rural, southern Indiana town of North Vernon, population 6,728. Roche looks more like the Butler students the women serve than the workers they toil alongside. Yet it is clear that Bradley, Gray, and Roche have grown close. "We lo-o-o-ve our Liam," Bradley coos, causing Roche to blush.

The oldest son of a small-town attorney father and a mother who is the second-generation publisher of the *North Vernon Plain Dealer and Sun*, Roche grew up focusing his attention on playing soccer, partying a fair amount, and listening to the Grateful Dead. His career goal was to become a small-town judge and farm some land in the country. But Roche's parents were also loyal Democrats, and his father's law practice included a fair number of pro bono cases and a consistent dedication to opposing government infringement of civil liberties. Roche's mother, before she was married, had been a union steward machinist at a General Electric plant.

The Roche household's liberal politics were an anomaly in rural Indiana, but they meshed well with the climate of Earlham College, the eastern Indiana Quaker school where Roche studied prelaw and philosophy. For his senior thesis, Roche decided to look into workplace drug testing. He did not come to the topic from a purely academic perspective. "I had a lot of friends who did warehouse and factory work in southern Indiana, and those places push people to the limit," he says. "You have to meet a quota like unloading three hundred boxes off a truck each hour, and if you miss it twice in a pay period, you get fired." Trying to get a boost, one of Roche's friends began taking over-the-counter stimulants—in Jennings County, they are called "trucker pills"—before heading to his work shifts. Roche's friend became reliant on the drugs, and then began using cocaine and other illegal stimulants. He failed an employer-administered drug test, and was fired.

While researching his paper, Roche attended a job fair in Indianapolis hosted by idealist.org, where he spoke to union representatives about drug testing and workplace conditions. At the fair, Roche met Mike Biskar. He found Biskar to be charismatic and far beyond Roche in political sophistication, even though the two were about the same age. "Mike had this grand vision of transforming the city and fighting for working class power. He was throwing out all these socialist buzz words I didn't know anything about but sounded really exciting," Roche says. Biskar convinced Roche to consider working for UNITE HERE. Roche attended a training held in the basement of an Indianapolis church, and was impressed by the union's focus on sharing individual life stories and nurturing personal growth: "It was really very moving stuff, and I was brought to tears listening to the personal stories. I'd never really experienced that kind of raw emotion before." Roche was graduating from Earlham soon, so he decided he would give the job a year while he took the Law School Admissions Test and prepared for law school.

Roche found a job providing room service at the Indianapolis Westin and was a part-time banquet staffer at the Hyatt. There, the exhilarating discussions about societal transformation and personal growth slammed up against the gritty reality of working at the lowest levels of the hospitality industry. Sometimes, Roche would finish a banquet cleanup shift at 4 a.m. and then start his other job just a few hours later. Exhaustion and humiliation went hand in hand. The upper-middle-class child of professional parents and graduate of a private liberal arts college was not used to being yelled at by managers and talked down to by hotel and banquet guests. Once, toward the end of an exhausting twelve-hour shift, Roche and his coworkers were sitting down to polish silver when the manager came in and ordered them all to stand and surrender their chairs. One of the crew had accidentally left a chair in the hallway while cleaning up a banquet room. The entire group would be taught a lesson by being forced to stand for the remainder of their shift. "We just looked at each other and were like, 'What the fuck?,'" Roche recalls. "But we did what we were told, and gave up our chairs." When Roche would see family and friends from his hometown or college, they were surprised at the honor student's line of work. They asked him if they could pass around his resume so he could find something more suitable.

Roche's pride was wounded, both on the job and off. But the experience gave him an understanding of the daily indignities faced by hotel coworkers who did not have one eye on graduate school. He realized now how workers could arrive at the point where they abandon any belief that things can get better. "The most difficult and frustrating part of organizing is when people simply have no hope that things can change. Fear can usually be overcome, but hopelessness is much more difficult," he says. By this time, Roche was struggling for optimism himself. The UNITE HERE hotel organizing he was helping with was not gaining much traction, and Roche often questioned whether his efforts were having any impact. The process of organizing was not always a natural fit for him, either. Roche does not have an aggressive personality, and he was often not comfortable encouraging a worker to take on a leadership role.

When Roche eventually quit the hotel jobs and was assigned to organize the Butler workers, his hesitancy proved to be a particular problem. The Butler workforce is well over 90 percent African American. Roche was acutely conscious of being a young, white man with a privileged background trying to encourage workers of color to take increasingly daring stands against their bosses: "I grew up comfortable and I did not have to go without, and my parents paid for my schooling. So how could I relate to a worker who was getting their lights cut off, who was getting evicted five or six times a year? That was really my biggest hang-up." Worried about coming across as too aggressive, Roche let a few Butler worker leaders slip away.

"To push a worker is to connect with them and really empower and inspire them to have the courage to do something hard," he says. "But when you are not doing it right, you just seem like an asshole ... another boss to them, this time the boss for the union." Eventually, Roche came to terms with his own self-consciousness and began forging bonds with Butler workers like Rebecca Bradley.

As engaging and eloquent as Bradley was, she nevertheless insisted to Roche that she was not equipped to be an example to her coworkers. She spent every day at Butler talking and laughing with students, faculty, and coworkers, but the idea of public speaking terrified her. She thought her grammar and word choice would embarrass her and the cause. "People at Butler would go to her for everything," Roche says. "She was a natural leader, but it took her awhile to realize that in fact she was a leader." Slowly, Bradley and the quieter Gray, along with longtime colleague Elmira Bowen, accepted larger roles in the union effort. They toured the IUPUI/Chartwells food-service operation, which was now unionized, and talked to the workers there. "The biggest thing we had to overcome in organizing in this city was the mentality that nothing was ever going to change," Roche says. "But when workers at Butler talked to James [Meyers] and saw the IUPUI contract, they knew this could happen."

The Butler workers started to take ownership of the process. Bowen overruled Roche on the best approach to persuade a fellow worker to join the union. The women met separately from the UNITE HERE staff and then insisted on a change of housing plans on a trip to union headquarters in Chicago. Roche was delighted: "When the workers are coming together and telling you, 'This is how we are going to do it,' that is when an organizer knows they are ready—it is their union now." On a late autumn weekend in 2012, the Butler union leaders formed teams to visit coworkers in their homes, regrouping regularly at a McDonald's restaurant near campus to compare notes. In a span of two and a half days, they signed up a remarkable 80 percent of their colleagues for the union.

The Butler union was recognized by Aramark in January 2013. But for several months afterward, Aramark rarely agreed to meet with the union representatives to talk about a contract. For the workers and the organizers, it was a worrisome pattern.

As the Butler workers were learning, winning union recognition is, at best, only half the battle. That membership is largely symbolic until and unless the union and the company reach an agreement on a contract. And that result is far from a given: research by Kate Bronfenbrenner at the Cornell School of Industrial and Labor Relations has shown that a majority of workers who won union representation still did not have a contract a year after voting to unionize, and 30 percent of them still did not have a contract three years after the union was formed.[1] U.S. labor law allows a union to be decertified by worker vote if no contract is in place one year after the union was recognized, giving employers a strong incentive to resist the first contract.

Union members and organizers often respond to this challenge by turning to community allies to help pressure employers into agreeing to fair terms. One of the reasons UNITE HERE chose to organize on college campuses in Indianapolis is that university settings provide an environment filled with potential supportive community members, including students and faculty. Reverend C. L. Day, president of the Concerned Clergy of Indianapolis, says he and his colleagues are very willing to support service-sector workers whenever they are asked. "As a minister, I can point to Scripture and cite 'Do unto others . . .' And I would want my neighbor to have an opportunity for a better life, because I want that life for myself," Day says. "But this matters to the broader community, too. These workers are taxpaying citizens who support our schools, our streets, our hospitals. Their kids go to school with ours, and they need parents to take care of them and get adequate health care."

In May of 2013, a delegation of Butler workers, buttressed by thirty students and community members, gathered in a huddle outside the campus's Atherton Union, the main dining area. The group then marched into the

Atherton Union building, aiming to track down and confront an Aramark manager named Michelle. Michelle tried to get away down a hallway into an empty room, but she was stopped by a locked door. With a sigh, she sat down to listen to the workers. Butler worker Mattie Cole, a short African American woman with close-cropped gray hair and wearing a blue work shirt, said her piece. "We would just like you to listen more, and appreciate us more. I've been here seventeen years, so I just want some justice."

Then Butler student Katie Burns, a young white woman in pig tails and a flower-print dress, spoke up, saying, "We are going to stand by the workers, you should know that." It was a good moment, and the workers left the demonstration smiling and laughing. But when the weeks continued to drag on without movement on the contract, the euphoria faded. A few more bargaining sessions had been held, but there was no contract agreement in site for either Butler or Marian workers.

At the UNITE HERE annual meeting held in midsummer in the community room of a Catholic church near Butler's campus, some workers' frustrations bubble to the surface. The meeting starts with a theme

Figure 8.2. A delegation of workers, organizers, and community leaders gather before making an unannounced visit to Aramark management at Butler University. Students, faculty, and clergy all participated in multiple displays of support for the workers seeking a union contract. Photo by author.

of optimism, as a parade of organizers and workers give prepared talks trumpeting the union's accomplishments during the past year. Unionized airport workers are being paid more than ever before, and their health insurance is cheaper. Hotel housekeepers are not unionized, but UNITE HERE's pressure clearly played a role in housekeeper pay increases and an end to widespread wage theft. Justin Moed, an Indiana state representative, pops into the meeting. "At the Statehouse they think that 'right to work' killed the labor movement," Moed says. "But you guys are still fighting, and you are winning. You guys are proving them wrong, and you are an inspiration to us."

Most of the workers clap politely in response to Moed's praise. But as soon as the floor is open for questions, the strain of five months of fruitless contract negotiations begins to show. Two Marian workers stand up and say they continue to be mistreated by managers. They do not see things getting better since the union was voted in, and they are tired of waiting for results. A Butler worker says a manager recently told her, "You all are a dime a dozen; you can just go work at McDonald's." Another Marian worker challenges the UNITE HERE organizers to change the venue for the fight. "They are breaking federal law. You just need to bring 'em to court—that's what they really care about," he says.

An IUPUI worker named Willa raises her hand and asks for a chance to respond to the Butler and Marian workers. She speaks about her own colleagues' successful contract negotiations. 'Stick with it!" she shouts. "I know it can be frustrating, but the union is worth it. Don't accept nothing you don't want, because you don't have to!"

The exchange goes back and forth a bit before Mike Biskar finally steps up to talk. "First of all," he says, "it is not a real union meeting until we have a disagreement." Most of the workers laugh. Then he gently challenges the use of the word "you" directed at him and the other organizers, along with the notion that a lawsuit will solve the impasse. "The whole point of the union is that it is *your* organization and *your* power," he says. "These companies are not nice and we can't underestimate them. So we are going to break up into groups now, by the companies you work for, and talk about what we are going to do next—together."

If the companies' representatives could witness this meeting, they likely would allow themselves a small smile of satisfaction. Employers' delay in contract negotiations does not just push back the date for any potential raises or benefit increases, it also accomplishes a broader goal that union-resisting professionals call "creating futility." As former SEIU organizer and contract negotiator Jane McAlevey has said, "This is what union busters go for in the end. If they can't win on any single tactic, they can still create an endless barrage of garbage until the workers decide that unless the union goes away their lives will simply never return to normal."[2]

Biskar does not show too much concern about the debate at the annual meeting. The naysayers are not the real worker leaders, for the most part, and most of the workers seem prepared to hang in there on contract fights for a while yet. But what Biskar does not tell the group is that he is frustrated by the slow bargaining process, too. Negotiations are going on for four different contracts simultaneously—the Butler workers, the Marian food-service workers, the Marian maintenance workers, and the airport workers for the company HMSHost. There are other local workplaces Biskar thinks UNITE HERE should be organizing, but instead he and others are stuck researching contract precedents, mastering the intricacies of changing health coverage laws, and crunching cost numbers. Biskar has a senior UNITE HERE bargainer mentoring him through the process, since he has never negotiated a contract before. It was not part of the job he took to naturally. "We have to find a way to do these bargaining sessions faster," he says privately.

But Biskar and most of the other UNITE HERE staff remain engaged with the workers and workplaces they helped organize the previous year, and they intend to stay connected until the contracts are completed. That is not always the case in service-sector labor organizing. Some unions have been criticized for elevating the process of winning the union over the oftentimes lengthy and tedious task of grinding out a good first contract. Jane McAlevey and others have criticized SEIU for the practice of parachuting in seasoned organizers to win union elections and swell SEIU's membership, and then pulling those organizers out when it is time to negotiate contracts. "All the talent is assigned to bring new workers into the union," McAlevey wrote in her 2012 book, *Raising Expectations (and Raising Hell)*. "The new members are then passed to a team with one-tenth the talent who are supposed to help them actually get a contract and build their union, which of course doesn't work, and SEIU ends up a hollow giant."

McAlevey and others have noted that in right-to-work states like Indiana, where workers can pull their financial support from the union at any time, organizing has to be a perpetual process. Indianapolis union advocates have criticized SEIU for removing staff of the local Justice for Janitors campaign after 2007, just when their presence was needed to enforce the contract. "The union got to declare victory, the community partners got to celebrate and go home, and the workers got the shaft," says IUPUI's Tom Marvin.[3]

In Indianapolis, at least, UNITE HERE does not erect the wall between organizing and bargaining that critics say exists at SEIU. Since winning union representation, workers at Marian have passed out leaflets on campus, multiple delegations and rallies have been held at Butler, and workers have turned to local media and elected officials to make their case for good contracts. All the activity seems to have an impact. When the union announces plans to picket on campus, the companies usually increase their offers and ask the union to hold off on the demonstrations. The multiple ongoing contract negotiations in the summer of 2013 provided more workers with the opportunity to be involved in the bargaining, which is helpful for building union strength. Sitting across the table from their bosses as equals boosts workers' morale and leadership skills. And more workers actively involved in the bargaining means the information flows better to the rank and file.

At the time of the UNITE HERE annual meeting, there were some positive signs coming from the Butler and Marian negotiations. Aramark was talking about paying more of the workers' health-care costs, contributing to a 401(k) retirement plan, and raising all cooks' salaries to at least ten dollars an hour. The parties were discussing potential solutions to the huge problem of campus food-service workers being laid off in the summer. The company suggested it might be willing to offer those workers first shot at shifts at Aramark's other local operations, including the concessions at the minor league baseball park. Even better would be if Aramark would continue its contribution to health care premiums during the summer months. Aramark had already changed its policy on assigning the limited summer work at Butler, agreeing to the workers' demands that the opportunities for work be assigned by seniority.

As the UNITE HERE annual meeting winds to a close, newly trained union stewards are brought up to the front of the room and presented with certificates. It is the moment when workers who had never been managers or bosses formally accept leadership roles, and there is much applause and laughter and good-natured teasing. The smiling steward group photo shows an age span from the twenties to sixty-plus, with men, women, African American, Latino, and white workers in roughly equal measure. Then the whole group gathers round for a clapping, foot-stomping rendition of the chant "*Sí se puede*!" (Yes, we can!), borrowed from the farmworkers movement.

The meeting is officially over. Men and women immediately grab the folding chairs and tables and haul them over to racks at the side of the room. I have been to a lot of meetings where the participants broke down the room in this way, but usually that happens only after some hesitation or when there is a reminder or request from the podium. There was no such request or hesitation here. This is a room filled with janitors and dishwashers and servers. They have no expectation that anyone else is cleaning up but them.

Wonderful Field, Awful Pay

When Kelley Erving was young, her grandmother was aging and had grown unable to care for herself. Erving and her mother both had jobs outside the home, so a home care worker named Lateisha helped Erving's grandmother. Lateisha performed tasks like bathing Erving's grandmother, feeding her, and helping her with her medications.

The total was much greater than the sum of the parts. "Lateisha was like family to us," Erving recalls. "She used to climb up in the bed with my grandma, watch TV with her, bring her stuff. She would do anything for her. She was a real comfort to my grandmother—my grandmother was so happy when that girl was coming over."

"That's me," Erving says. "I'm that same person now. I am there doing what I do as a home care worker, and I like seeing people's faces light up when I walk in the door. They say, 'Girl, let me tell you what happened last night.' Once you have people who have entered your heart, that makes you good at your job."

That job is a demanding one. When the Bloomington, Indiana-based Erving arrives at her client's home in the morning, she greets the woman and starts preparing a sponge bath. The client suffers from muscular dystrophy and is confined to a wheelchair. "That is my hardest client, because she can't walk at all anymore. With help, she can stand up on her legs, but she can't move from there." So Erving kneels down and cleans her client as much as possible while the woman sits in her wheelchair. Erving, thirty-three years old with strong arms and wide shoulders, then squats, leans, and helps the 185-pound woman stand up and brace herself against an end table so Erving can wash the rest of her body. "Once you learn how to use body mechanics, you don't get hurt—unless you have to jerk out of position to help prevent a client from falling," Erving says. Following the morning bath, Erving helps the client get dressed and sets out her morning medicine. Next, she prepares the day's meals, and cleans up around the house. Then Erving has to rush out the door, heading to two more clients' homes to perform similar duties. One was in a serious accident and has a debilitating back injury; the other is ninety years old and needs Erving's help with various daily activities. "The clients are amazing, and as long as you keep them happy, they'll make sure you are happy too," she says.

Erving is part of an industry that is already huge and quickly getting bigger. There are an estimated 2.5 million home attendants and aides in the United States already, and the aging of the baby boom generation is making the profession one of the fastest growing job categories.[1] The U.S. home care industry is estimated to collect more than $84 billion in revenue annually.[2] A recent report from the Indiana Governor's Commission on Long Term Caregivers looked at the demographics of the aging Indiana population and concluded, "The growing need for long term care represents an amazingly stable source of jobs long into the future."[3]

Yet those jobs are usually not very good ones. Like many home care workers in Indiana and beyond, Kelley Erving provides health care for others but cannot afford medical treatment for herself. In the winter of 2012, Erving picked up the flu from her two young sons. The virus developed into a sinus infection. Or at least that is what Erving thinks happened, because she could not afford to go to a doctor or get antibiotic medication. The health insurance program offered by her employer is prohibitively expensive and provides limited coverage, so Erving and most of her colleagues go without. When she is ill, Erving cannot go to work.

"If I would have brought a virus to one of my clients that is on oxygen and has COPD [chronic obstructive pulmonary disease], then that is pneumonia right there, and it could kill them," she says. Her job provides no sick leave; when she missed work, Erving missed her paycheck, too. A single mother when she fell ill (Erving has since married) she had to cut back on food and gas, but still fell behind on the bills. The family had its electricity cut off for two weeks.

Nichole Paschal has faced similar struggles. A native of Fort Wayne, Paschal works as many as seven days a week as a certified nursing assistant (CNA) for an Indianapolis-area home care agency. Paschal took the CNA training because she was told that health care offered good job prospects. Sure enough, positions were available. But it took Paschal awhile to come to terms with the gritty challenges of the work: "I will admit: at first, I thought it was gross to wipe butts and clean up vomit." A large woman with long hair extensions colored a bright red, Pachal laughs theatrically at her admission, and mimes her reaction the first few times she had to perform these tasks. "Oh my God!" she says, and covers her mouth with her hand. "But then I started realizing I was really providing help, and that I really do like caring for people," she says. "You never know when you'll need this kind of care, so you want to treat people the way you would like to be treated. Wiping people, changing people—that does not bother me anymore."

But Paschal discovered the job comes with other challenges. She has high blood pressure that caused her to be hospitalized in 2010, but she has no health coverage. Like Erving, she cannot afford to pay the high premiums and co-pays on her employer's insurance plan. Despite sixteen years of experience and a recent raise, Paschal earns only $10.45 per hour. On those wages, she says, she can't fill her current blood pressure prescription and still make ends meet for her twin twelve-year-old daughters.

Erving makes less than $11 per hour, too. Like most home care workers, Erving strains to get full-time hours by shuttling between short two- or three-hour shifts at multiple clients' homes. When a client goes to the hospital or to stay with a family, Erving simply does not get paid for those hours she would have spent at the client's home. For the past several years, Erving has not been able to get her average hours up high enough to qualify for any vacation time.

The low wages Erving and Paschal earn are common in this profession. The U.S. Bureau of Labor Statistics reports the average wage of home health aides in Indiana to be just over $10 per hour, with an average annual income of $21,030, barely over the federal poverty level for a family of three.[4] The national averages are about the same. Nearly 90 percent of home care workers are women, who are vastly overrepresented across the spectrum of low-wage service-sector positions.

In real terms, those low wages translate into home care workers skipping doctor visits and not filling prescriptions, cutting back on groceries so that the kids can get school clothes, and missing time with their families because they are picking up extra hours caring for someone else. Paschal is worried about her daughters as they become teenagers, especially the one who has been diagnosed with attention deficit hyperactivity disorder and hearing loss. As she describes the challenge of making ends meet, Paschal's frustration grows. She is not laughing any more. "How can we work effectively for our clients when we are getting so little pay that we are not sure that the rent is paid or food is put on the table?" she asks. "People caring for others should get a good steady rate of pay. When you have someone's life in your hands, your pay should not be so low."

One of the reasons many home care workers have struggled with low wages and limited benefits is that they have been excluded from some of the most basic protections of U.S. labor law. In the 1970s, the U.S. Congress decided to place home care work in the same category as babysitters, thus denying them coverage by federal minimum wage and overtime pay requirements. As recently as 2012, Republicans in the U.S. Senate introduced the Companionship Exemption Protection Act, which aimed to block any change to the rules exempting home care workers from labor law protections. Yet, if those workers performed the same services in a nursing home setting—Erving and Paschal, like many home care workers, have nursing home experience—all the terms of the Fair Labor Standards Act would have applied. In September 2013, a change to U.S. Department of Labor rules finally brought home care workers under the full protection of workplace laws.[5]

Historically, workers that are being treated poorly often found relief by banding together into a union. Home care is a difficult industry to unionize, with solidarity hard to come by when workers have little interaction with each other at their wide-ranging workplaces. Yet home care workers in several states have come together in unions to bargain for the terms of employment the law does not guarantee them. In California, for example, the Service Employees International Union, which represents 180,000 home care and nursing home workers, has partnered with disability advocacy groups and other unions to lobby to protect home care funding at the state level. In Illinois, unionized home care workers have bargained for access to health care. SEIU has a limited membership in Indiana so far, but union home care workers here get overtime pay, have seniority protection, and can only be disciplined for just cause, all protections that go beyond state law. Paschal once was fired from a nonunionized care facility for speaking up about the treatment of residents. She and the 2,400 other Indiana unionized home care workers think they can get even better pay and working conditions if others join their ranks.

A morning press conference in front of the Julia Carson Government Building has broken up, but four women remain talking in the parking lot. Three of the women are African American. They wear the purple and gold T-shirts of SEIU and happily recount what they told the gathered media about the need to raise the federal minimum wage. One of the women makes plans to call in to a radio talk show that afternoon to continue the minimum wage conversation. There is a fourth woman wearing the same T-shirt. But this woman had studiously avoided talking to the media, and she stands out in both her appearance and her accent. Being a bit different is an advantage in organizing with SEIU Healthcare, Yin Kyi says. "I'm usually the only Asian in the group and certainly the only Burmese," she says. "The workers are usually interested in figuring out who I am and knowing my background."

Kyi spent the first two decades of her life in Burma. Beginning at the tender age of eleven, she participated in prodemocracy meetings and demonstrations. This was in the 1980s, and activism under the country's military rule was anything but child's play. Some of Kyi's friends were among the many Burmese students jailed or killed for protest activity. "There were rallies across the country, and I found it so inspiring to see a huge group of people demanding freedom," she says. "That is what actually changed my life and brought me all the way to this work." A lifelong commitment to social justice is not always associated with a sunny personality, but Kyi is beloved by her worker colleagues for her seemingly indomitable cheerfulness and self-deprecating humor. Even surviving the deadly Burmese military rule is fodder for a joke. "I probably got away with it because I was so short; they did not think I could be an activist," she says with a laugh.

At age twenty-one, Kyi came to the United States to study at California State University San Marcos, near where an older brother was living. She eventually received political asylum here, a ruling that recognized the danger she would have faced as a former youth activist returning to Burma. Because of that status, Kyi has never returned home to Burma. She was unable to see her mother before she passed away in 2001. Kyi earned her degree at Cal State San Marcos and a master's in political science at Northern Arizona University, where she prepared to write her PhD dissertation on human trafficking. But Kyi's grad school mentor suggested she take a break after she earned her master's. Kyi quickly agreed. "I really wanted to learn community organizing, because I had only been studying theory up to that point. I wanted to have that connection to real events and real people," she says. "I read about SEIU being a very diverse union that helped organize the janitors, so I applied." She laughs again. "I guess now it has been a ten-year sabbatical from graduate school!"

Kyi's mother was a physician and her sister and other relatives are also in the health care field, so Kyi gravitated toward SEIU's health care organizing. She worked in a Chicago-area hospital union campaign before switching over to devote most of her time to home care workers in Indiana. Most of the high-level SEIU organizers for Indiana are based in Chicago, site of the union's regional meetings and a vastly more cosmopolitan setting than any Indiana has to offer. ("The one condition I put on working on an Indiana campaign is that I would not have to move here!" one SEIU organizer told me.) Kyi also lived in Chicago for several years, but decided to move to Indianapolis full time in early 2013. "I just wanted to take the challenge," she says. "I think that we have to invest in rural areas to actually change the dynamics of the state and the country."

One of the challenges Kyi faces is building class consciousness and solidarity among Indiana workers. In her Indiana organizing, the well-chronicled observation that every American thinks they are middle class comes to life. Once, Kyi visited a home care worker near La Porte, Indiana. The woman's employer would assign her only twenty hours of work each week, and the woman lived in a decrepit trailer that was slated for demolition. But the worker told Kyi that she had no interest in the union: "I'm middle class. The union is for the blacks."

As the comment suggests, there is a racial divide to be bridged among Indiana home care workers, too. In Indianapolis and the Chicago metropolitan area in northwest Indiana, known as the Calumet Region, the home care worker demographic is about 50/50 African American and white. In the rural parts of the state, whites are a solid majority of home care workers. Since the workers do not share a common job site, Kyi often tries to build solidarity by pulling them together in meetings in person or by phone. Some of the ensuing discussions can be tricky. Kyi has found that rural white workers and urban African American workers can hold sharply differing views on hot-topic issues like abortion and gun control. Like Mike Biskar of UNITE HERE, Kyi does not talk much macropolitics with the workers she organizes. But, like Biskar, her politics are far to the left of the typical Hoosier. (The distinctions are not surprising. Noncynical faith in a communist or socialist vision of an idyllic future may be a good trait for an organizer. As one successful labor activist told Julius Getman in a 1986 interview, "I think you have to have a belief in happiness. You wouldn't ever, I think, become a union organizer if you didn't believe there was a potential for happiness."[6])

Kyi tries to provide home care workers with opportunities to advocate in campaigns for minimum wage increases or immigration reform. Those advocacy experiences help build strong Indiana worker leaders, Kyi says, while also pushing legislation that would directly benefit many health care workers in the state. Union members also help lead house visits to fellow workers, pitching the value of union membership. Such visits are a well-established way to both grow the movement by increasing membership and to identify leaders among the workers who can lead or host a successful house meeting.[7] Kelley Erving has become so adept at communicating with her fellow workers that she took a short leave of absence to help SEIU organize Vermont home care workers into the union.

Kyi says that Erving and other Indiana home care workers will benefit if they can build up their union "density," growing in the state's larger cities like Indianapolis and Fort Wayne while also bringing rural workers into the fold. Toward that end, Kyi will continue to drive around the state—she puts thirty thousand miles on her car each year—quietly pushing home care workers to expect more from their jobs and to believe in their own worth. "I once read a parable where a man walked through a village that has been cast under a spell. He simply asks the villagers questions," she says. "He does not make any statements himself, but his questions cause the villagers to wake up and take action. That is basically what an organizer does: ask questions that cause workers to think about how they can make things better."

Organizers like Yin Kyi prefer to remain behind the scenes, preferring instead to encourage home care workers to go in front of the microphones and cameras. But the organizers are also thrilled when home care clients join the effort as vocal and visible advocates for the workers. Linda Muckway, a fifty-five-year-old Muncie, Indiana, resident who has cerebral palsy, has testified in the Indiana General Assembly and spoken at public rallies many times, all as a passionate advocate for the rights of people with disabilities. Muckway sees home care workers' rights as fully intertwined with the goal of active and independent community living for persons with disabilities, so she invited me to her apartment to discuss home care worker issues. When I arrive, I watch as her care provider, Kay Romaine, helps Muckway pull on compression socks and ankle and leg braces over her severely swollen lower legs. Romaine then heads to the kitchen to prepare meals of spaghetti and taco salad for Muckway to keep ready to reheat in the next few days.

Muckway is pleased with both Romaine and the agency she works for. But Muckway and other advocates express concern about the overall turnover rate in the industry, which some estimates put as high as 60 percent annually.[8] "You would not have as much turnover if they were paid more," she says. The numbers back her up. A University of California study conducted from 1997 to 2002 found that significant wage increases for home care workers in San Francisco led to a 31 percent decrease in worker-initiated turnover.[9]

The increased wages in San Francisco were due in part to a change in the law, specifically living wage legislation. Advocates such as Muckway, the SEIU, and consumer-focused organizations such as the Indiana Home Care Task Force say that changes to Indiana law could also benefit home care workers. Health care for seniors and persons with disabilities is the very opposite of a free market, with services largely funded by government programs such as Medicaid. So lawmakers hold the power to readily adopt changes that can make a huge impact on the field. For example, some Indiana home care workers get paid little more than half what their agencies receive in government reimbursement for the care they are providing. Indiana could require that home health agencies spend a fixed percentage of its government reimbursement on worker pay and benefits, a provision that has boosted worker salaries in states such as Illinois. And some states have established provider networks that allow home care workers to receive health benefits through the state government.

Currently, though, Indiana officials use their power mostly to provide benefits to the nursing home industry. "Indiana has far too many people in nursing homes who could be in home-based care and would rather be in home-based care, which is more cost-effective, too," says John Cardwell of the Generations Project and the Indiana Home Care Task Force. Indiana does provide home and community-based services such as the CHOICE (Community and Home Options to Institutional Care for Elderly and Disabled) program and a Medicaid waiver program to support home-based care. But, as of 2011, Indiana was forty-eighth in the nation in funding such options. At the time of this writing, these programs have thousands of people on their waiting lists.

Home care providers say they are not surprised by the demand. "My clients don't want to go to nursing homes, and I don't blame them," Erving says. "Sometime my clients are crying because it hurts to turn over, and you just need to hold their hand. In a nursing home, they [workers] are not going to have time to hold your hand. They are going to throw you over whether it hurts or not, clean you, and then they are out of there."

The Generations Project hosted a multiyear statewide roundtable discussion on long term care in Indiana, issuing its findings in 2011. The report concluded that home care is both the preferred and most cost-effective form of care, saying that "nursing home care is simply the wrong model for virtually anyone needing long term care services." Advocates like Cardwell and Muckway say that Indiana is missing the opportunity to sharply reduce its Medicaid spending by expanding home care options. They point to the state of Washington, which emphasizes home care options, has a population slightly larger than Indiana's, but nearly two-thirds fewer nursing home residents.

In the 2013 session of the Indiana General Assembly, Republican representatives Tom Saunders and Ron Bacon sponsored legislation to expand home care options in part by funding the growth with Medicaid savings created by avoiding nursing home costs. The bill did not receive a hearing.

Home care workers like Kelley Erving and Nichole Paschal would like to see the importance of their jobs affirmed by government priorities. But they do not need a lawmaker to tell them their work has value. "Everybody

Figure 9.1. SEIU home care worker Alecia Cox demonstrates in front of the Indiana Statehouse in favor of Medicaid expansion. Unable to gain favorable contracts, some Indiana unions of low-wage workers turned their efforts toward advocacy of an increased minimum wage and broader access to government health insurance. Photo by author.

that breathes is at some point going to die," Erving says. "It's sad to say it like that, but it is the truth. The normal way is either getting sick by some type of disease or getting older, and your body starts to deteriorate. And when that happens, you need help. Period. There is no way around it."

"The people who are not thinking about that are going to make it to that place regardless," Erving says. "So our job is to give these people the best quality of life possible. You can't do home care just because it's a job. You have to have your heart in it."

Paschal agrees. But she also considers going back to school for accounting or starting her own business one day. She wishes those plans were less attractive options, because she cares deeply for her clients, and feels that providing home care is part of her better self.

"It is a wonderful field," she says. "But the pay is just awful."

10

Trying to Secure a Union

Tiara Johnson and Tonya Yarborough have a lot in common. Both women are mothers, and both are security guards with several years of experience. Johnson works for a Wishard Health Services contractor at the construction site for a new Eskenazi Hospital in Indianapolis. Yarborough works in the financial district in Chicago.

But when Johnson arrives at her worksite at 6 a.m. and puts on her neon yellow high-visibility vest, her hard hat, and her safety goggles, differences begin to emerge. Johnson is paid just $10 per hour, significantly less than Yarborough's near $13-per-hour wage. Yarborough has been thoroughly trained in handling emergencies, Johnson has not. Beyond viewing a short safety video required of all Wishard staff, Johnson says security guards at the construction site are provided no special training. "We are pretty much given a uniform and told to stand there and open a gate," she says.

Through her work in Chicago, Yarborough has health insurance that allows her and her son to see a doctor and get discounted prescriptions. She has not had a co-payment for eight years. Johnson says the health insurance offered by her direct employer in Indianapolis, a company called Securatex, is all but worthless, covering only a fraction of health care costs in return for large employee contributions. Johnson and most of her colleagues choose not to pay for the policy, instead paying out of pocket for whatever care they can afford.

But health crises have a way of ignoring such budget planning. When Johnson suffered from heat exhaustion after a twelve-hour work shift in August, her emergency room bill added up to almost $4,000. Now, collection agencies are calling her home and writing threatening letters. After making the rent and car payments and buying groceries, there is no money left over from Johnson's paycheck to cover that kind of debt.

Johnson and Yarborough agree on the reason why, despite their similar jobs, their lives are so different: Yarborough is represented by a union at her workplace; Johnson is not. Yarborough's employer has a contract with SEIU Local 1 that includes annual raises, a grievance procedure, and seniority rights even when security guards need to switch employers. "It is strength in numbers," Yarborough says. "We got all this through the union. The company is never going to give us that on our own as individuals."

In contrast, SEIU Local 1's efforts to organize Johnson's Indianapolis employer Securatex have not yet been successful. Also, the state of Illinois mandates initial training, background checks, and refresher training for security guards like Yarborough, where Indiana law includes no such requirements. An SEIU-backed 2010 proposal to require minimal training for security guards in Indianapolis failed to pass the City-County Council.

Workers going without health care while helping to erect a state-of-the-art hospital presents an irony that Johnson and others guarding the hospital construction site do not shy away from invoking. They have held demonstrations outside the building, brandishing giant Band-Aids lettered "Working Without Health Care at Wishard Hurts." They marched in front of the Health and Hospital Corporation of Marion County, Wishard's parent organization, with a giant pill labeled "No Healthcare is Hard to Swallow."

Wishard's current hospital is patrolled by security guards who are direct Wishard employees receiving better pay and benefits than the Securatex guards. And Johnson is quick to praise Wishard's commitment to its low-income patients and the community's overall health. "This situation with Securatex is not up to Wishard's good reputation," she says. "Their responsibility is to hire a contractor who shares their values. Wishard needs to do its homework a little more, instead of saying, 'You are the cheapest, so I'm going to go with you.'"

It is no accident that Johnson, an active supporter of the union campaign, focused her statement on Securatex's client Wishard. On the wall of SEIU's sparsely furnished office near downtown Indianapolis is a large sign labeled "The Three 'C's' of Winning." The sign is directed to the security guards trying to win a contract. After "Co-Workers: Lobby Them," and "Contractors—Pressure Them" is number three: "Clients—Pressure Them, Too." The clients are the high-profile companies and institutions, such as Wishard, that engage security contractors like Securatex. In the summer of 2013, SEIU security guards held a noisy demonstration outside the annual meeting of the National Collegiate Athletic Association (NCAA), which uses a nonunion company to provide security at its Indianapolis headquarters. "We passed out some leaflets and ruffled some feathers," says Jade Lee, the SEIU organizer leading the Indianapolis security guards campaign. "Our goal there was to get the NCAA to call Universal [the nonunion contractor] and say, 'Hey, treat your workers right or we're going to drop you and go with a different contractor.'" SEIU did not invent Securatex's poor record of training and worker treatment—a local government official overseeing a Securatex contract told me that the company did an awful job in fulfilling its security obligations—but it certainly spread the word.

Indianapolis is a challenging environment for a campaign like this. With the exception of a few security guards at manufacturing sites, unionized because of past insistence by the United Auto Workers, which dominated the plants, there is no recent history of unionized security guards here. But SEIU has won some private agreements with local security companies that serve commercial office buildings, where SEIU already represents the janitors. And it has secured promises of cooperation from managers of public buildings such as the Indiana Statehouse and local libraries. The union is seeking to win over enough additional companies to achieve sufficient "density" to trigger National Labor Relations Board recognition. That recognition would give SEIU the right to bargain for a contract that will cover security guards at multiple Indianapolis companies and sites. "We have to win this campaign," Lee says in the summer of 2013. "And we are real close." Indeed, the security workers won union recognition in early 2014 and were preparing in late summer of 2014 to begin bargaining for their first contract later in the year.

Labor lawyer Thomas Geoghegan, in his book, *Which Side Are You On?*, describes a romantic, Hollywood-inspired version of a union organizer, conveniently with an Indiana setting:

> I would like to think of an organizer as someone who can spend six weeks at a Holiday Inn in Kokomo, Indiana, reading novels like *The Day of the Jackal*, and then going out after dark to organize a ten-man machine shop; who sneaks around on private property; and who, after losing an election, can stub out his last cigarette, get in his car, and then, emotionless, drive down to Terre Haute, as if nothing happened.[1]

That is not Jade Lee. For one thing, she is certainly not smoking cigarettes, since she was eight months' pregnant with her second child at the time of the NCAA demonstration. Instead, she shifts her weight around uncomfortably, cusses at the heat, and complains that the campaign she has led to the near-finish appears unlikely to conclude before she goes on maternity leave.

Lee is also the opposite of the image of an organizer as a rootless loner. She was born in Indianapolis to teenage parents and raised here, largely by her grandparents. Lee and her husband and daughter now live in a modest neighborhood on the city's near-east side, where her home sits on the same block as those of her mother, grandparents, brother, sister, and cousin. Lee's fifteen-month old daughter plays every day with Lee's eighteen-month-old sister, the child of her father and stepmother, who live across the street. The family, along with the few nonrelated neighbors who managed to somehow sneak onto the block, maintain a thriving community garden on an open lot. Since the melons get stolen and smashed if they are in the open garden, Lee grows them for the community in her fenced-in backyard.

Lee cheerfully admits to bossing around her family members, in both how they tend the garden and how they approach public affairs. "My brother is not really a political person, but sometimes he thinks he's a conservative," Lee says. "I'm like, 'Dude, we're poor. No, you're not [a conservative].'" I think it is because my stepdad watches Fox News, so I tell him he's not allowed to watch Fox News." She laughs as she recalls her orders,

Figure 10.1. SEIU organizer Jade Lee helps prepare the Indianapolis Worker Justice Center for its grand opening. The first-ever worker center in the area brought together union and non-union advocates for low-wage workers. Photo by author.

but it is not hard to believe that her brother follows them. Jade Lee is a veteran of the National Guard, she spent several years as a security guard herself, and she is solidly built even when not pregnant. After graduating from Warren Central High on Indianapolis' far-eastside, Lee spent six years juggling her military duties with private security work and college classes. Many local security guards are former military like she is, and her mother and several other relatives still work security jobs in Indianapolis.

Lee comes from a die-hard union family. The grandfather who raised her was a UAW member and shop steward. After the Chrysler plant he worked for in Indianapolis closed, he got up every morning and drove fifty miles to a plant in Greencastle, Indiana. Lee attended St. Phillip Neri elementary school in a working-class neighborhood not far from where she lives now, and remembers regularly attending UAW family picnics. Her first political conversation occurred the day she returned home from second grade and informed her grandparents that the class was going to hold a mock election to coincide with the U.S. presidential election. When the seven-year-old Lee asked her grandparents who she should vote for, they looked at her as if she was crazy. "Well, you vote for Bill Clinton, honey," they said. "You don't have a choice."

Even at a young age, Lee had a well-established and specific career goal: she would become an anthropologist studying the indigenous people of the Amazon Basin in South America. Through high school and two years of classes at Ivy Tech Community College, Lee held on to that vision. But when she enrolled at IUPUI and began taking anthropology courses, she found no professors there focusing on the South American people. Instead, she found plenty of faculty and students keenly interested in the people living in the neighborhoods where Lee grew up, many of them doing the same kind of work as her family members and friends. Lee switched her studies to urban anthropology, and soon landed an internship with SEIU, where she was assigned to the local Justice for Janitors campaign. On one of her first days, Lee joined dozens of local janitors conducting a singing, drumming, sign-waving demonstration on Monument Circle in the heart of Indianapolis' downtown. "It really had a profound effect on me," she says. "I was like, 'Wow, this is grassroots action, people standing up to the government and the powers-that-be, and this is really cool!'"

Lee devoted her senior project to SEIU work, too, and was hired by the union after graduation. She traveled the country for a year and a half, organizing what the union calls "property service" workers, including janitors and security guards. Those are Lee's favorite workers to organize, and she enjoyed the new towns and new experiences. But soon she was ready to settle down and start a family. When SEIU said they were going to launch a drive to organize security guards in Indianapolis, Lee jumped at the opportunity to lead it. "I'm your girl for that," she said. "That is me all the way."

Many organizers and unions are tight-lipped about the process of recruiting and inspiring workers. But, when asked, Lee is willing to provide a minitutorial on union organizing. When she and a worker first meet, the organizer introduces herself and openly discloses what she is up to. "Then you want to find an issue," Lee says. Questions about what the worker would like to see improvements on their job could lead to a discussion about low pay or expensive health care costs or even poor-fitting uniforms. Then the "agitation" process begins, with questions such as, "How would your life be different if you had health insurance?" or "What would be better if you made an extra $2 per hour?"

The conversation soon steers to a "plan to win," such as gathering coworkers together, confronting the boss, and demanding a union contract that addresses the identified issues. Organizers sometime say they are in the business of raising expectations, encouraging workers to both articulate their goals and envision a process for achieving them.[2] If workers think they can expect nothing better than their current treatment, the boss is free to impose whatever pay and conditions he wants. Just like a good salesperson is measured by her ability to close the deal, union organizers need to be effective in making the ask, which they sometimes refer to as "calling the question." Are you ready to stand with your coworkers and demand a union? If so, sign the union card and attend the next meeting.

But organizing does not conclude in a single conversation, nor does it operate in a vacuum, without resistance. So organizers need to "inoculate" the worker against the inevitable push back from the employer. Open-ended questions yield predictions about how the boss is likely to react ("Don't talk to union people!" or "They just want your dues money" are the most common responses). The workers practice responses to the resistance they will face from above. Organizers have countless subsequent conversations with the workers, always reiterating the plan to win and identifying short-term tasks—leafleting, recruiting two more coworkers, a delegation confronting the boss—that move the process toward victory. If the worker falters or wants to skip an action, the organizer takes them back to their initial issues: I thought you wanted to get health care coverage? Remember how you told me it was important for you to get full-time hours?

Unions like SEIU train and retrain their organizers on all of these steps: introduction to issues, agitation, plan to win, call the question, inoculation, and follow-up. Good unions demand the same kind of adherence to process from an organizer that the military does from a soldier, Lee says. "At first, I thought the organizing training was kind of silly, because I know how to talk to people," she says. "But it helps you keep on track and it helps to motivate the workers. I fancied myself a leader in the military, and I'm a leader in this union with my members. And to do either role well takes training and discipline."

Lee and other organizers say even the strongest relationships with workers have to be supplemented by alliances with community members, including elected officials, clergy, and other unions. "These clients and these contractors don't see this activism as a workers' rights issue, they see it as the union just trying to get more members," she says. "So it's important that we have that moral voice from the church, it's important that we have that authority from the [unionized] sheriff's department, it's important that we have elected officials invested."

SEIU has been criticized for sometimes neglecting the contract bargaining process after a union is formed. But, during the 2013 Indianapolis janitors' negotiations, Lee's colleagues who are Local 1 organizers seemed to be defying that characterization. SEIU maintained an active presence throughout the community and on social media. For example, a few days before a bargaining session, the union led a group of workers, community members, and media to visit the headquarters of Indianapolis's most prominent corporate citizen, the international pharmaceutical company Eli Lilly and Company. The unannounced delegation marched past arching fountains surrounded by the flags of two dozen countries and into a gleaming, hushed lobby. The security guards there, both male and female, wore crisp navy blue blazers, white oxford shirts, and red ties. An SEIU janitor says that the group wants to see a vice president. He is not available, so they leave a letter. The tone of the visit was polite—the message was to thank Eli Lilly for using a company that employed unionized janitors—but the demonstration carried a message, too: if negotiations don't go well, they will be back, and the visit will not be so polite next time.

Once the security guards advance to the contract stage, Lee intends to do the same. "We just have to make noise in the streets, noise on the TV, noise through the media, so that when these contractors come here—we call them 'the suits'—from Los Angeles or New York City or Chicago, they know they better offer us something good or we'll go on strike." But the process is neither easy nor foolproof. The initial SEIU janitors' campaign in Indianapolis took five years to win, and a recent yearlong Indianapolis janitors' strike with one contractor ended with defeat for the union. "At first, this work seems all good and exciting, but it's hard work, it's stressful, and it can be heartbreaking," Lee says. "Too often, the workers don't realize that if we stick together, we can accomplish so much more than we can ever do on our own."

Even though she grew up in the bosom of trade unionism, Lee acknowledges that her hometown is not always fertile ground for that kind of collective action. "The Chryslers, the Fords, all that manufacturing went away, and people in town blame the union for it, even though it was the companies deciding they would leave the country to get cheap labor," she says. "But there is more than that. I get in trouble when I say this to my union management, but this is not Chicago. There is so much more union history and density there, and people's ideologies are different."

There are some positives in the local union scene, though. The two most active organizing unions, SEIU and UNITE HERE, work well together in Indianapolis, despite a history of deep conflict in other regions and at the national level. Lee does some SEIU work in Cincinnati, where she sees a much more pronounced racial divide than in Indianapolis. "And I think the [Indianapolis] community is starting to see that there are people out here organizing the service sector and that we are getting some wins," she says.

Lee fears that things will get worse for Indianapolis workers before they will get better: "I think the labor movement is going to come back in a strong way. But I think it is going to be out of absolute necessity, where people are going to see that if we do not organize then we are completely screwed. I mean, if you look at a chart that is the decline of union membership and one that is the decline of the middle class and real wages, it is the same chart. The union is like having another family, like having a safeguard. It's my job to make people understand that."

Like Tiara Johnson, Tony "Coach" Young also worked for Securatex at a local government site. Young was a security guard at the Duvall Residential Facility, a near-eastside work-release center that houses over three hundred inmates. Young was among many guards, all encouraged by Lee and SEIU, who echoed Johnson's critique of Securatex for its treatment of its workers and failure to train its guards. Young began work at Duvall in 2010, but never received any self-defense or conflict resolution training through the job. A part-time wrestling coach at Emmerich Manual High School, Young says CPR and first-aid training was required of him before he was allowed to coach, but not before he was assigned to guard the 340 inmates at Duvall.

Young and other guards say that as few as five security officers are assigned to oversee all of the Duvall inmates on an overnight shift. The Securatex contract with the City of Indianapolis calls for an armed guard with special deputy arresting powers to be present on-site at all times, but guards say there are many times when no such deputy is present. One night in September 2012, during Young's shift, several inmates got into a fight. Quickly, another two dozen inmates joined in, and the situation appeared on the verge of escalating into a riot. Young radioed for backup, but no one ever responded. The situation cooled down, but Young worried that the next time might not end so peacefully. "Eventually, someone is going to get hurt," he told me. "And that is because the City of Indianapolis made a decision to hire a contractor that is cheap, but does not train their employees."

I printed Young's statements in an article for a local newspaper, and he said essentially the same thing in a report broadcast on WRTV-6, a local television station. Securatex did not return my calls seeking comment. However, company president Patricia DuCanto told WRTV-6 that Securatex was meeting all the training standards set by its contracts. DuCanto also told WRTV-6 that the negative attention directed to Securatex was the product of the SEIU organizing campaign. Young readily admitted to being an advocate for union recognition at Duvall Center. "We are dealing with all walks of life there, so we need better training, better wages, and better healthcare," he said, again in a statement published in the newspaper. Shortly after the publicity, Young was fired by Securatex. He and SEIU said the action was a clear case of retaliation for his union advocacy. The union helped Young file a complaint with the National Labor Relations Board, where he received a favorable ruling and an order for Securatex to pay him for the period after he was fired.

Tiara Johnson hung on to her job, even though she also openly cited the need for benefits and a wage that would allow her to pay her rent, car payment, and groceries. In 2013, Johnson and her husband agreed to adopt two-year-old twin girls whose mother faced legal trouble, so money was tighter than ever. But Johnson has the focus of an experienced security guard, not to mention the backing of her union organizer. In conversation about the job challenges, she circles back from economic concerns to the issue of safety, clearly the focus of the SEIU's campaign. "We need the training," Johnson says. "Right now, we are out there just hoping to get through difficult situations so we can go home to our families at the end of the night."

11

Prayers for Citizenship

It would take a stone not to be moved by Cinthia Torres's story. The hopes of the more than six hundred people packing the gymnasium at St. Monica's Catholic Church on the northwest side of Indianapolis are that Congresswoman Susan Brooks is not a stone.

It is September 2013, and it is the middle of a meticulously scripted Sunday afternoon event called "A Prayer for Citizenship." The sixteen-year-old Torres approaches the microphone and faces the crowd. To Torres's right, Brooks sits at a table by herself. Torres explains that she grew up in Indianapolis and is a student at George Washington High School. Then she pauses, and takes a deep breath. "When I was twelve, my mother was deported," she says. She tries to begin her next sentence, but can't quite get the words out. Tears well up in her eyes, but she gulps and starts in again: "No twelve year old should have to care for her three year-old and six year-old siblings. But I was all we had."

Torres's voice is cracking a bit, but she rushes on, using the momentum of her words to keep from breaking down: "I pray that the congresswoman will make the right choice and support a pathway to citizenship that supports family values. I don't want anyone else to have this pain and suffering."

The rest of the afternoon's agenda is no less subtle. Torres was preceded at the podium by two Catholic priests, both Anglos, who cite to Brooks their own families' immigrant backgrounds and the biblical mandate to be welcoming to the stranger in our midst. Torres is followed by a tiny, adorable eight-year-old Latina girl, who looks directly at Brooks and, in a thin, high voice, asks her to support a path to citizenship. The gymnasium is decorated with U.S. flag-themed banners reading, "Keep Us United." The masters of ceremonies are Rolando Mendoza Sr., speaking in Spanish, and teenage Rolando Mendoza Jr., speaking in English. Both are parishioners of St. Gabriel Catholic Church in Indianapolis. And, they disclose to Brooks and the gathered crowd, both are undocumented immigrants.

The goal is for Brooks to publicly pledge to support the Border Security, Economic Opportunity, and Immigration Modernization Act, known as H.R. 15. The bill would allow the Mendozas, Cinthia Torres, and the more than eleven million other undocumented immigrants in the United States to get legal residency, permission to attend school, drive a vehicle and work, and move toward a day when they would earn full citizenship. At the end of the Prayer for Citizenship program, Brooks, a first-term Republican, will be invited to respond. Each of the persons in attendance holds a small battery-operated candle. They are instructed to light it only if Brooks agrees to support a path to citizenship. It is an agenda designed to create tension, and the design is being realized. It is hard not to feel sorry for Brooks, sitting up front alone with the eyes of hundreds—and the hopes of millions—trained directly on her.

Among those holding the small candles and sitting in the crowd are several local organizers for UNITE HERE, SEIU, and the local living wage and worker center efforts. Most of the people living as undocumented immigrants in Indianapolis are low-wage workers, so the union and immigration activists work hand in hand, cross-promoting each other's initiatives and events. Roman Catholic activists help form the core of both the labor efforts and the citizenship campaign. Although the unions helped turn out people for today's citizenship campaign event, they are not able to produce this size of a crowd for one of their rallies. Clearly, the most vibrant and broad-based local movement for working people in Indianapolis is the immigration reform movement.

The labor-focused campaigns for food-service workers and janitors in Indianapolis likely could not pull the suburban-based, business-sympathizing Congresswoman Brooks out to one of their rallies. In fact, it is hard to understand at first why Brooks would agree to attend such a presentation at all. She represents the 5th Congressional District, which spans north and east of Indianapolis's center, pulling in the most affluent suburbs. Her statements on immigration have focused on bolstering the country's borders, not welcoming the undocumented in our midst. But when Brooks finally takes the microphone to respond, she quickly points out that this setting is a familiar one for her. She and her family have been members of St. Monica's parish for decades, and the invitation to attend today was issued in part by her own pastor, the same priest who had started the agenda by delivering a strongly proimmigrant invocation.

Yet, even though she is no stranger to the setting, the Latino-dominated crowd itself may not be all that familiar to Brooks. Since she and her family joined the parish, its Latino membership has swelled, and multiple Spanish-language masses have been added to the weekend schedule. The world around Susan Brooks has shifted in recent years, as it has for all Americans. The United States is the world's leading destination for immigrants, with a record forty million-plus people living in the country now having arrived during the recent decades' wave of immigration.[1] One of every twenty Indiana residents is foreign-born, with almost half of those coming from Latin America.[2] By 2050, the Hispanic population in the United States is expected to comprise 29 percent of the population.[3]

And that puts Susan Brooks in a tough spot. On one hand, anyone in the business of winning elections ignores such obvious demographic trends at their peril. In 2013, the Growth and Opportunity Project of the Republican National Committee issued recommendations that highlighted the party's need to embrace comprehensive immigration reform.[4] One of the report's cochairs, Ari Fleischer, who served as White House spokesperson during the George W. Bush presidency, cited the meager 27 percent share of the Hispanic vote earned by Mitt Romney in the 2012 election as "a clear two-by-four to the head" to the Republican Party.[5] At a local level, Brooks is well aware that the business community, including the Indiana Chamber of Commerce, Eli Lilly and Company, and other traditional Republican supporters, favors the legislation that passed the Senate. A 2013 poll for the Public Religion Research Institute showed two-thirds of Hoosiers support a path to legal citizenship.[6]

Yet such surveys pull in a much broader group of respondents than the population of likely GOP voters in an off-year congressional primary. In those Indiana elections, Tea Party and other conservative activists carry more influence than the Chamber of Commerce. Just ask former Senator Richard Lugar, who was sent into unplanned retirement in 2012 by Indiana primary voters who chose his Tea Party–backed opponent. That challenger's campaign was launched with an attack on Lugar's support for the DREAM Act, which would have provided a pathway to citizenship for young immigrants brought to the United States as children.[7] "Immigration is one of those really tricky political issues for an Indiana candidate," says Purdue University political science professor James McCann. "Indiana is a newer destination area for migration, so we do not have the large base of voting-eligible immigrants that other communities do. And we do have entrenched right-of-center constituencies that, in tough times, come out against immigrant rights."

For the activists pushing Brooks to defy anti-immigrant constituencies, there is some helpful precedent to draw from. When U.S. Senator Joe Donnelly was a Democratic member of the House of Representatives representing a northern Indiana district, he voted against the DREAM Act that helped sink Lugar. He also criticized the Obama administration for trying to stop Arizona from enforcing a state law that would have led to wider arrests of undocumented immigrants.[8] Donnelly actively promoted these anti-immigrant positions when successfully campaigning to win Lugar's seat in 2012.[9] But, soon after his victory, immigration reform activists held prayer vigils outside the new senator's office and paraded in downtown Indianapolis under banners reading "¡*Todos Somos Americanos*!" (We Are All Americans). Phone banks were arranged for Hoosiers to call Donnelly's office, eventually turning calls from 20 to 1 against a path to citizenship to 15 to 1 in favor. Business and religious leaders met with Donnelly individually, pressing for his support for H.R. 15.

It was not clear how Donnelly was going to vote until just before the June 2013 roll call, when he joined sixty-seven other senators in supporting the bill. Donnelly's official statement after the vote contained so many qualifiers that it sounded more like he had voted against it—he referenced border security a half-dozen times in just three paragraphs. But Indiana's new senator had come over to the side of immigration reform.

So has Rep. Jeff Denham, like Susan Brooks a Republican member of the House. In his district in Northern California, Denham sat through church-based immigration reform forums that mimicked the format of the Indianapolis event. Then, in October 2013, Denham announced that he would join 185 Democrat House members who support H.R. 15. Two other House Republicans have since also signed on as cosponsors, and immigration reform activists say there are two dozen more House Republicans who have publicly supported a pathway to citizenship. As of this writing, though, House Speaker John Boehner has not brought H.R. 15 to a vote.

Both the local and national campaigns for citizenship have strong ties to the Roman Catholic Church. The Prayer for Citizenship event in Indianapolis was part of a national Catholic "Day of Prayer and Action for Immigration Reform." The agenda and the crowd were dominated by members of local Catholic parishes. Clergy like St. Monica's pastor, Fr. Todd Goodson, regularly issue statements that call for a change in the law. "We are all created in the image and likeness of God," Goodson told the *Indianapolis Star* in November. "Immigrants should have the same rights as everyone else to be able to live and work and raise families."[10]

Indeed, many Catholics see a clear biblical mandate that they create a "preferential option" for the poor. (To wit, "Whatever you did for the least brothers of mine, you did for me." Matthew 25:40.) But the Catholic Church, and most U.S. faith-based organizations, usually choose to fulfill that obligation to the poor through acts of charity rather than advocacy for justice. It is a trend that cuts across the U.S. culture. The Archdiocese of Indianapolis, for example, spends considerable resources operating a homeless shelter and transitional housing, feeding the hungry, and, yes, aiding recent immigrants.[11] That legacy was noted by Kim Bobo, founder and director of the Chicago-based Interfaith Worker Justice, when she visited Indianapolis in the fall of 2013 to help open the city's first worker center. "The faith community generally does a good job with soup kitchens and food pantries, which are certainly important," she said. "But the people in those lines are usually there because they or their loved ones have a job that does not pay enough or they are being mistreated on the job." In her remarks, Bobo singled out the need to advocate for the oft-exploited population of undocumented immigrant workers.

Indianapolis archbishop Joseph Tobin does not disagree with Bobo's observation about the tendency to elevate charity over justice. "I'd say there is probably some truth to that. Exercising what Catholics originally called the corporal works of mercy is part of our history, and on a personal level it can be much more satisfying," he says. Tobin is a large man, with a ruddy complexion and girth that suggests a retired offensive tackle more than a parish priest. The oldest of thirteen children and raised in Detroit, he speaks five languages and came to his post in Indianapolis from a prestigious position in Rome. There he served in a position with a voluminous title, the archbishop secretary of the Congregation for Institutes of Consecrated Life and Societies of Apostolic Life, which is the church's number-two position for religious life, overseeing over one million men and women in religious life worldwide.

Once in that role, Tobin appeared to come into conflict with the Vatican's controversial investigation of the Leadership Conference of Women Religious, a support organization for U.S. nuns. The scrutiny was initiated after some in institutional church leadership concluded that the nuns were too independent and progressive. But after he was appointed to his position, Tobin issued public statements that seemed to disagree with the process. Tobin said that it was important for church leadership to acknowledge "the depth of anger and hurt that exists among the sisters" due to the investigation.[12] The newspaper *Vatican Insider* reported that Tobin was not happy with the subsequent report criticizing the nuns.[13] Soon after, barely two years after putting Tobin in the Vatican post, Pope Benedict XVI reassigned him to Indianapolis. Many Catholics privately speculate that Tobin's dissatisfaction with the investigation of the nuns may have led to his placement in central Indiana. But his stance has only endeared Tobin to Indianapolis Catholics who want to see a stronger role for women in the church. "We have a genuine rock star here!" gushes one local Catholic activist.

Given that track record of dissent, perhaps it is not surprising that Tobin has no trouble with the archdiocese calling on government leaders to change immigration law. In an interview, he points out that Jesus instructed his followers to turn the other cheek, but also demanded an explanation when he himself was struck by an official. Tobin too does not hesitate to ask political questions. He was part of a delegation that visited Donnelly in April 2013 when the new senator was still on record opposing a path to citizenship for undocumented youth and adults. Tobin told Donnelly, a Roman Catholic and Notre Dame graduate, that he assumed the senator was Native American. No, Donnelly replied with surprise, his background was Irish American. "Mine, too," Tobin said with a smile. "So you must know a little something about immigration!"

Tobin cites several reasons why immigration reform is a central issue to the Catholic Church. First, Christian orthodoxy is that Jesus himself was an immigrant whose family fled his home country because his life was at stake. There is also the core instruction to embrace the stranger in our community. Tobin says that U.S. Catholics have a special obligation in this area. "In this country, except for Native American Catholics, every one of us is a child or grandchild or great-grandchild of immigrants," Tobin says. "My grandparents lived with the 'Irish Need Not Apply' signs, and that is still very ingrained in the memory of my family. If we are uncaring about the new Irish in our midst—the Hispanics, the Africans, the Asians—on the day of judgment it won't be them who condemn us. It will be our grandparents." Senator Donnelly declined a request to be interviewed for this book, so it can only be guessed whether a reminder of his Irish American ancestry tipped the scales in favor of his June 2013 vote for a pathway to citizenship. But, Donnelly's official statement about his vote included the sentence, alongside the multiple references to border security, "The United States has a rich tradition built upon the work of immigrant citizens."[14]

Of course, issuing calls for justice to accompany less controversial acts of charity exposes the church and its leaders to criticism. Tobin was told by the editors of the *Criterion*, the archdiocesan newspaper, that his advocacy for the rights of immigrants generates more negative responses than any other action he has taken. One local Catholic wrote to the paper in November, "To imply that not supporting said [pathway to citizenship] legislation is anti-immigrant, anti-poor or anti-Catholic is reprehensible."[15] Another wrote, "Those who are here illegally are not immigrants, but are illegal aliens. To call them immigrants gives them a 'belonging' they do not deserve since they have not followed our laws to get here."[16] Pushback after embracing a justice agenda is not a new story for those in Tobin's position. As the twentieth-century Brazilian archbishop Dom Helder Camara famously said, "When I gave food to the poor, they called me a saint. When I asked why the poor were so hungry, they called me a communist."[17]

More recently, another Catholic leader's outspoken advocacy for the poor has earned him remarkably similar criticism. Pope Francis too has been accused of Marxist intent, most notably by conservative commentator

Rush Limbaugh.[18] In fact, Francis can sound a bit revolutionary, especially in the context of the twenty-first-century global embrace of free market ideology and recent pontiffs' lower profile on social justice issues. The former Jorge Bergoglio has labeled unfettered capitalism "a new tyranny," condemned the "idolatry of money," and denounced structural inequality that sentences so many millions of the world's citizens to abject poverty.[19] The first-ever Latin American pope has championed the rights of immigrants, invoking his own family's struggles in emigrating from Italy to Argentina. Francis made his first papal trip outside Rome to the Mediterranean island of Lampedusa, near where thousands of African migrants have drowned in desperate attempts to reach Europe. In case there was any confusion about what that trip indicated about his priorities, Francis tweeted that day, "We pray for a heart which will embrace immigrants. God will judge us upon how we have treated the most needy."[20]

Francis's social justice theology is firmly rooted in Catholic tradition, a legacy often obscured by the church's recent focus on issues such as contraception, abortion, and homosexuality. Francis himself has said that the church has appeared to be "obsessed" of late with those below-the-belt topics.[21] But there is a connection between his statements on poverty and immigration and the church's hardline positions on issues like reproductive freedom. The same Catholic rejection of individualism that frustrates pro-choice advocates also leads to a skeptical view of the free market's Darwinian sorting out of economic winners and losers. Max Weber, writing in *The Protestant Ethic and the Spirit of Capitalism*, claimed an affinity between Protestantism and capitalism.[22] For Catholics, whose doctrine embraces a more collective responsibility for the general good, the relationship is more chilly.

Francis's statements echo those of his predecessors as far back as Pope Leo XIII. In his 1891 encyclical *Rerum Novarum* (On Capital and Labor), Leo issued the Church's first formal statement on the rights of workers in the then-new industrial society. Citing the teachings of Thomas Aquinas, the encyclical did not reject capitalism outright but said that its rough edges have to be smoothed out by the state guaranteeing workers a living wage: "[There is] a dictate of natural justice more imperious and ancient than any bargain between man and man, namely, that wages ought not to be insufficient to support a frugal and well-behaved wage-earner."[23] Forty years after *Rerum Novarum*, Pius XI issued his own Depression-era encyclical expanding on the Church's embrace of workers' rights to organize into unions, earn a living wage, and receive state assistance when necessary.[24] Later in the century, when John XXIII ushered in modernizing Vatican II reforms, he also walked the walk on worker justice. When the pontiff learned that the Vatican gardeners struggled to support their families on low wages, John ordered their pay increased. Told that the raises would lead to a reduction of funds available for charity, the Pope responded, "Then we'll have to cut them. For justice comes before charity."[25] His successor, Paul VI, famously said in 1972 that those who want peace have to work for justice.[26] And even the noted conservative Benedict XVI, Francis's immediate predecessor, explicitly reaffirmed the right to a just wage.[27]

In the United States, the first Catholics were largely working-class immigrants disconnected from governmental and capital power. They arrived here ready to troop together in large numbers to Mass and union meetings both. The leader of the late nineteenth-century Knights of Labor, Terence Powderly, was an Irish Catholic, and Catholic parishes operated over one hundred "labor schools" in the basements of urban immigrant churches, teaching workers about their rights and potential collective power.[28] So-called labor priests mentored the organizers of unions at all levels. [29] Archbishop Tobin tells of hearing former United Auto Workers president Douglas Fraser eulogizing a Detroit monsignor by saying the UAW was built on the social teaching of the Catholic Church, sometimes delivered to the non-Catholic union leaders during late night discussions over coffee at Holy Trinity church in Detroit. That Detroit monsignor, George Higgins, later became one of many visible Catholic supporters of the Cesar Chavez–led United Farm Workers movement.[30]

There was often an explicit connection between Catholic social teaching and electoral politics, too. Pius XI's 1931 promotion of workers' rights and a state that would build a safety net to catch the victims of capitalism served as a de facto position paper for Franklin Delano Roosevelt's 1932 presidential campaign. Roosevelt explicitly linked the New Deal to Catholic orthodoxy, telling a cheering campaign audience of Detroit workers that year that the encyclical was "just as radical as I am" and "one of the greatest documents of modern times."[31]

The driving intellectual and ethical voice of the U.S. minimum wage movement was a Catholic priest and economist, John Ryan. In 1906, Ryan published his doctoral dissertation, *A Living Wage: Its Ethical and Economic Aspects*, which became the foundational document for decades of living wage activism by Ryan and his mentees.[32] The argument that a living wage is a moral right that supersedes laissez faire capitalism—Ryan used the phrase "sacred and inviolable" when referring to a living wage—laid the groundwork for early twentieth century minimum wage legislation in states such as Oregon and Ohio.[33] In Depression-era New York, Governor Franklin Roosevelt and future secretary of labor Frances Perkins, then serving as commissioner of the New York Department of Labor, cited Ryan's work as an inspiration for passing state minimum wage laws. They would later do the same when promoting the federal Fair Labor Standards Act in 1938.[34] (Like today, minimum wage advocates did not always enjoy enthusiastic support from labor leaders, who then and now are usually focused on the benefits of collective bargaining. In the early twentieth century, Samuel Gompers and most other leaders of the American Federation of Labor opposed minimum wage legislation.[35])

Today, the U.S. Conference of Catholic Bishops' "Seven Themes of Catholic Social Teaching" still embraces a message that echoes the New Deal: "The economy must serve people, not the other way around. . . . If the dignity of work is to be protected, then the basic rights of workers must be respected—the right to productive work, to decent and fair wages, to the organization and joining of unions, to private property, and to economic initiative."[36] Viewed in a historical political context, it is not surprising that positions like these voiced by Francis startle GOP supporters like Rush Limbaugh and Fox News's Andy Shaw, who said Francis "will prove to be a disaster for the Catholic Church."[37] The Republican Party–Catholic Church alliance forged on issues like abortion and same-sex marriage is a relatively recent phenomenon. A growing Democratic Party–Catholic bond built on immigration reform and worker justice raises echoes of the potent political pairing of the New Deal era.

Pope Francis seems not to be bothered by the criticisms directed his way. Neither does Archbishop Tobin. They see no option but to follow the biblical directives: The poor must be fed, the stranger must be welcomed, and justice must be fought for. As Tobin says, "As a disciple of Christ, the Gospel is not just one datum among many, it represents the determining value."

Advocacy for Citizenship

Isaias Guerrero greets me at the door of the converted convent that hosts the offices of St. Anthony parish, Holy Trinity parish, and the Indianapolis Congregation Action Network, known as IndyCAN. Guerrero leads me up a narrow staircase and past a six-foot tall statue of the Virgin Mary. A snake is depicted below her bare feet, symbolizing the crushing of the serpent devil prophesied in the book of Genesis. Some of the tiny offices on the second floor still have sinks on the walls, installed decades ago when the rooms were living quarters for the nuns.

Guerrero is the coordinator of the immigration justice campaign for IndyCAN and the Archdiocese of Indianapolis. Today, he is excited after a good meeting to enlist the support of Bishop Timothy Doherty of the Lafayette Diocese. Like Archbishop Tobin, Doherty proved to be quite willing to throw his support behind the advocacy movement. Politics and religion were nailed together on the cross, he told Guerrero. That is the idea of IndyCAN, Guerrero says. "We want to create a culture where people of faith can act on their values in the public arena," he says.

Immigration laws are not an abstraction for Guerrero. A thin young man of twenty-eight, with dark curly hair and moustache, he came with his family to central Indiana without permanent residency. Guerrero was fifteen years old when his father lost his job in Colombia, and Guerrero suddenly found himself transplanted from a Jesuit high school in Bogota to being just one of five Latinos in Greenwood High School south of Indianapolis. Shortly after he saw the father of one of his new U.S. friends get deported to El Salvador, Guerrero joined the Indiana Undocumented Youth Alliance. He had the chance to meet Senator Lugar and thank him for supporting the DREAM Act. That legislation never passed, but in 2012 President Obama used an executive order to create the Deferred Action for Childhood Arrivals program, which allows Guerrero and others to get temporary work permits and driver's licenses. But the program does not provide any permanent status, nor does it create any route to citizenship.

IndyCAN includes over twenty Indianapolis congregations from different Christian denominations. In addition to the citizenship campaign, it embraces issues such as increased public transportation and ex-felon reentry opportunities. The citizenship effort is cosponsored by the Archdiocese of Indianapolis and funded in part by the Catholic Campaign for Human Development. IndyCAN is affiliated with the PICO National Network (PICO stands for People Improving Communities through Organizing), founded in 1972 by Father John Baumann, a Jesuit priest trained in the Saul Alinsky community organizing model. In Indianapolis, the manifestation of that approach has included a series of clergy-packed community events in churches, a business-oriented briefing hosted by Eli Lilly and Company, and demonstrations and vigils calling out individual lawmakers. "At the Statehouse, you mostly see people getting paid to represent the views of corporations," Guerrero says. "You do not see people who are poor. We are out to change that."

All the while, IndyCAN engages in aggressive media outreach, holding camera-ready events and lining up undocumented youth to share their struggles, often while standing alongside priests who deliver the faith perspective. As Guerrero recently told the archdiocese newspaper, the campaign invites church members to "see in the immigrant the face of Jesus Christ."[1]

There is plenty of suffering to analogize to the Christian narrative, Guerrero insists. Over a thousand persons are deported every day across the country, some of them based only on traffic violations.[2] Guerrero tells of an Indianapolis ten-year-old girl whose father faces deportation because he missed a hearing in traffic court. He describes speaking to some of the one hundred immigrant workers who recently lost their jobs at a steel mill in Anderson, Indiana, due to their undocumented status. Even for the immigrant families who have not yet faced deportation proceedings or job loss, uncertainty weighs heavy, he says.

But Guerrero finds hope in the growing coalition dedicated to reform. "One of the most beautiful things is seeing Anglos and immigrants coming together to talk about the law in a safe and welcoming place, which so often is inside a church," he says. When I visited an IndyCAN organizational meeting, it is actually down the hall from the church, in a classroom of St. Gabriel School. After an impassioned bilingual opening prayer, African American pastors and residents talk about mass transit problems and advocacy plans. Then, the Latino residents deliver an update on the citizenship campaign. Later in the meeting, a middle-aged white man in a blue oxford shirt and khakis joins Guerrero at the front of the room. He introduces himself as Ed Witulski, and he leads a discussion of voter registration and turnout in the next election cycle. The highlighted districts include those of Congresswoman Brooks and several state legislators who have been particularly rough on immigrants. Witulski is not a polished speaker, but he projects sincerity. "We only have as much justice as we have the power to compel," he says to the group. "So we need to create the power ourselves."

It is somewhat jarring to hear the philosophy of radical grassroots organizing being delivered by someone who looks like a career banker. In fact, Witulski is just that, currently working as an underwriter for PNC Bank. But he is also a cradle Catholic who found his commitment reenergized five years ago while participating in the "Just Faith" program that calls for Catholics to embrace the roles of advocates for justice. Like Brooks, Witulski is a longtime parishioner of St. Monica's, where he helps lead the social justice committee. When Fr. Goodson, his pastor, asked the committee to get involved in IndyCAN, that was reason enough for Witulski. Roman Catholicism is built on obedience to church leadership, so Witulski sometimes thinks that the only response he should have to give to fellow parishioners who oppose a pathway to citizenship is that the Catholic Church supports it. That should be that. But Witulski also began talking with some of the hundreds of Latino families that swell attendance at Spanish-language masses across the city. He learned that many are undocumented and suffering as a result. "How can we not look at our past and see that we are all immigrants? How can we forget that the Statue of Liberty stands for 'Bring me your poor, your tired, your hungry?,'" he asks.

Witulski admits that plenty of his fellow Catholics do not agree with him or IndyCAN. And there are many more who do not seem very engaged with social justice questions at all. His committee sometimes struggles to get much of a turnout to their presentations that discuss separate tenets of Catholic social teaching. He looks with envy at the large numbers of parishioners who sign up for charity projects. But Witulski is heartened by the calls for justice issued by both Pope Francis and Archbishop Tobin. There has been a spike in the number of St. Monica's parishioners signing up for social justice work since Francis began speaking out, Witulski says. He attended the IndyCAN event at Eli Lilly, where a PowerPoint slide presentation outlined multiple anti-immigration U.S. laws that have been struck down or repealed over the years, including once-popular racist attacks on Chinese and Japanese workers and their families. Witulski is confident that the current exclusion of millions of U.S. residents from legal status will eventually join the list of conditions that future generations will be surprised ever existed. "And I think Susan Brooks wants to do the right thing, too," he says. "I think Susan Brooks is praying for IndyCAN to change the minds of her voters."

Sure enough, as soon as she got the chance to respond at the September 2013 event at St. Monica's, Brooks did say that she was pulling in divine consultation on the issue. "I am opening and listening," she said, as Rolando Mendoza Jr. translated her remarks into Spanish. "I am discerning and praying about how to fix the system." But she did not commit to support H.R. 15, nor did she support in principle any law that provides a clear path to citizenship for undocumented residents. Purdue political science professor McCann says he is not surprised that Brooks refused to take a stance that could trigger a serious challenge from within her own party. "She is in a safe Republican seat, and in an age of gerrymandering and incumbency advantages, general elections can pose a much less significant challenge than a party primary challenge from the right," he says.

Although the Prayer for Citizenship event failed to deliver a dramatic statement of support from Brooks, IndyCAN and the Archdiocese kept up the pressure. In November, several dozen people marched the forty-eight miles from St. Monica's to Brooks's office in Anderson, carrying a "Pilgrimage for Citizenship" banner. They stopped at multiple churches along the way, and held prayer services outside a county jail that detains immigrants on the way to deportation.

Jesus Ramirez was one of the marchers, and he shared his own story with Brooks and with church groups along the route. Ramirez was born in Mexico. In the wake of an uncle being killed and his parents threatened, the family moved to the United States when Ramirez was seven years old. Now a sixteen-year-old student at Perry Meridian High School on Indianapolis's south side, Ramirez went without food for twenty-three days as part of a national Fast for Families set up to gain attention to the suffering of undocumented persons. "I stopped [my fast] only when I felt pretty sure that one more day would put me in the hospital," he says. During the time he abstained from food, Ramirez sat in the high school cafeteria drinking only water while his classmates ate their lunches. But he explained to them why he was fasting, and directed some to a YouTube video he had posted about his own undocumented situation. Soon, thirty-two of his classmates decided to show their solidarity by joining in Ramirez's fast for a day.

Ramirez is one of several eloquent and daring undocumented youth in the Indianapolis community. They follow in the footsteps of five undocumented college students who risked deportation by staging a sit-in at Governor Mitch Daniels's office in 2011. The five were arrested in protest of Daniels signing new Indiana laws that block undocumented students from access to in-state tuition and penalize businesses for hiring undocumented workers. Dramatic sacrifices like these, and retail communication by youth like Ramirez, seem to be having the desired effect among their peers: national polls show a strong majority of young people support comprehensive immigration reform.[3]

The November pilgrimage reached thousands of people directly and attracted significant local media coverage. "God walked with us," Fr. Mark Walter, associate pastor at St. Mary and St. Ambrose parishes in Anderson, told the marchers at the end of their journey. "God was with you on this pilgrimage. He will not let go of your hands."[4] But those hands were still not being grasped by Brooks and her fellow House Republicans. Brooks did meet with the marchers, but refused again to commit to support their goals.

In response to my request for comment, Brooks's spokesperson, Alex Damron, said, "Congresswoman Brooks favors a step by step approach to the immigration discussion that allows us to give various complicated topics the attention they deserve. Along with the debate surrounding a pathway to citizenship, we must pay attention to a number of other pressing issues including border security, our legal immigration system, and our temporary worker programs." That response echoes the House GOP leadership position, which seems most likely to propose legislation that elevates border security and possibly guest worker provisions over a route to citizenship. In reference to IndyCAN's advocacy, Damron pointed out that the congresswoman and her staff had met with the group several times, but had also met with others with opposing immigration views. "The congresswoman will always keep in mind the thoughts of constituents who feel passionately about issues that are important in their lives," Damron said.

Several weeks after the march, and nearly four months after the Prayer for Citizenship event, I reconnected with the masters of ceremonies that day, Rolando Mendoza Sr. and Jr. Like they did at St. Monica's, the elder Mendoza spoke mostly in Spanish, the younger in English. Their family of five came to the United States from Oaxaca, Mexico, in June 2002, fleeing violence and heading to join relatives in Indianapolis. They arrived in town on a Sunday and attended Mass the same day at St. Gabriel's. The priest asked for any visitors to stand and be welcomed, and the congregation prayed over the Mendozas. They have been active members of the parish ever since.

The next day, the elder Mendoza found work as a dishwasher. He later moved to jobs in a meatpacking plant and then making mass-produced furniture. For seven years, he worked in an industrial bakery in Hendricks County, driving a forklift and doing maintenance. It was a good job, but in early 2013 Mendoza was abruptly fired for not having legal status, a situation he is convinced the company knew since the day he was hired. He has since found work at a recycling plant, but his pay is far less.

The younger Mendoza attended Indianapolis public schools, graduating sixth in his class at Crispus Attucks High School after playing four years on both the soccer and wrestling teams. His dream to attend Indiana University was made financially impossible by the 2011 law that denies him access to in-state tuition. But his excellent record earned him scholarships to the private University of Indianapolis, where he is majoring in biology and business. He plans on becoming an optometrist. Both Mendozas are enthusiastic participants in IndyCAN, and have grown comfortable sharing their personal stories as part of the advocacy. The younger Mendoza invited his parish's youth minister, an Anglo, to an IndyCAN event where Mendoza spoke about life as an undocumented teenager. The minister had not been involved in citizenship activities before, and she cried as she listened. Then she promised to talk about the campaign with other Anglos in the parish. "Once they get to know us, they begin to support us," the younger Mendoza says.

So they both were willing to participate in the Prayer for Citizenship event, which meant disclosing their undocumented status to more than six hundred people, as well as to TV cameras and a member of Congress. "It is not just a problem for us, it is a problem for 11 million people. Even though I was talking about my situation and my feelings, I was in a way talking about everyone else in the same situation," Mendoza Sr. says. His son nods, and says he got a good vibe from Rep. Brooks, despite her reluctance to sign on to a pathway to citizenship. Like Ed Witulski, the Mendozas believe Brooks wants to do the right thing for undocumented families. So they push on.

"There is still sometimes a lack of knowledge, even in religious communities," says Rolando Mendoza Sr. "Sometimes we forget that it is not enough just to go to church. We are told to love our neighbor as we love ourselves."

13

Contracts on Campus

This is a good work night for James Holder. It is around 10 p.m. in a concrete-walled storage room in the basement of St. Francis Hall on Marian University's campus, and he is using a clear plastic hose to empty water from a floor stripping machine. Tonight, Holder has been assigned to a special floor-cleaning project, work that he enjoys more than his usual task, known as "general cleaning." When a custodian is on general cleaning duty, he has solo responsibility to sweep, mop, dust, wipe down drinking fountains, and take out the trash for his designated building. And clean the bathrooms, of course. "I don't mind scrubbing toilets," Holder says. "I've scrubbed plenty. But it is not as rewarding as making a floor shine."

Holder and a colleague will strip and wax a hallway on the first floor of this building, which houses faculty offices and a small chapel. The machine is drained now, so Holder reattaches the end of the hose to the floor stripper. He and his colleague begin hauling the mops, buckets, and equipment they need from basement storage rooms to the first floor. Once a few straggling students leave a late chapel service, the two men will scrub the baseboards and spread the stripper solution on the floor. Then they will affix coarse stripping pads to the dark gray machine, plug it in, and strip the soiled wax from the beige-colored linoleum floor. They will then use a mop to spread three separate coats of fresh wax, using a figure-eight motion to distribute the wax. They do other tasks while they wait for each coat to dry. It is cool outside tonight, so the wax coats should dry in about forty minutes each. On warm, humid nights, they have to wait hours for each coat to dry.

Both men wear short-sleeve light blue polo uniform shirts, with gold name tags over the front pocket and heavier long-sleeve shirts underneath. Holder is sixty years old now, and he has added a black Velcro back brace to his work uniform. If he doesn't wear it, he will be in pain for days. Holder's colleague appears to be about the same age. As they pull together their equipment for the floor job, they answer my questions about working the assigned shift from 9:00 p.m. to 5:30 a.m., with a "lunch" break at 1 a.m. They both say they are used to it. But that turns out to mean that they can't sleep at night on weekends, either, not that they get enough rest during the week. Holder's colleague sleeps about four or five hours during the day. That seems pretty good to Holder, who often can get only two or three hours of sleep between work shifts. The two men trade notes about blocking out harsh daylight from their bedrooms and the losing battle to keep multigenerational households quiet in the middle of the day. They laugh as they recount how often they have been awakened by someone yelling, "Hush! Grandpa's trying to sleep!"

The lighthearted conversation stops when they pull the floor stripping machine down the basement hallway. The building's elevator is out, and the two have to lug the 120-pound machine up a flight of stairs. Holder takes the bottom, which gives him more weight to bear but spares him the bending over that his colleague up top has to do. The process is awkward and halting. The stripper's wheels occasionally bounce off the steps as they climb. Somewhere, a workplace ergonomics expert is cringing.

It could be worse, though. Holder says there have been some nights when he has had to handle this bulky equipment on his own. "A night like that can get to you," he says. If a union contract can be reached, these are the kinds of issues he would like to discuss with management. This should always be a two-man job, for example. And, when the elevator is out, perhaps work like this could be switched to another building.

In the late summer of 2013, three Indianapolis union contract negotiations reached breakthroughs almost simultaneously. First, the airport services company HMSHost reached an agreement with UNITE HERE on an initial contract with its Indianapolis International Airport workers. HMSHost operates airport Starbucks stores, a Wolfgang Puck restaurant, and some other restaurants and retail shops. Its agreement with UNITE HERE followed the lead of airport service companies SSP America and Areas USA, who had entered into Indianapolis contracts with the union in previous years.

City politics were intertwined with the airport union negotiations. Indianapolis's airport terminal opened in 2008 with a construction price tag of $1.1 billion, the largest civic development project in the city's history. Ten thousand people work at the airport each day, and local officials were not pleased to see attention paid to the fact that many of those jobs were food-service work that paid poorly. "This is our government running the airport," community activist and blogger Pat Andrews told me in February 2013. "The airport is generally known for having low-paying jobs, and you would hope our Indianapolis Airport Authority could do more to address that."[1] Government involvement in private industry, whether in licensing, subsidies, contracts, or zoning, provides unions with opportunities to build pressure on the government-dependent employer from outside the workplace. In the spring, when the union held a public meeting for airport workers to discuss job pay and conditions, several members of the City-County Council, including the body's president, appeared and expressed support for the workers.

Perhaps in part because of the local lawmaker attention, and HMSHost's relationship with the local government those lawmakers direct, there was limited drama in the negotiations. HMSHost opened talks by offering raises of just fifteen cents per hour. In response, dozens of workers signed postcards demanding higher wages. The company's offer improved. By late August, the workers approved a contract that raised wages by several dollars per hour over the course of four years, reduced workers' health care costs, and recognized seniority rights for new positions and transfers. By the end of the new deal, no HMSHost worker would be making less than $10 per hour. At the meeting where the workers ratified the contract, a longtime clerk at the airport who had been skeptical of the union showed up. She asked for a card, signed up as a dues-paying member, and then thanked the organizers for their work. As union advocates say, nothing organizes like winning.

The negotiations between Butler and Marian workers and the company Aramark were less straightforward. Shortly after the union won recognition on the campuses, Aramark gave most of its workers a small raise. The implicit message to the workers was that the union would not get them a better deal than the company would provide on its own accord. The message to the workers and union representatives at the negotiating table was more explicit: the company had given raises, and it had no intention of giving any more. Negotiation sessions were rare, and unproductive when they occurred.

Soon, the workers received more bad news. As the school year drew to a close and laid-off university workers began asking to get summer work at other Aramark locations in the city, they found themselves apparently blackballed from those jobs. The company would not confirm it, but it appeared that Aramark was worried that unionized Butler and Marian workers would infect an organizing virus into its nonunionized workplaces, locations that included the local minor league baseball park and an in-patient mental health treatment facility. Some Butler and Marian workers were frustrated with the union: not only were they not getting a new contract, they were now being blocked from interim jobs they once could count on. The union was making things worse, not better.

The worker leaders remained loyal to the union, and they and UNITE HERE staffers decided to expand their advocacy beyond the negotiating table. The workers passed out leaflets at Marian and held demonstrations at Butler, recruiting students and faculty to join them. Both Butler and Marian are small private schools that pride themselves on providing a quiet, isolated academic setting even within a major city. Noisy labor disputes did not fit that image, particularly when they highlighted a race and class divide on campus. Most of the universities' food-service workers were persons of color, and the students were overwhelmingly white. When an article about the contract impasse was published in a local newspaper, one of the reader comments was, "Butler students=haves; Butler food-service workers=have nots. Quite the dichotomy."[2]

"Butler University values all workers' rights," the university's director of public relations Courtney Tull said in that same newspaper article. "We are committed to being an employer of choice in Indianapolis, and providing a fair and just workplace for all employees, including contract vendors who provide services to our campus." Based on statements like these and off-the-record comments relayed their way, workers and union officials believed that university officials were telling Aramark to resolve the contract before it overshadowed the start of the 2013–14 school year. So far, the workers had held off from picketing the school's graduation ceremonies or high-profile events. But such demonstrations were clearly possible if there was no agreement by the time the school year began. Butler was hosting South African archbishop Desmond Tutu in September, and word was that the university was concerned that a labor protest by mostly African American workers could mar the event.

Sure enough, by the time students returned to campus, Aramark and the workers' negotiating committees had agreed to terms for both Marian and Butler. But the workers still had to decide whether to accept the contracts their committees had agreed on.

In a dimly lit, overcrowded room in the basement of Butler's Jordan Hall, Biskar explains the proposed agreement to several dozen workers. The cooks, cashiers, and dishwashers gathered here wear black uniform shirts and pants. Some still have on their chef hats or hairnets. For many, streaks of sweat on their faces and smears of food on their clothes show the effects of a long shift on their feet, cooking and serving meals and then cleaning up afterward.

Biskar begins by laying out the contract terms that promise to bring some job and income security to the workers over the length of the four-year contract. The agreement largely tracks the terms of the Marian-Aramark contract agreed to at the same time, he says. Seniority will be respected when workers apply for open positions and if layoffs occur, thus blunting the favoritism some workers say managers show to workers they most identify with. (The Butler workforce is overwhelmingly African American. U.S. labor history shows that workers of color have often been highly motivated to avoid the capriciousness of an unregulated workplace, where prejudiced decisions about promotions and pay could be masked by subjective evaluations about "attitude" or "initiative."[3]) The company promised to create as many full-time jobs as possible and to limit the student workers to no more than 15 percent of the workforce. Workers can take up to a full year leave of absence and still return to their work. That means that the firing of Marian worker Herb Latigne after a four-month sick leave would be barred under this contract.

As Biskar describes the deal, heads nod in approval. The nods become more energetic as he explains how the contract addresses some widely shared concerns. Management will no longer be allowed to ask workers to stay several hours late on busy days, and then avoid paying overtime by sending them home early on the final day of the week. (Federal law on overtime pay applies to work in excess of forty hours per week, not a certain number of hours in any given workday.) "Oh, yeah!" says one man in the back row, slapping palms with the man to his left. Work schedules must be posted a week ahead of time, allowing workers to plan for their child care and outside commitments. In the past, employees had been called in to work on off days, only to have managers send them back home after deciding they are not needed after all. Under the new contract, if management calls an employee in to work, she must be paid a minimum of four hours. Workers who have been misclassified in lower-paid positions—apparently a lot of de facto cooks have been paid as dishwashers—will be bumped up. "I guess I really am a cook now," says one woman.

Biskar smiles at this, then adds a note of caution. "We may have to push them on some of these contract terms," he says. "Just because we have a contract does not mean the company will not break it—in fact, I am sure they will." So he outlines the new grievance procedure, and points out that the company has agreed to recognize the rights of union stewards to represent the workers in disputes.

The contract includes the company's first-ever commitment to make contributions toward the Butler worker's retirement. Aramark has agreed to contribute an amount equal to 3 percent of a worker's salary into a 401(k) retirement plan if the worker puts in 1 percent of her salary. "Now, let's be honest here," Biskar says. "They agreed to this because they don't think you will make your contribution. And I know most of you are living paycheck to paycheck. But we should all figure out a way to make this contribution, not just the ones who are getting ready to retire soon. The company match is like extra money for the taking."

Biskar offers a similar pitch urging workers to take advantage of the new contract's health care coverage. "Currently, you have a very bad health plan," he says. An older woman in the front row says, "I know that!" Only five or six of the nearly one hundred Butler Aramark workers ever signed up for the existing plan, which has high premiums and only covers 60 percent of health care costs. The new plan will cover over 80 percent of costs and save workers over $100 a month in premiums. Biskar says that the phasing in of the coverage requirements under the Affordable Care Act, aka Obamacare, will eventually grab workers' attention to this provision of the contract. "A lot of you have not cared about health care plans before, but Obamacare means you will be paying a big fine by 2016 if you don't sign up," he says. "This is going to be a big issue for you all soon, and your family and friends who are not in a union are going to be paying a lot more than you for health care."

The health care talk has drained some of the energy from the room, but everyone perks up when Biskar turns to the topic of wages. The contract calls for seven raises over all, with most workers getting $1.55 more an hour over the course of the contract. All cooks are bumped up to $10 an hour immediately, as are campus operations workers at Marian. Aramark has been bringing in new employees at salaries as low as $7.25 per hour, but by the end of the contract no one will be paid less than $9 per hour. The raises will go into effect as soon as the contract is ratified. A large man with a shaved head and a dark beard interrupts Biskar. "Are you saying that if we vote 'yes' today, I get a forty-five cents an hour raise tomorrow?" Biskar says that is correct. The man smiles, mimes shooting a jump shot, and says in falsetto, "Ballin'!" Everyone laughs. Biskar decides it is a good time to protect against any future misunderstanding. "I guarantee you that sometime over the course of this contract, management is going to tell some of you that they would love to give you even bigger raises, but the union won't let them. That is a damn lie. This contract only sets out the minimum raises you can count on; the company can always go higher if they want to."

On the question of summer work, Aramark and the union reached a creative settlement. When the school staff is cut during academic year breaks, the company agrees to offer university workers the first opportunity for hours at other Aramark locations. In return, UNITE HERE agrees not to organize unions at the other locations for at least a year after Butler and Marian workers are placed there. The provision gives Aramark a strong incentive to annually find positions for Butler and Marian workers at all of its locations, since their placement inoculates the workplace from union organizing. Also, summer university work will not be offered to students, and all available work will be offered on a seniority basis. A worker hears all this, holds up his voting card, and says, "Hell, let's just vote 'yes' right now!"

But first, Elmira Bowen has something to say. A member of the negotiating committee that hammered out this deal with Aramark, Bowen started out the unionization process as a very shy person. But she was also frustrated by a lack of respect from her managers and by tiny raises from Aramark that were as little as two or three cents per hour. "It was time for someone to do something, and I finally decided that I couldn't always look for someone else to do it," she said. Bowen became a member of a prounion team that included workers like Tanya Gray and Rebecca Bradley. They met several times as a group and with UNITE HERE staffers, and then committed to spending the long weekend in late 2012 visiting Butler workers at home and asking them to sign them up for the union. "I feared that most would say, 'I don't want to do that, I don't want to lose my job,' but they were happy about the union," Bowen recalls.

The strength that was built through efforts like that led to the contract the workers were voting on today, Bowen says. So, even though she still prefers to let other people talk most of the time, Bowen decides that it is now the time to address her colleagues. "We told everyone we were 'In it to win it,'" and that is just what we did," she says. "Now we have a voice and they can't just treat us any kind of way. They have to treat us with respect!" The workers fill out their cards and place them in a cardboard box. On a secret ballot, the final vote to approve the Butler contract was 72–0.

Liam Roche was not present at the triumphant Butler contract approval meetings. Shortly after the Butler workers voted to join the union in late 2012, Roche quit UNITE HERE and reenrolled in school. He took a full load of science classes at IUPUI and got a job at the university cancer center, all in preparation for seeking a nursing degree. Roche had recently married a former high school classmate. Even amid all the changes that his new life as a union organizer brought, he had retained his dream of returning to small-town family life, a life he envisioned as all but impossible to achieve while working as an organizer.

Roche remained close to the Butler workers, and credits them with inspiring him to dive into a whole new career path. "I had the chance to see people overcome the mentality of 'I'm just a dishwasher, nothing's ever going to change,' and then one day, the spark comes alive in them and they are a different person," he says. "I had the chance to see Tanya, Elmira, Rebecca, and all of them do these amazing, brave things, like walking in and confronting their boss. It gave me courage, and I felt like I needed to put up or shut up about pursuing my own dreams."

The Aramark contract is ratified at Marian by an overwhelming 43–1, with the tally 24–0 in James Holder's campus operations division. After the ballots are counted, Holder confesses to being tired. He is ready for a time of healing at Marian and a chance to unwind personally. But his important role in the union campaign's success means that Holder will not be allowed too much free time. He is already being asked by UNITE HERE and other local groups to talk about the Marian and Butler struggle, and to share his story with workers who have yet to earn a union contract. The union even flew him to Los Angeles to talk with campus workers there. It was Holder's first trip to the city. He has mixed feelings about the travel, but he is inspired by the work: "It is normal now for me to go around and talk to people; to ask them how their jobs are going. And there are a lot of people who are hurting."

But there are fewer workers hurting at Marian University than there used to be, he says. In the spring, one of Holder's longtime colleagues had withdrawn his union membership, weary of the contract fight and intimidated by management's discouragement of union activities. On the day of the contract ratification vote, that same worker walked into the room where ballots were being collected. "I am back, and I am joining the union," he announced. Four more of Holder's colleagues signed up for the union that week. A similar pattern occurred at Butler and HMSHost.

After months of arguing for the union at Marian and across the city, these conversions pleased Holder. And he had his own pain addressed in this process, too. "I got into all this because I did not see job security, and there was a lack of respect," he says. "That is all taken care of now."

14

TURNED AWAY AT THE HOTELS

For better and for worse, the scene outside the downtown Indianapolis Hyatt Regency spoke volumes about the state of UNITE HERE's efforts to organize hotel workers in the largest U.S. city without a unionized hotel. The occasion was West Hollywood, California, Hyatt housekeeper Cathy Youngblood's visit to Indianapolis, part of a 2013 national tour for the union's "Someone Like Me" campaign to get a hotel worker added to the Hyatt board of directors. "I am a Hyatt housekeeper, and yes, I do windows," she told the gathered crowd. "I clean toilets, too. There is no shame in being a housekeeper, but shame on Hyatt for not wanting to talk to someone like me."

From one perspective, the event was a success. A good-sized crowd of about one hundred people picketed the hotel and garnered some attention to the hotel workers' struggles. Youngblood, a thin, dignified woman of sixty-one who holds multiple college degrees, gave several media interviews and was an articulate spokesperson for the cause. "Thousands of housekeepers and cooks and doormen go to work every day for Hyatt, and we are the front lines of the company," she said. "Most of us are women, people of color, or immigrants. Having a real hotel worker on Hyatt's board would benefit the company and the employees both."

For observers in Indianapolis, the strong event was no surprise. In its years of efforts to organize the Hyatt and other Indianapolis hotels, UNITE HERE had shown time and again its capacity to put together a good demonstration and to present articulate hotel workers and community spokespersons. The union had proven its ability to organize airport and university workers and win good contracts for them—often with the help of former local hotel workers turned organizers. But what it had not yet accomplished was real progress toward the goal it set upon its arrival in Indianapolis: winning the union for hotel workers.

Understandably, lead organizer Mike Biskar preferred to put a positive spin on the situation. "You know, we've done a lot of pickets outside the Hyatt over the years but I thought that one was particularly special because we have real members now, and so it wasn't just the students and the typical Indianapolis community activists," he said a few days after the event. "We had twenty Aramark workers there and a handful of airport workers. I kind of feel like it's the beginning of a new era here where when we are taking on companies like the Hyatt or other hotels, it's going to be this movement of workers and union members." At the same time, though, union leaders privately conceded there was not an active or strong committee of workers inside the Hyatt. The demonstration did not include a single Indianapolis Hyatt employee.

I circled back to Keisha Johnson, the Westin Hotel housekeeper, a few times after her City-County Council testimony in 2012. She and her husband were evicted again in early 2013. At their new home, she now had a longer walk to the bus and a longer bus ride downtown. Johnson still made less than $10 per hour at the Westin, but she was hoping to figure out how to squeeze out money to pay for health insurance premiums. "Truthfully, I am pretty discouraged," she said in late 2013. Morale was low inside the hotels. In the Westin, the temp agency housekeepers outnumbered the permanent employees five to one, Johnson said, and the two groups were not getting along. She felt that she was the only person in her workplace willing to make sacrifices to get the union. "They [the other workers] want the union, but they are not wanting to put their name and face out there, and to speak out like I have." Johnson sighed. "I feel like I am the quarterback that has to hold up the entire team."

UNITE HERE organizers did not dispute the grim picture painted by Johnson, but they pointed toward the difficult environment they encountered when they arrived in Indianapolis, especially the widespread subcontracting. "Hotels were able to run wild and basically do whatever they wanted with workers," Biskar said. "They can raise room quotas for housekeepers, send their workers to Wishard [the community-supported hospital] when they are sick rather than provide health care, and basically save millions of dollars because there is no union here. So we knew that the hotels would fight hard to resist the union." The UNITE HERE-led legislative campaigns against blacklisting and for hotel worker tax relief, along with the wage theft litigation, had curbed some excesses. The union efforts even seemed to have boosted local hotel worker wages a bit.

But the organizers did not pretend that these indirect victories, and the smaller-scale success in organizing other hospitality workers in the city, were a substitute for victory in the hotels. "We have to organize the hotels," UNITE HERE organizer Stuart Mora told the union's university and airport workers at their annual Indianapolis meeting in the summer of 2013. "That is where the power is in this city, with the convention and tourism industry."

That industry was what brought UNITE HERE to Indianapolis in the first place. As the union argued for good wages at other hotels across the Midwest, it found its proposed pay rates reliably undercut by the much lower wages that major hotels were paying their nonunionized Indianapolis employees. In particular, national union organizing campaigns for Starwood and Hilton hotels were being harmed by the example of Indianapolis, where the downtown hotel market was dominated by the staunchly antiunion White Lodging Inc. A similar wage-depressing effect was being felt within the city of Indianapolis itself, as low pay in the hotels pushed down the pay rate of hospitality workers across the community. "Indy was a fast-growing hotel and convention market that thrived by being cheaper than anyone else," says Antony Dugdale, director of research for UNITE HERE. "So what was happening in Indy was not staying just there. It affects what the standards are in places like Minneapolis or Nashville or Houston and many places where we have big convention hotels. Indianapolis is like the Walmart of the convention industry, and we worked to figure out if we could change that."

The opportunity for change seemed to present itself in 2005, when the mayor of Indianapolis announced support for the construction of a large new downtown hotel, a facility deemed necessary to buttress the city's bid to host a Super Bowl. Indianapolis would ultimately set aside over $60 million in tax breaks and other subsidies to support the development of the new hotel.[1] UNITE HERE is well known for using this type of intersection of government decision making with private investment to exert pressure on hotels to welcome union presence among their workforce, or at least to promise to remain neutral if an organizing campaign occurs. Dugdale, one of many former Yale students in the UNITE HERE leadership cadre, explains that his team is tasked with uncovering the many ways in which taxpayer dollars backstop companies in the hospitality industry: "Our research is all about understanding the complex web of mutual accountability that exists between all different institutions in our society. You use it right, the workers can have power. If you don't, workers get totally lost in the shuffle."

In other words, private companies wanting to get government subsidies for their hotel developments need to agree to the terms set out by elected officials. And if the elected officials are Democrats, whose voters and funding are often closely connected to union activism, UNITE HERE can often persuade those officials to include prounion terms in the funding agreements. The Indianapolis mayor who would be choosing the new hotel's developer was Bart Peterson, Indianapolis's first Democratic mayor in almost forty years. From UNITE HERE's perspective, the stars seemed aligned for Indianapolis to finally have its first unionized hotel. "We thought, let's figure out how to work out a partnership where we will talk about the positive impact a union hotel will bring," Dugdale says. "If Indianapolis finally has a unionized hotel, you can bring in for conventions all the progressive groups that were not going to Indy at all."

Peterson appointed a committee to choose the developer, and the bidders were narrowed down to two companies. The union began speaking with one of the finalists, a partnership led by Indianapolis-based Browning Investments. The talks went well, and Browning leadership indicated it would be willing to work with UNITE HERE and not oppose a campaign to unionize the new hotel's workers. UNITE HERE never spoke with the other finalist, White Lodging. Not only did it seem pointless to attempt talks with a company that is one of the most antiunion hotel management corporations in the country, it seemed impossible that Peterson's committee would choose White Lodging. The company was closely tied with

Republican politics, with its billionaire founder, Dean White, consistently assuming the spot as the top donor to Indiana GOP candidates. His company, Whiteco Industries, would in 2011 give $1 million to a Republican political action committee.[2]

But, in late 2006, Peterson's committee did choose White Lodging to develop what would become a 1,005-room J. W. Marriott Hotel, the largest J. W. Marriott in the world. UNITE HERE's leaders were stunned. They recovered enough to recruit City-County Council members to push Peterson to require that the developer not resist union organizing. They also enlisted progressive groups to pledge to bring conventions to Indianapolis if the hotel included a union workforce. But Peterson followed his committee's recommendation, approving the White Lodging deal with no union strings attached. The perceived opening for hotel union organizing in Indianapolis had slammed shut.

Dugdale says now that UNITE HERE had been "naïve" to assume that the Indianapolis mayor would support a union hotel just because he was a Democrat. After all, Peterson was the son of a real estate developer and a former staffer to centrist Indiana governor Evan Bayh. But the White Lodging choice still puzzles UNITE HERE organizing director Jo Marie Agriesti. "A lot of our hotel work, especially in new developments, is built around having political support for the idea of having good jobs in the city," she says. "I just find Indianapolis to be a very complicated place. Even when the Democrats get in power, they are fairly conservative and not necessarily supportive of hotel workers." In 2007, Peterson was defeated for reelection by Republican Greg Ballard.

The union leaders also express frustration at the structural weakness of the City-County Council, Indianapolis's legislative body. Across the country, city councils are often UNITE HERE's best allies in new hotel development unionization efforts, but the Indianapolis council has relatively limited impact on such decisions. The Indiana General Assembly has created an unelected entity called the Metropolitan Development Commission that it empowered to grant the tax abatements and make zoning decisions that drive economic development policy in Indianapolis's Marion County. In every other city in the state, the local Council makes those decisions. In 2013, the Republican-controlled General Assembly gave the mayor, also a Republican, five appointments to the Commission and thus majority control.[3] The Democratic-controlled Council was reduced to four appointments. The Council can overturn a Commission decision, but the process is so difficult that it is almost never done. One former Council member, Joanne Sanders, recalls only one or two Council overrides of the Commission in her dozen years in office. "It is astonishing to me how dramatically the Indiana legislature has radically disempowered the city council," Dugdale says.

With the effort to secure a union hotel contract through the political process now blocked, UNITE HERE turned to more traditional organizing in Indianapolis. Mora and several colleagues inside the Hyatt, including Hakiim Ejjair, pushed for the union. Keisha Johnson and others argued for representation in their hotels. Mike Biskar and Becky Smith built community support that led to demonstrations and even civil disobedience outside the hotel. By organizers' reckoning, at one point, as many as 65 percent of the Hyatt workers would have supported the union if a card check was allowed. A 2009 video produced by the union, entitled *Raising Indianapolis: Hotel Workers Rising in Indianapolis*, depicts the heady days when the union organizing movements at the Hyatt Regency, the Westin, and the Sheraton Keystone Crossing all went public.[4] Enthusiastic worker committee members are shown persuading a strong majority of workers to sign a petition calling for a "fair process." That process included card check and a management pledge to remain neutral as the workers decided whether they wanted to be represented by a union—the same deal that UNITE HERE hoped Mayor Peterson would compel as part of the J. W. Marriott development.

In the video, tearful housekeepers talked about being forced to rush through dozens of rooms in each shift, and insisted that it was time to come together as a union. UNITE HERE hotel worker members from Chicago joined Indianapolis workers for a raucous march to the Statehouse, and state and local officials joined the workers in delivering the petitions to hotel management. "This is the beginning, only the beginning," one hotel worker said on camera. "This is a powerful group of people and it is beginning to snowball. It is just going to get bigger." A city-county councilor echoed those sentiments, saying, "It is to a point where [the movement] cannot be stopped. It cannot!"

But the Indianapolis hotels had no intention of going along with a card check process. And UNITE HERE generally avoids NLRA elections, believing that U.S. labor law does not allow the union to effectively respond to a management-led inside campaign to erode workers' union support. A stalemate ensued. In hindsight, Biskar says now that he did not recruit a large enough committee of worker leaders supporting the union, and that he did not prepare the workers for how difficult the challenge would be. With little progress being made, the union decided to launch a local boycott of the Indianapolis downtown Hyatt.

It was a mistake. The union struggled to find enough groups and individuals whose shunning of the Hyatt would affect the hotel's bottom line. Meanwhile, hotel management told the workers that the boycott would deprive them of tip money and work hours. "The boycott allowed the Hyatt to run the antiunion campaign they always wanted to run, which was that the union is taking money out of your pocket, they are stealing from you," Biskar says. Hotel managers supported the creation of an antiunion committee of workers who persuaded dozens of their colleagues to sign a petition opposing the union. Becky Smith tells of a Hyatt worker who went from a passionate union supporter to an opponent almost immediately after the boycott was announced. A bartender, the worker felt that the boycott was causing her already meager income to take a hit. Smith also found some of her community contacts recoiling from the confrontational nature of a boycott. "Before the boycott, we were really moving," she says. "We had workers excited, we had community support, we even had civil disobedience, which was a big deal in Indiana."

Sensing the momentum in its favor, the Hyatt gave some workers generous raises and lifted the caps on salaries for longtime employees, supporting its argument that a union was not necessary for the workers to be treated well. At the same time, the Hyatt also fired an active supporter of the union, a former employee of the year. (The worker had sleep apnea, and a video surveillance camera caught him with eyes closed on his shift.) Hotel managers pointed out to employees, especially older workers and workers of color, that the most passionate union supporters included a disproportionate number of young white workers like Mora and Liam Roche. Inside the hotel, union support among the workers began to erode. By late 2011, UNITE HERE began pulling back on its Indianapolis hotel campaign.

Since UNITE HERE came to Indianapolis in order to organize hotels, I have asked union staffers why they did not leave town when the organizing campaigns fell apart. The initial decision to send organizers to

Indianapolis was Agriesti's, and it appears she was the one who decided the union should not leave town, either. She cites the workers' continued desire to unionize, young organizers' commitment to Indianapolis workers, and the community's enthusiasm as demonstrated in rallies and demonstrations. But it is also clear that Agriesti and other UNITE HERE staff simply could not stand the thought of giving credence to the hotels' antiunion rhetoric, which was often based on the goal of creating a sense of futility among the workers. "The idea of these corporations is to demoralize people and tell them they are never going to win, and that is just not true," she says.

Dan Abraham, a Chicago-based food-service organizing director for UNITE HERE, says that after the Indianapolis hotel campaigns had clearly gone sour, there was a logical time for the union to walk away from the community. He says there is definitely an argument to be made that the union sticks with struggling campaigns too long, when it would be more efficient to switch resources to more promising areas. But he also points out that, by the time the hotel organizing had run aground, Indianapolis Airport workers had launched their own union campaign. "I think something we do culturally as a union is that, if a group of workers stick their necks out, we are not going to leave them behind when there are setbacks," Abraham says. UNITE HERE is also known for striving to gain traction in nonunionized markets such as Atlanta, San Antonio, and Phoenix, as well as Indianapolis. Even when the initial efforts failed, the union continued to see value in resisting the wage-depressing effect of the nonunionized Indianapolis hospitality and convention industry.

Interestingly, it was the union's commitment to its own Indianapolis staff leadership that may have tipped the scales toward staying in town and picking new fights. The union had high hopes for Mike Biskar, Abraham says, and pulling him out of Indianapolis after a losing hotel effort was not going to be good for Biskar's development as an organizer. "It's fairly easy to say that a campaign is not going anywhere, and to pull resources," he says. "But sometimes the thing that makes us stick with campaigns is the training of the people. We wanted Mike to succeed."

So the Indianapolis UNITE HERE effort turned to food-service organizing, which proved to be much lower-hanging fruit than the hotel efforts. "In Indianapolis, each hotel is in a nonunion sea in their industry, and they don't want to be the first ones to be singled out to go union,"

Dugdale says. But industry consolidation in food service means that the dominant companies in Indianapolis are multinational firms that have already entered into union contracts all over the world. Those companies include Aramark, Chartwells, and the airport food and retail companies like HMSHost. For universities, a hike in the cost of food service is a fraction of their total operating budget, compared to hotels where a unionized payroll would significantly impact the cost of doing business. As was proven at IUPUI, Marian, and Butler, faculty and students can be natural allies for union-seeking workers. As for airports, they are strongly tied to municipal governments, which provide the opening for political pressure to support union jobs.

None of that makes unionization in food-service settings a slam dunk, of course. But it certainly improved UNITE HERE's chances, and thus set up a different Indianapolis union challenge: bringing a campaign to a successful conclusion. Abraham helped oversee the initial Indianapolis food-service organizing that Biskar and others led on ground. "I don't feel like I taught them how to organize," Abraham says. "But I do feel like I taught them how to win, which is not the same thing." He points out that winning a contract requires compromises. "We [can] maintain a high level of ideological purity in a long-term battle we never win," he says. 'We don't have that luxury when we want to hammer out a real contract." For example, he says, the Butler and Marian workers did not achieve everything in their contracts that they deserved, nor did they get all that the companies and universities could afford. But that does not mean they did not win. And those Indianapolis victories, he and others at UNITE HERE believed, helped build the momentum to allow the union to turn its attention back to hotel organizing. In fact, just as the Butler and Marian campaigns were coming to a successful conclusion in the summer of 2013, the union reached a national agreement with Hyatt. The long-sought deal promised a chance to finally organize a hotel in Indianapolis.

15

BACK TO THE HYATT

In the late twentieth and early twenty-first centuries, UNITE HERE achieved remarkable success organizing North American hotel workers. Where the union is strongest, in cities such as New York, Los Angeles, and San Francisco, its members make over $20 per hour with good bene-fits packages. As discussed in chapter 7, UNITE HERE achieved historic gains in Las Vegas's huge hospitality industry. By 2013, the union reported that it represented over one hundred thousand hotel workers working in nine hundred hotels across the United States and Canada.

But little of that strength is reflected in Midwestern cities like India-napolis and in union-resistant Sun Belt communities, where hotels engage in widespread outsourcing and workers are poorly paid and have little or no job security. By 2012, UNITE HERE was struggling to form unions in Hyatt hotels in cities such as Indianapolis, San Antonio, and Baltimore. At the same time, the union faced Hyatt resistance to contract renewals for its workers in area strongholds such as San Francisco, Honolulu, Los Angeles, and Chicago.

The union responded by conducting a campaign that included high-profile one-day strikes in Chicago and San Francisco and aggressive international public relations outreach under the banner "Hyatt Hurts." The union singled out the Hyatt for its outsourcing practices, highlighting a notorious 2009 decision by three Boston Hyatt hotels to outsource one hundred housekeeper jobs to Hospitality Staffing Solutions. (HSS is the same company sued for engaging in wage theft from hotel temporary workers in Indianapolis.) The union also alleged widespread mistreatment of Hyatt workers, including managers forcing a San Francisco dishwasher to return to her job three days after undergoing a C-section. "Hyatt has abused workers, replacing career housekeepers with minimum wage temporary workers and imposing dangerous workloads on those who remain," UNITE HERE's "Hyatt Hurts" website proclaimed.

In mid-2012, the union announced a global boycott of the hotel chain and recruited the support of the AFL-CIO, the National Organization for Women, and the National Football League Players Association. The International Union Federation, which represents hotel workers internationally, signed on to the boycott, too. UNITE HERE launched a companion online campaign to have Hyatt voted "The Worst Hotel Employer in America." When President Obama nominated Penny Pritzker, whose family owns the Hyatt chain, to be his commerce secretary in 2013, the union organized a protest picket in Chicago, the hometown of Obama and the site of Hyatt headquarters. UNITE HERE workers also packed a Senate committee hearing to show opposition to Pritzker's nomination.

UNITE HERE claimed that the hotel chain lost more than $25 million in business due to the boycott. There is no way to verify that figure, but it was clear that the negative campaign was landing significant blows to the hotel chain's image. A week before Pritzker was confirmed 97–1 by the U.S. Senate (Vermont senator Bernie Sanders cited the Hyatt's treatment of its workers in his dissenting vote), there were reports that the hotel and the union had reached an agreement. One week after Pritzker was confirmed, Hyatt and UNITE HERE announced the deal.

Neither party provided many details about the terms, but the workers in San Francisco, Honolulu, Los Angeles, and Chicago were to get a new, favorable contract, and the union would drop the global boycott. Most important for workers in Indianapolis and other cities where Hyatt organizing campaigns have not yet broken through, the company agreed to

Figure 15.1. A demonstration in front of the Indianapolis Downtown Hyatt Regency hotel. Several years of efforts to organize hotel workers in Indianapolis have not yet proved successful. Photo by author.

what is commonly called a "neutrality agreement," pledging not to actively oppose union organizing efforts. Also, unionized Hyatt workers in cities such as San Francisco retained the ability to strike in support of nonunionized Hyatt workers if those workers do not have a union contract after a year. It was an unusual concession by the company, as union contracts usually bar workers from striking during the length of the contract.

If Indianapolis hotel workers were ever going to get a union, this was the time.

Stuart Mora enters a downtown Indianapolis coffee shop, grabs a table, and opens up a manila folder filled with various notes about the Hyatt. He puts down his phone, an out-of-date flip version with silver duct tape holding in the battery in the back. From 2008 to 2011, Mora worked in various positions within the food and beverage division of the downtown Indianapolis Hyatt. His last two years were spent working at the Starbucks in the lobby. Now, Mora is a full-time organizer. In recent months, the union has assigned him to help with the university campaigns and the Indianapolis effort to push immigration reform, but now his focus is back

Figure 15.2. UNITE HERE organizer Stuart Mora and IUPUI worker-turned-organizer James Meyers lead Indianapolis union workers in an organizing session. Photo by author.

on building support within the hotel workforce. "The national Hyatt settlement is wonderful, but none of it is going to mean anything here if a majority of workers in the hotel do not realize that the union will be good for them," he says.

Union organizing campaigns are not launched with press conferences or ribbon cuttings. Under current U.S. law, employers have the ability to block union organizers from holding meetings at the workplace, or even from providing information to workers on-site. Employers certainly do not disclose the identity of their workers, so unions rarely even know the names of the employees they seek to organize, much less their contact information. Thus, organizing begins as a quiet, "underground" affair, as union supporters inside and outside the shop work to spread the word and build support. By the fall of 2013, the underground efforts to organize the Indianapolis Hyatt Regency were ramping up, and Mora was leading the charge.

Maria Garcia arrives at the table a few minutes after Mora has set up. Garcia is not her real name—she fears employer reprisal if her union support is known. She comes from a deep union background: her mother is a local leader for another union, and her grandparents were union activists back in Mexico. A close friend recently helped lead the union organizing efforts at the Indianapolis International Airport. Garcia was a proworker student activist in college and is active in the local citizenship campaign— she herself is an undocumented immigrant. By the time she met with Mora, she had worked for several months as a housekeeper at the Hyatt. Like many of the staff, she is actually employed by a subcontractor. But she is immersed in the hotel, where she does laundry, fulfills guest requests for extra towels or pillows, and sometimes cleans the rooms.

Actually, Garcia admits, she does not clean the rooms very often anymore. It turns out that Keisha Johnson's description of the pressure on hotel housekeepers was no exaggeration. Garcia simply could not clean rooms at the pace that management required—"It is the most stressful, difficult job in the hotel," she says—so she was moved to laundry and guest services. Unlike many of the subcontracted workers, Garcia is an excellent English speaker, which makes her ideal for the guest interaction. In her guest services role, Hyatt management gives her a strict fifteen-minute limit to field the request, complete it, and call a manager on the radio to confirm. Some days, Garcia works in the laundry room, where dirty sheets and towels arrive after being dumped down a chute. The room is actually quite small, perhaps the size of two parking spaces, and the soiled laundry stacks up in enormous piles that need to be sorted between linens—sent out for cleaning—and towels, which Garcia and colleagues wash, dry, and fold in-house. The linens can contain "gross stuff," Garcia says, and I do not ask for elaboration. She shows me a cell phone photo that demonstrates that the piles of laundry grow to twice her height and dominate the room, making the setting claustrophobic. Several of her coworkers struggle to keep up with the cleaning duties. During their mandatory breaks, they will clock out as instructed, only to spend the off-the-clock time back at work catching up with their tasks. If they don't work the extra unpaid time, they fear they will be fired for not finishing their duties.

Garcia is staunchly prounion. As time permits, and if she can get herself to work early, she talks to her colleagues, getting a feel for the mood and the social structures of the workplace. Garcia is one of three Hyatt workers who Mora meets with weekly. Four others are also committed union supporters, likely to become members of a future workplace committee to push for majority worker support of the union. Fearing reprisal by management, they have not yet openly disclosed their prounion stance.

Their numbers are not large, especially compared to the 120 employees at this Hyatt. But, to union organizers, this ratio is neither surprising nor particularly discouraging. Social science research shows that most workers fear conflict in the workplace,[1] and the history of union organizing shows that most successful campaigns are led by a small core of workers and activists. For example, the iconic Flint, Michigan, sit-down strike of 1936 and 1937 that fueled the growth of the United Auto Workers was triggered and sustained by a distinct minority of workers.[2] In Flint in 1936 and in Indianapolis in 2013, most workers are understandably wary about getting involved in the earlier and more risky stages of union organizing. But they happily jump on board once the workers' strength is demonstrated. "They are willing to fight, but they don't want a war," says Wade Rathke, founder of the Association of Community Organizations for Reform Now (ACORN) and SEIU Local 100, summarizing research about the attitudes of most workers today. "They want agreements, but the majority of workers surveyed want to figure out a way to work with the company on some mutual program, rather than be in a contentious relationship."[3]

The UNITE HERE organizers say there are both benefits and costs to following the previous unsuccessful Indianapolis Hyatt organizing effort. The positives come from knowing many of the workers already and having a sense of how management will respond once the organizing becomes public. The negative is represented by the lost enthusiasm of some workers who have already fought once, only to be defeated. Mike Biskar points to the growth of some of the Butler and Marian workers into union leaders during the course of their successful campaigns and contract negotiations, but he bemoans the fact that none of the Hyatt workers have had a similar chance to develop. "There were people at the Hyatt who were much stronger than almost any of the Butler and Marian workers, but they totally fell off the map because we were not winning," he says. Biskar describes one particular hotel worker, a young African American bartender who was politically engaged and a natural leader in the workplace. But, as the campaign dragged on without showing results, the worker slowly disengaged from the union. "Winning really matters for developing organizers," Biskar says.

The good news for the union is that the Indianapolis Hyatt campaign does have some time to build momentum. UNITE HERE's plan for following up on the national agreement with Hyatt is to proceed, nonunionized city by nonunionized city, toward public announcements of majority union support. After the public announcements, elections mandated by the Hyatt agreement will be held. In that queue, hotels in cities such as San Antonio and Baltimore are lined up before Indianapolis. As of the meeting between Stuart Mora and Maria Garcia in September 2013, the hope is for Indianapolis to go public with a Hyatt worker union majority in early 2014. As events unfolded, that date would be pushed back indefinitely.

Mora and Garcia begin speaking about which workers inside the Hyatt may be supporters of the union. Mora does most of the talking. Garcia's manner is reserved, and it is hard to envision her pumping coworkers for information. But she seems to get the job done. "Maria is very soft-spoken and very genuine, and she shares stories in a real direct way that is very effective," Mora says. In fact, Garcia has made a lot of contacts inside the hotel. She knows who thinks there should be two persons assigned to clean each room, and she knows who is frustrated by the uncertain hours assigned by management. She also knows which workers are upset because the hotel's Housekeeper Appreciation Week replaced bonuses with group arts-and-crafts projects. (For her gift that week, Garcia received a bag with an apple and an orange. She thinks the actual Hyatt employees' bag included a lottery ticket to accompany the fruit.)

One of Garcia's connections has been a woman who moves well between the permanent Hyatt room cleaners, who tend to be African American, and the contractor employees, who tend to be Latina. Another work friend is a young maintenance worker who shows concerns about workplace problems and low pay but does not get upset daily like some of the Hyatt workers. "Good," Mora says when he hears this description. "There is a difference between just being an agitated person and a leader—a leader knows how to see what is important."

Stuart Mora was sixteen years old when the attacks of September 11, 2001, occurred. The next Sunday, as they always did, Mora and his parents and two younger brothers went to Mass at their neighborhood Roman Catholic parish in Lansing, Michigan. But this time, something was different, at least for Mora. As he listened to the sermon, he grew increasingly upset. "It was not our regular priest, it was an older guy," Mora remembers. "And he gave this sermon that was anti-Muslim and antiliberalism. I thought to myself, 'I definitely disagree with what you just said. I don't know exactly what I think, but I know I disagree.'" The next Sunday, as the rest of the family prepared for church as usual, Mora informed his parents that he was not going. Shocked, his parents insisted he had to go. There was screaming and there was crying, but the teenager refused to budge.

Mora's reaction to 9/11 spilled over into arguments with classmates who advocated retribution against "towelheads" and even into debates with teachers who pushed for war. Mora can cite no role model as inspiration for his reaction or for his sudden willingness to go against the grain of the consensus opinions in his community. His mother is a pediatrician without strong political views, and his father is a stay-at-home dad and Reagan-admiring Republican. Ironically, Mora realized later, the seeds of his discontent with the jingoistic sermon and its aftermath were sown in the same church pew where he rejected the faith. He attributes his reaction to the teachings of the Catholic school he attended from kindergarten through eighth grade and to the hundreds and hundreds of Masses he sat through. "We went to church every Sunday and heard the message, 'Love everyone, love your enemy, turn the other cheek, stand up for what is right even if it causes harm,'" he says. "Those messages are just very fundamental, and they obviously stuck with me from a young age." But this was the first time that Mora, a top-ten student in his class and captain of the school's football and baseball teams, had ever challenged authority. He bonded with the handful of fellow students who shared his views, and he became even more politicized when the United States invaded Iraq during his senior year of high school.

Suddenly, Mora found himself in a different place politically than his family and most of his community. He decided he wanted to be in a different place geographically as well. He applied for admission to University of Notre Dame largely to appease his parents, but Mora had his sights set on California. After high school graduation, he deferred his enrollment at Notre Dame and signed up for an AmeriCorps program that placed him in a bilingual literacy program in Salinas. Salinas is a migrant community in the fertile valley region called the "Salad Bowl of the Nation," which was made famous by the books and stories of its native son John Steinbeck. Mora did not know a soul when he arrived in California, and he loved it. He worked as a tutor and found plenty of time to hitchhike around exploring the state. Mora's initial plan was to stay and enroll at one of the campuses in the University of California system. But he balked at the requirement that he take another standardized test before admission. He was also finding California a little too welcoming politically, and he missed the challenge of defending his views in the more conservative Midwest. "I knew that going to a place where people thought differently was going to challenge me, and I also thought very arrogantly, 'Hey I want to challenge them.'" He accepted his deferred admission to Notre Dame.

Once on campus, Mora fully embraced the college party scene. By the time he was a sophomore, he had got into enough trouble on campus that he avoided a suspension only by agreeing to take a voluntary leave of absence. Kicked out of a university program that would have allowed him to study in Chile for a semester, Mora decided to go to Mexico on his own. With money saved from his year working in California, he spent seven months traveling around the country, watching election rallies and immigration demonstrations. He set a personal goal to talk to at least six people each day.

"As my Spanish got better, I had deeper conversations, and we would talk about politics and religion and work and faith and family, you name it," he says. Some of the conversations turned into lengthy stays in the homes of families he met. Throughout, Mora took notes, with the intention of writing a book about his experiences. The book did not materialize, but Mora says he took away something more valuable:

> I finally got my head straight. I'd been fucking up for two years [at Notre Dame], and I wasn't being who I wanted to be. A couple of things became very clear to me. One, I'm not Mexican. I say that kind of tongue-in-cheek, but it was me saying, "It's OK to be white and middle class and American." That is my community, and I needed to go back to it. And two, everyone in Mexico had someone in their family or close community who went to the U.S. to work, and they do it because they want to build up their community. That's why they risk their lives to cross the border and work two crappy jobs and live in a place where they don't speak the language. People would say, "We just want to work. We just want to support this family, this community. That's it."

Mora returned to Notre Dame determined to build on those lessons, but having no idea how he was going to do so. He started volunteering at a South Bend homeless shelter and rejoined a student organization that had been advocating for a local living-wage law. The group had lost direction, so

Mora suggested they imitate what seemed to work for him in Mexico: "I'd never heard the word 'organizing' at this point, but I just figured we should go out and talk to [poor] people and figure out what they want. If it's a living wage, let's do a living wage. If it's not, we'll do something different." The group ended up advocating for workers at the university, even winning a worker's job back after he was fired for being gay. A friend suggested Mora join an annual Notre Dame seminar that introduces students to community and labor organizing, in part through a trip to Chicago to meet with workers and organizers there. Mora went to Chicago, and was enthralled. "That was the first time I realized that organizing was a job. I was like, 'Holy shit, are you kidding me? This is exactly what I want to do!'"

At the same time Mora was discovering organizing, he was rediscovering Catholicism. All of his colleagues in student organizing at Notre Dame were Catholic, and he learned that many Catholics found organizing to be the perfect expression of their beliefs. Mora was introduced to the writings of Dorothy Day, founder of the pacifist, activist Catholic Worker movement, and to the social-justice-oriented theology of the Trappist monk Thomas Merton. Mora finally found a vision of the church that lined up with the "love your neighbor" lessons of his parochial-school childhood. "It was a long journey back, and I still share more in the Catholic tradition than the theology sometimes," he says now. "But I learned that it is OK to have my views and still be Catholic." His parents would have never guessed it, but the teenager who boycotted Sunday Mass would turn out to be the most devout of their three sons.

Before graduation, Mora made two trips to Indianapolis for organizing trainings with UNITE HERE staff. During the first trip, in the spring of 2007, he sat in a room with several young people about his age and was not particularly impressed: "This is my arrogant streak, and I apologize for it, but I thought I could organize as well as any of the people in the room." But when he returned in the fall for another session, these former students had been training with the union and working hospitality jobs full-time, and Mora's arrogance dissolved. "It was like they were transformed: they were leading the meeting and really teaching me things," he says. "I was like, 'I want that training that they have been getting. So if that is what they are doing in Indianapolis, I am here.'"

He got hired at the Hyatt, and plunged into a demanding schedule that combined his hotel server duties with union organizing. Mora was put in charge of building Catholic community support for the hotel workers, and he was instrumental in turning out people for rallies and city council hearings. He discovered a lot of antiunion sentiment in Indianapolis, inside and outside the workplace. But he also discovered that patience and persistence often paid off. "People move in baby steps," he says. "They only get from here to there a little bit at a time. So you learn to celebrate when you get someone to move even a little bit." He learned that giving speeches to Catholic groups was not as effective as quietly persuading the group's leader to bring the group along in active support of workers. He learned the value of building bonds by sharing stories, both among workers and in the community. He learned that it is more valuable to recruit a single worker leader than a roomful of followers.

But as the Hyatt union effort began to unravel, Mora found himself exhausted and discouraged. By now, Mora, his future wife, and several friends had started their own Catholic Worker community in a working-class neighborhood on the near westside of Indianapolis. For over three years, Mora had been working at the Hyatt as a regular job, organizing the Catholic community for the union, and putting in long hours fixing up the house where the Catholic Worker would be located. Disappointed at the fading prospects of organizing a hotel union, Mora quit the Hyatt in November 2011. He considered quitting union work, too. He eventually decided to stay, but he moved away from the hotel organizing toward duties organizing college students across the Midwest to support UNITE HERE workers, including on the Marian and Butler campuses. UNITE HERE leadership says that the deep roots that Mora is sinking in Indianapolis will be a real benefit for their organizing in the community.

Now reassigned to the Indianapolis Hyatt, Mora feels he is better equipped to organize workers this time around. Reflecting on his collaboration with Garcia and other workers, he freely admits to pushing them beyond their comfort zones. "People want to be challenged, and if they don't, they don't come find us, that's for damn sure," he says. "They have to be able to respond to a challenge in a way that is healthy and positive, because some people don't." Mora is confident that the second Hyatt campaign in Indianapolis will be more successful than the first. The national agreement between the union and the hotel is a big boost, as is the momentum created by the union victories at universities and the airport. But, this time, Mora refuses to define his own success solely by the creation of a hotel union in Indianapolis. "Long term, it can't be only about the campaign. It has to also be about the leaders we are training, and where they are going to be in three to five years, or even ten to twenty years," he says. "If we get out of this [campaign] that Maria and other Hyatt workers end up being strong leaders of the movement, then it all keeps going."

"BRING LISA BACK!"

As of late fall 2013 it was not clear when the Indianapolis Hyatt organizing campaign would go public. After UNITE HERE's summer 2013 national agreement with the hotel, the Hyatt organizing was going well in such cities as Baltimore and Greenwich, but moving more slowly in places such as San Antonio and Indianapolis. The deadline in the back of organizers' minds was October 2015, the date when Hyatt workers at unionized hotels in Chicago, San Francisco, Honolulu, and Los Angeles can strike in solidarity with Indianapolis and other nonunionized workers. Privately, Indianapolis organizers wondered if it would take the prospect of those walkouts—or the sale of the Indianapolis hotel—to put the campaign over the hump here.

But the union's organizing in Indianapolis moved forward, informed by the unsuccessful effort a few years earlier. Biskar says the union has to be stronger in the housekeeping department this time around, with a broader base of leadership rather than just one or two vocal supporters. He looks forward to publishing a photo petition showing the faces of union-supporting workers, a tactic that worked well in building coworker support during the Butler and Marian campaigns. The Hyatt has made some decisions that may help the organizing, he says. Management has capped senior employee salaries, returning to an unpopular policy they abandoned during the last union campaign. And the hotel has responded to union and community pressure by hiring more African American staff. Given that UNITE HERE's successful Indianapolis campus organizing has often been led by African American workers, this is good news for the union.

Union organizers discussed how they should reengage with the Hyatt workers who openly supported the union the last time around, only to be disappointed when the campaign failed. To Biskar's way of thinking, it is important for UNITE HERE to demonstrate to its former leaders that the union can recruit new supporters, and that the result will be different this time. "Because we are doing this a second time around, there is going to be a lot of fear," he says. Then he stops and edits himself. "Not a lot of fear, probably, but probably a lot of hopelessness. So my personal opinion is that we should make sure there is some new blood supporting the union before we go back to the people who were our leaders last time."

With the Butler and Marian contracts won, James Meyers was joining Stuart Mora on the UNITE HERE Hyatt organizing team. By now, Meyers had made the transition from IUPUI and food service to full-time union organizing. He was quickly learning the organizing trade, and he filled a need: Meyers is the only African American on the local organizing team, he is significantly older than the other organizers, and he is the only one who grew up in Indianapolis.

It is clear that Meyers connects better with some Indianapolis workers than do the younger white organizers who grew up in other communities. "When I started as an organizer, I gave lip service to the idea that the workers should be the real leaders in organizing, but I am not sure how much I believed it," Biskar says. "But I soon realized that workers are more effective at communicating with fellow workers than I can ever be. James is the real deal, and you just can't fake that." Meyers's hometown status helped, too. When IUPUI professor Tom Marvin conducted his study of twenty-first-century service-sector organizing in Indianapolis, every interviewee mentioned that the Indianapolis community has a higher-than-usual distrust of outsiders.[1]

Becky Smith agrees with those observations. When she joined the local UNITE HERE organizing team in 2007, she was the only staff member who had grown up in the state. "When I was representing the union out in the community, the first question I would get was, 'Where are you from?' When I responded that I was from Indiana and lived here before doing the union work, people immediately became more at ease." In strategy discussions, Smith found that she often had different views from her colleagues, with Smith arguing that Hoosiers do not respond well to aggressive tactics like the local Hyatt boycott. It was not the only area of disagreement. Smith respected her UNITE HERE colleagues, but she felt she had broader goals for community change than her fellow organizers who were more focused on the particular workers being unionized. "I understand why the labor movement relies so heavily on low-paid young organizers you can send anywhere, but I also think the movement needs to learn how useful hometown advocates can be," she says. During most of her tenure Smith was also the only woman on the UNITE HERE team in Indianapolis, and she felt her style of organizing was not always respected by her younger, male colleagues. Shortly after coordinating the Adopt-a-Worker campaign in 2011, Smith left UNITE HERE to join the staff of the Indiana AFL-CIO.

During that late fall 2013 period, on a Friday morning in the UNITE HERE offices, Meyers, Mora, and Maria Garcia gather in the conference rom. Meyers is still learning about some of the Hyatt workplace issues, so he quizzes Garcia about her duties and those of the workers around her. It turns out Meyers had once worked as a "houseperson" at the local Westin. ("I hated it," he recalls.) Mora turns their attention to the upcoming week's big event. In midweek, the union would be holding a press conference in front of the Hyatt to announce a new wage theft lawsuit.

Ramón Silva, a former security guard for the company that provides security services to the Hyatt, says he worked as many as seventy-two hours per week but was not paid for many of his extra hours. The Hyatt subcontractor, C. G. Security, says Silva was a supervisor and thus not eligible for overtime pay. In fact, in October 2011 the company did switch Silva from a hourly rate to a salaried position. The Fair Labor Standards Act requires workers to be paid the minimum wage of $7.25 per hour and overtime at 1.5 times the workers' hourly wage, but the law exempts workers holding certain executive and administrative positions. Silva says the promotion was an illusory effort to avoid paying him overtime, and he says repeated twelve-hour days left him making an hourly rate far below minimum wage. Other security workers at the hotel were making similar allegations. The plan was for the press conference to be followed by a delegation of Silva and community supporters going into the hotel to personally serve the lawsuit on the head of security.

The event offers an opportunity for Garcia and other prounion workers to learn where some of their coworkers stand, Mora says. "This announcement is going to be a big deal at the hotel, since it will be on TV and in the newspaper," he says. "What are you going to say when a coworker asks you, 'Have you heard about all that going on in front of the hotel today?'" They role-play a few scenarios, with Mora portraying a back-of-the-house employee. Garcia tries a response to a coworker bringing up the lawsuit. "Yeah, since I am subcontracted too, I am worried that will happen to me."

It was not exactly what Mora was looking for. "How do you turn that into a question back to me?" he asks. "You got to get me to talk. Maybe say, 'Are you surprised?'" The desired approach, he says, using organizing terms Garcia is familiar with, is both "agitational" and "pro." Agitational means that the discussion should reveal what bothers a worker about the Hyatt. It is a concept deeply rooted in social movement history, indicating a moment when the worker sees a conflict between the workplace as it should be and the current situation.[2] "Pro" indicates a chance, if it comes up, to deliver a message that the union is one way to resolve that tension in favor of the workers. Since Garcia's parents are in unions, she has an obvious answer to any coworkers asking about her views. If a coworker echoes strong prounion views, she becomes someone Garcia and organizers will follow up with.

UNITE HERE organizers prefer not to disclose whether Garcia—or workers-turned-organizers like Mike Biskar and Stuart Mora—are or were "salts." Salting is a widely used technique where paid or unpaid union organizers obtain a job at a targeted nonunion company with the intent of helping form the union from within. This method of peer-to-peer organizing, with young activists usually performing the role of salts, is a core component of the strategy of UNITE HERE and many other unions.

But that doesn't mean they want to talk about it. When labor activist and journalist Steve Early published an article on salting in the September 2013 issue of *Working USA: The Journal of Labor and Society*,[3] he was publicly taken to task by a UNITE HERE organizer. "Anyone with the slightest familiarity with 'colonizing' [salting] understands that its success depends largely on companies not suspecting any 'colonization' . . . This piece can only put more companies on the lookout."[4]

In fact, salting is often vigorously condemned by employers and their trade organizations. The National Right to Work Committee calls salting "an underhanded method of intimidation designed by Big Labor bosses to blackmail employers into handing loyal employees over to union officials without the employees' consent."[5] And although the U.S. Supreme Court has ruled that salting employees should be protected from discrimination,[6] the term's likely origin comes from the deceptive practice of "salting" a mine by placing valuable metal inside to falsely suggest that the mine contains the metals naturally.[7]

So why do unions turn to salting? In considering the motivation, it is useful to view the constrictions of U.S. labor law as defined by an oft-cited National Labor Relations Board decision from 1972.[8] The Retail Clerks Union was trying to organize workers at Dexter Mills, a retail store, but was struggling to get access to the workers. The employer had barred the union organizers from the company property, including the parking lot, where the union had wanted to distribute handbills about the potential for workers to organize. Since the union had no way of obtaining accurate information on workers' names and addresses, efforts to reach workers at home were not successful. Union organizers then tried to stand outside the company parking lot to distribute handbills. That did not work well, either, since the only place they could stand was in a ten-foot-wide, tree-filled easement that stood between the parking lot and a public highway that had a speed limit of forty miles per hour. Both customers and employees whizzed past the organizers, who felt they were in danger of being struck by the cars when they tried to pass along the handbills.

Citing the U.S. Supreme Court's 1956 decision in *Babcock v. Wilcox*,[9] the union pointed out that the company could not block organizers from its premises if there was no reasonable alternative means of communication. "The right to self-organize depends in some measure on the ability of employees to learn about the advantages of union membership from others," the *Babcock* court had written.[10] But the NLRB refused to order the employer to allow organizers on the premises, saying the union should instead place staff on the easement and write down the license plate numbers of all the cars—customers and employees alike—entering the premises, and try to determine contact information by researching the identity of the license holders.

This kind of "access" to workers under U.S. labor law, union organizers say, leaves them with little choice but to place workers inside the facility. There, the workers/union activists can directly observe who works there and how they can be reached for a discussion about the union campaign. For most union campaigns, the organizers' first task is to compile "The List." Since union organizers are not allowed to formally communicate with the workers at their workplace, they need to know how to reach the workers outside the job. Employers are not interested in providing this information, of course, so organizers—and salts—are usually forced to resort to some backdoor methods for gathering phone numbers and addresses. Sometimes a sympathetic worker registers his colleagues to vote or even gathers addresses for party or wedding invitations, thus starting the list.

Salting dates back at least to the turn of the twentieth century, when the Industrial Workers of the World placed workers inside the lumber industry.[11] And it was the strategy employed to great effect during the 1930s heyday of U.S. organized labor. Union activists, who included Communists and Socialists, took jobs inside auto plants, coal mines, and steel mills in order to organize workers from within. Even the iconic Flint, Michigan UAW–General Motors sit-down strike of 1936–37 was led by a small number of activists-turned-workers.[12]

At varying levels of intensity and centralized coordination, salting has continued ever since. In the early twenty-first century, some union activists responded to organized labor's declining membership by calling for a renewed surge in salting, as in the 2002 appeal by International Longshore and Warehouse Union's organizing director Peter Olney:

More than hiring young people as organizers, [salting] is the way to promote large-scale organization. Nothing can replace the presence of these politicized organizers in the workplaces of America. Nothing can replace this experience in teaching young organizers, largely from a nonworking class experience, what the working class is about and how to talk and especially listen to workers. Salting needs to become fashionable again for young people politically committed to reinvigorating the labor movement.[13]

UNITE HERE and SEIU activists inside and outside Indianapolis will not be as explicit as Olney, at least on the record, but Olney's statement represents a rough consensus among almost every organizer I have ever spoken to. College-educated Indianapolis organizers like Biskar, Jade Lee, and Liam Roche are among those who say they could never have fully connected with workers if they had not spent hard days on the jobs themselves.

Part of the rationale for the underground nature of salting is that union activism exposes workers to risks of retaliation, up to and including being fired from their jobs. The union's response to that kind of retaliation presents an existential moment, according to former SEIU organizer Jane McAlevey. "When the employer starts firing workers for their union work, either the union steps right up to the plate that very minute, or it immediately starts to die," McAlevey says.[14] In late 2013, both the Indianapolis UNITE HERE team and the local Fight for 15 fast-food-worker campaign faced the firing of key worker leaders. Both met the test of fighting back, but the differing results revealed that the movements were not at equal stages of their development.

Lisa Massing is a forty-eight-year-old waitress who began working at the Champps Americana restaurant at the Indianapolis International Airport in 2008. Massey is a veteran server—she dropped out of school after becoming pregnant at age fifteen, and has been working as a waitress ever since. She has raised four daughters on the money she makes waiting tables, and she is proud that all her girls were able to finish high school, something she never had the chance to do.

UNITE HERE came to the Indianapolis airport in 2009 to organize Champps and other airport restaurants operated by Areas USA, an international-travel food-service company. During the initial campaign, Massing signed a union card, then promptly forgot about it. A union sounded OK to her, but she was used to relying on herself. In all her years as a waitress, Massing never made more than the federal minimum wage for tipped employees, which was $2.13 an hour in 2013. She never had her seniority recognized when shifts were assigned, and never had a grievance process if she had a dispute with management. But after UNITE HERE won the new union contract at Champps, she noticed the boost in her wages and the even bigger bump in pay for the nontipped cooks and dishwashers. For the first time in her career, Massing was able to exercise seniority to get her preferred schedule. Intrigued, she started to attend union meetings, and soon was asked to be a shop steward.

Massing likes a lot of things about working at the airport. It is a better atmosphere than a "street" restaurant, she says. There are a few regular travelers who are customers, but mostly she gets to meet new people, which she enjoys. Her 1 p.m. to 9 p.m. weekday shift allows her to spend time with her kids and grandchildren—a total of ten people in Massing's extended family live in her house in a working-class neighborhood on the west side of Indianapolis. Business at the restaurant is steady, and spikes up when flights are delayed. "We hate it for the travelers when the weather is bad, but that sure is good for us," she says, smiling a little sheepishly. "People come in and they are ready to eat and ready to drink!"

But there is one thing Massing does not like about her job: the restaurant seems to bring in new managers every few months. Massing finally stopped counting after she tallied fifty-two different managers and supervisors who started during the course of her five years at Champps. Experienced servers were being told to change procedures by managers who had just arrived on the scene, only to have a new set of rules imposed by that manager's replacement a few months later. Predictably, tensions rose in the workplace. During one of those tense periods in November 2013, Massing was on her scheduled break, talking on her cell phone in the back of the restaurant. One of the managers confronted Massing and chastised her. The restaurant had a rule against servers speaking on the phone during work hours, but it was a rule routinely ignored by previous managers. And, Massing pointed out, she was on her break. She did not think much of the encounter, and worked the next day without incident. But a week later, two days before Thanksgiving, Massing was called in to talk with the general manager. Citing the cell phone incident, the general manager fired her on the spot.

Several of Massing's Champps coworkers told me they believed the stated reason for the firing was a façade, and that Massing was being punished for her advocacy as a union steward. "They fired Lisa because she actually stood up to them and spoke up when need be, and the managers just didn't want anyone questioning them," one waitress said.

Massing was devastated. She certainly knew how to wait tables, but feared starting the process of trying to find a new job in her late forties. "They want younger, prettier faces as waitresses, and I understand that," she says. She immediately began putting in applications at other restaurants, but she was worried that a new employer might not be willing to take a chance on a waitress with diabetes and arthritis in her feet.

Massing also called UNITE HERE's Eva Sanchez, who in turn called Mike Biskar, who was out of town on another union assignment. They quickly helped Massing file a grievance and asked for the post-termination meeting with management that is guaranteed by the union contract. The meeting did not go well. The union representatives and Massing told the Champps manager that they had witnesses prepared to say that the no-phone-calls rule was inconsistently enforced. The manager was unimpressed. "I am standing my ground, and I am not changing my mind," he said. "Lisa is terminated, and you can get all the witnesses you want."

While preparing for that meeting, Sanchez and Massing made the rounds of other union restaurants in the airport, telling other workers what had happened. They quickly put together a handwritten petition captioned "BRING LISA BACK!" and collected dozens of signatures from Areas USA airport workers. Then they asked workers to join them in a delegation to Champps managers, where they would demand that Massing be rehired.

The delegation was scheduled for the morning after the unsuccessful grievance hearing. I arrive ten minutes before the action is to begin. Massing, Sanchez, and Biskar are gathered near the designated meeting spot in the airport baggage claim area. But no other workers are there yet, and they are not sure what kind of turnout to expect. The Champps manager had been openly hostile at the hearing, and had been cracking down on workers after Massing was fired. The union activists are worried that workers will be afraid to publicly speak up. After all, Massing apparently lost her job for doing so.

Then, just after Biskar excuses himself to take a phone call, a group of a half dozen Champps waitresses burst in from the parking garage. The women immediately engulf Massing in hugs. Massing is clearly moved. "Thank you so much for coming here for me!" she says.

"I could not believe it when I heard they actually fired you," one of the waitresses says. "You always take such good care of your customers."

"If it happened to you, it could happen to any of us," another says.

Several more Champps employees and other airport workers arrive. As they surround Massing, Biskar puts away his phone and whispers to Sanchez. Sanchez smiles broadly, and calls for everyone's attention. The phone call was from Champps' management. They had been told that the delegation was on its way, and they wanted no part of a public confrontation with their workers. Massing had her job back.

Massing is again swarmed by her coworkers, and several people wipe away tears. Massing's final hug is for Sanchez, who only recently left hospitality work to be on union staff. "I love you," Massing says quietly.

Massing is eager to tell her family the good news, so I give her a ride home. I ask her what she thinks would have happened if she was not part of a union. "Oh, no way would I have had my job back," she says. "But I had faith, because I have seen the union work before. I always say, 'The union is job security, as long as you do your job right.'"

By late 2013 the Indianapolis fast-food activism was clearly getting on Reginald Jones's nerves. Jones, who owns and operates a half dozen McDonald's franchises in Indianapolis, has been recognized by both the local United Way and the McDonald's corporate offices for his business success and community service. But noisy demonstrations about low wages paid to his workers was not the kind of attention he was seeking. On the morning of the August 2013 strikes, Jones stood in the parking lot of his restaurant, which is located at a high-traffic intersection just north of downtown Indianapolis, yelling angrily into his cell phone.

Later, Jones had a shouting match with a Fight for 15 organizer and submitted complaints to the police about the actions held outside his store. Jones's restaurant did receive a disproportionate amount of the activists' attention. The restaurant was a featured spot for the fast-food actions in part because of its high visibility, but also in part because it was the workplace of Dwight Murray. Murray was perhaps the most eloquent and reliable spokesperson for Indianapolis fast-food strikers.

In October, the National Employment Law Project released a study showing that fast-food jobs cost taxpayers billions in subsidies paid to workers being paid low wages. A full 52 percent of frontline fast-food employees rely on some kind of public assistance, with McDonald's employees alone receiving an estimated $1.2 billion in public subsidies each year.[15] New demonstrations were held to attract attention to the report. Again, the Indianapolis Fight for 15 action calling attention to the report was held in front of Reginald Jones's McDonald's restaurant. Dwight Murray was in attendance, wearing his McDonald's uniform and responding to requests for interviews. The demonstration was held in midday, and that afternoon Murray reported for his assigned shift. Within just a few hours, he was fired.

A manager told Murray he was being fired because he sexually harassed several female coworkers, supposedly all in the same afternoon. Murray says the allegations are not true, and he was never allowed to see any statements by any accusers. He applied for unemployment benefits and was found by the state agency to have been fired without just cause. But his unemployment check was just $64 per week. Murray's girlfriend had always opposed his involvement with the Fight for 15. Now, with money even tighter than usual, they began arguing regularly, and she threw him out of their shared apartment. The most visible Fight for 15 worker in Indianapolis was now unemployed and homeless.

Like Lisa Massing, Dwight Murray was eager to get his job back. Like Massing, he had support he could call on. The Fight for 15 campaign helped Murray file an unfair labor practice charge with the National Labor Relations Board and organized a delegation to confront Jones and demand that Murray be reinstated. The delegation included two dozen members of the community and SEIU Healthcare union members and activists. All signed a letter to Jones calling for Murray to be rehired. I participated in the delegation and signed the letter.

But unlike the group aligned behind Lisa Massing, the delegation did not include any of Dwight Murray's coworkers. One of the August strikers was on duty at the time the group marched into the restaurant to see Jones, but the striker ducked his head and looked in the opposite direction. Jones refused to speak to the delegation and summoned the police, who instructed us to leave. We did so, chanting "We'll be back!" But it was clear that Dwight Murray would not be back any time soon, at least as a paid worker.

"That Is What the Union Does for Me"

In 2013, Indiana governor Mike Pence announced that he would not expand Medicaid health insurance to the state's poor, even though the expansion was enabled and funded by the federal Affordable Care Act, aka Obamacare. In the following months, plenty of health care experts came to the Indiana Statehouse to express their opinions on the decision. But only one group did so by braving subzero wind chill temperatures, marching down the sidewalk through the snow, and chanting, "Up with justice, down with hate / Hoosiers need a healthy state!"

The frontline experts were SEIU Healthcare members, who rallied on the east steps of the Statehouse before going inside to meet with legislators. "We are asking Governor Pence to extend Medicaid so that it can cover workers like us," Theresa Johnson, a home health care worker from South Bend, told me once the group finally sought out some warmth inside the Statehouse. Johnson struggles with an autoimmune disorder, a pinched nerve in her back, and arthritis, all of which make it difficult for her to care for her patients. If Johnson was a resident of states surrounding Indiana, she would qualify for Medicaid under the new law. Instead, she struggles with chronic pain and makes do with over-the-counter medications. She hopes for a day when she can receive some of the professional health care she provides her patients. "Maybe one day Governor Pence or someone in his family will need the kind of health care we provide, and he will want someone healthy to give them the care they deserve," she said.

Johnson and her fellow SEIU Healthcare workers in Indiana, still led by organizer Yin Kyi, were at the Statehouse because they do not yet have the power to secure a strong union contract that provides good wages and benefits. So they and their union actively support Medicaid expansion and proposals to increase the state minimum wage. The hope is that demonstrations, lobbying, and support for progressive Indiana candidates can win them better working conditions, since they do not yet have the bargaining strength to achieve concessions directly from their employers.

As of early 2014, these home care workers and other low-wage workers have an increasing number of Indianapolis allies. The local Community Faith and Labor Coalition launched the city's first-ever worker center in late 2013 with an opening reception at the site of a former Carpenter's Union local. The enthusiastic standing-room-only crowd included many who wrote checks and donated cash to give the center a boost. "Do you think the community has been waiting for something like this?" a former city-county councilor asked, laughing. The center started its work by advocating for victims of wage theft and conducting community outreach on workers' rights. At the same time, union members and community supporters continued to march regularly with the fast-food strikers and with SEIU janitors and security guards pushing for new contracts. A coalition called Raise the Wage Indiana began working in 2013 with the state's Jobs with Justice chapters on a campaign to support federal, state, and local efforts to raise the minimum wage.

Butler and Marian workers settled into the long game of enforcing their newly won contract terms. Rebecca Bradley at Butler, who once had to be convinced that she had leadership potential, is now so well versed in the collective bargaining agreement that she is referred to as "the Lawyer" by her coworkers and even some managers. Herb Latigne, who had been fired from Marian's staff after he suffered a stroke, was offered his job back during the union negotiations. He decided to stay retired, but he was glad that, this time, the decision not to work any longer was his to make. At Marian and Butler, as well as at the Indianapolis Airport, the food-service companies began hiring more workers to comply with the union contracts that require fully staffed workforces. One airport food-service company, HMSHost, had grown from seventy to ninety-eight workers since the contract with UNITE HERE was finalized.

But Indianapolis hotel workers continued to struggle. Keisha Johnson's financial troubles dogged her, and Hakiim Ejjair still worked two jobs to support his family. In December 2013 he was working at the Hyatt when he received a call from his wife that she was rushing their daughter to the emergency room. He asked to leave work to join his wife, who speaks little English. Ejjair's manager checked with a supervisor, who allegedly said, "We're busy and we're running a business. He can't leave." In fifteen years on the job, Ejjair had never before asked to leave work, but he was forced to stay. He is filing a complaint against the Hyatt, and continues to advocate for a union.

Since the Butler and Marian contracts were finalized, UNITE HERE in Indianapolis has focused on the internal campaign at the Hyatt and a handful of still-underground campaigns at food-service sites. As of this writing in mid-2014, it has been more than two years since the union has coordinated any large display of community support like the Adopt-a-Worker campaign in 2011. That concerns former UNITE HERE organizer Becky Smith, who still lives in Indianapolis. "The union is more focused on the workers than mobilizing the community now. That is a common problem for the labor movement, where there are always limited resources," she says. "But I think there should be a balance. I worry that when they will want the community to come out for them again, the ties won't be as strong as they need to be."

It is New Year's Eve, 2013, and Mike Biskar and his girlfriend, Kate, are packing up their near-eastside home in Indianapolis. In a few days, on his twenty-ninth birthday, Biskar will board a plane and move to Seattle. He has long wanted to live closer to his family on the West Coast. He also wanted to take on the task of organizing workers in a city that is not already well-established union territory, which ruled out Los Angeles and San Francisco. Seattle, it turns out, has a very supportive political environment for working people but surprisingly little union density in the hotel and food-service industries.

It is a challenge that plays to Biskar's strengths. His seven years in the unexpected destination of Indianapolis has built Biskar into one of UNITE HERE's most seasoned organizers of workers in decidedly non-union settings. "One of Mike's best attributes is his very high capacity to see things that are not yet there, like imagining a working-class movement in Indianapolis," says Dan Abraham. "Having a vision of that is one thing, but it also takes a lot of guts to push that vision in spite of evidence to the contrary." When Biskar and the union look at Seattle's meager 15 percent union density in its hotels, along with unorganized food-service workers at massive companies such as Microsoft and Amazon, they see an opportunity to organize thousands of workers to pursue contracts that give them better pay, benefits, and job security. "If we can get the workers moving forward, they can win there," he says.

Biskar also plans to help with the Hyatt organizing campaign in Seattle, and thus hopes to push over one of the dominoes that need to fall on the path toward Indianapolis finally getting a unionized hotel. He does not try to hide his disappointment that he is leaving town without that goal already being accomplished. "For hotel organizing, it has definitely been a tough seven years that I have been here," he says. Over the course of multiple conversations, he has talked several times about the Indianapolis mayor's decision on the new hotel development in 2006. Again, Biskar explains how that single union hotel could have triggered a wave of hotel organizing in the town. Again, his frustration is evident. "Things could have broken a little differently, but they didn't," he says.

But he is glad that the union sent him to the unfamiliar Midwest, and to the town where he would face such a difficult struggle: "When I came here, I was very young, but I had a lot of confidence because we had won our hotel in Virginia. What the union leaders knew was that I really needed to be in a big fight, to see how hard it can be. Indianapolis was the right place for that." He is glad that a byproduct of the hotel struggle is some improved conditions for subcontracted workers, and he is proud that the union succeeded in building a foundation in the city's food-service industry. Biskar leaves town with contracts in place for several years at IUPUI, the Airport, and Marian and Butler Universities.

On a personal level, Biskar says he learned to appreciate the history of the region, often learning about Indiana's union legacy from service-sector workers whose parents and grandparents worked in the once-plentiful union manufacturing jobs. And Biskar learned to appreciate the people of Indianapolis, too: "I think about, when I get to Seattle and people ask where I am from, what do I say? I don't really feel like I am from Los Angeles anymore, because I have been in Indianapolis so long. Almost everything I know in terms of organizing is from here."

Biskar leaves behind a team of UNITE HERE organizers that includes Stuart Mora, James Meyers, and Eva Sanchez. They will focus on the Hyatt campaign in the near future, but they also want to organize more Indianapolis food-service workers. There is talk of the city making another Super Bowl bid, which would trigger another downtown hotel development and another opportunity to use the workers' growing political influence to secure a unionized hotel. Jo Marie Agriesti says the union's commitment to the community remains strong. "We are going to do more organizing in Indianapolis, period," she said in early 2014.

Biskar hopes to return to help with that, but this time as an outside supporter rather than the leader. "All things considered, I feel like we did great work here," he says. "But this is just the end of one chapter. The next chapter is the team here leading more fights, winning the hotels, and growing the union membership by big numbers."

As of this writing, in the late fall of 2014, it is unclear whether Biskar's optimistic predictions will come true. The campaign to unionize the Indianapolis hotels has been quiet. UNITE HERE will not concede this publicly, but it appears that the union will not be able to mount a sufficiently strong local worker movement to organize the downtown Hyatt. Instead, UNITE HERE will likely rely on the threat of strikes in other cities to trigger the unionization of the Indianapolis hotel in late 2015, per its multicity agreement with Hyatt. It is hard to conclude that Indianapolis is becoming a robust union town when its workers need to look to brothers and sisters in stronger union cities to win the day here.

The workers at Butler and Marian universities are undeniably better off because of unionization, but most of them still earn wages below any calculation of a living wage for even a small family in Indianapolis. The increase to $10.10 per hour contemplated by the Fair Minimum Wage Act would give many of these workers a substantial raise, so some of the university workers have served as spokespersons for the local iteration of the national campaign.

Local security guards and janitors represented by SEIU are on the verge of a new contract. Like the UNITE HERE contracts, it will improve the workers' pay but not lift them out of poverty. For the community's home care workers, there has been no visible traction gained in the local efforts to raise wages or improve work conditions. Since Senator Donnelly switched his position on immigration reform in the summer of 2013, no more Indiana lawmakers targeted by the Catholic-led citizenship campaign have followed suit. That includes Congresswoman Susan Brooks, who was re-elected without difficulty.

By contrast, the new local worker center and the movement to raise the minimum wage seem to be building momentum. The center is conducting know-your-rights trainings for nonunion workers throughout the community and connecting many of these workers to attorneys for wage theft prosecutions, some of which have achieved notable success. The Raise the Wage Indiana campaign is working to persuade local lawmakers to sign on to a proposed ordinance that would mandate higher pay for all city workers and the employees of city contractors. The ordinance is likely to serve as a rallying cry in 2015 as Democrats try to take back the local mayor's office from the Republican incumbent, who is expected to oppose the wage hike. As part of the wage campaign, several Indianapolis small-business owners have taken individual pledges to pay their nonunionized workers in excess of the proposed $10.10 per hour minimum. The campaign has the active support of local workers and organizers for UNITE HERE and SEIU, in part because many of their unionized workers still earn below the proposed minimum.

As some observers of the twenty-first-century labor landscape have argued, "if we can win here" in Indianapolis may mean winning at the ballot box or in the halls of the local legislature, rather than on the picket lines or at the negotiating table.[1] But others just as passionately argue that workers in Indianapolis and beyond will earn fair wages and conditions only when they organize into unions in the tradition of the early to mid-twentieth century U.S. movement.[2] The recent events in Indianapolis serve to illustrate the current wave of organizing and political activity surrounding service-sector and low-wage workers, but they have not settled that ballot-box-versus-workplace debate. In truth, workers and their advocates here do not seem interested in picking sides in the argument. Union members are enthusiastic participants in local minimum wage activism, and nonunionized advocates join the picket lines for the union campaigns. In Indianapolis, at least, advocates for low-wage workers seem content to pursue parallel tracks of political and workplace organizing.

For James Holder, the setting is slightly different from what he is used to. Instead of a union hall in Indianapolis, he is sitting in the cramped living room of a one-story house in a working-class neighborhood in Richmond, Indiana. The people gathered around him are different folks, too. The fifteen workers and students here are from Earlham College, not Butler or Marian or IUPUI. The organizer at the front of the room is wielding a magic marker and scribbling lists on large white Post-it notes. But Mike Biskar is two thousand miles away now. This time, Stuart Mora is leading the meeting.

Yet, on this Saturday morning in early March 2014, as one of the coldest, snowiest winters in Indiana history lingers on, James Holder feels like he has been here before. To his left is Anita. She works in the coffee shop at Earlham. But Anita echoes the cafeteria workers at Butler when she says, "If it was not for the kids we serve at the school, most of us would definitely be trying to find work somewhere else." Across the room, Todd talks about struggles to afford health care and find work in the summer months, just like the IUPUI workers did. And Charles, who has been at Earlham the longest, sounds like James Holder circa 2011 on some of the bad days at Marian. "This used to be a great place to work—all smiles," Charles says. "But it just isn't like that anymore."

Fifty-eight workers on the campus of Earlham are employed by the multinational food-service company Sodexo. In late 2013, Sodexo executives called the workers into a campus auditorium and announced that half of them would be cut to part-time status. They would lose their health benefits, too. The company representative said the workers would see raises that they should put away to use at a later date. But the raises were usually just ten to fifteen cents an hour. Since the announcement, managers seemed to be pushing workers harder than ever. A new chef belittled one sixteen-year veteran cook in front of her coworkers until she broke down in tears.

Now, Earlham workers can't find doctors who will see them in Richmond, so they travel to another county to get care—or go without. Anita is one who lost her company health insurance and does not qualify for Indiana's Medicaid program. "I'm either too poor or too rich," she says, laughing and shaking her head. She has bought into the new Obamacare insurance exchange, but no local health providers will accept her plan. She has to pay cash up front to get an appointment with her doctor of thirty years.

Earlham is a Quaker school that prides itself on its Peace and Global Studies program and its service to the broader Richmond community. Its mission statement emphasizes "a concern for the world in which we live and for improving human society." It didn't take long for Earlham's students and faculty to hear about the problems with Sodexo, and to offer the workers their support. Soon, workers and students alike were talking union.

This Saturday morning meeting starts with a few introductions. Each of the workers present has deep roots in Richmond, a town of thirty-six thousand people next to the Ohio border, seventy miles east of Indianapolis. Anita is in her fifties, and is content not to talk much at first. But she eventually offers observations and comments that show she is both perceptive about her coworkers and deeply angry at the company. Charles, the only African American worker here today, speaks when he is spoken to, usually when Mora draws him out. But it is clear that the others look to him for leadership, and he too feels betrayed by Sodexo.

Todd is a cook now, but evidence of his background as a former political science graduate student peeks out. He talks about the "misery index" in the kitchen and his calculation that the benefits cut equals a de facto 40 percent reduction in compensation. Marc is beloved by Earlham students, who see him as the embodiment of small-town Indiana. A small, hollow-cheeked man with a thick gray beard, Marc is wearing a Pink Floyd T-shirt and a U.S. flag baseball cap. He points out that some of his younger coworkers are the children of men and women he partied with decades ago. Marc is fiercely anti-Obama and just as fiercely prounion. "The company pulled the rug out from under us," he says.

James Holder is meeting all these Earlham workers for the first time, but he has worked with people just like them for decades. After the successful Marian election, Holder became a union steward. In October 2013, he was called on to represent a coworker at a contract-mandated grievance hearing. It was Holder's first-ever experience as a formal advocate. On the day of the hearing, as he held his colleague's termination papers in his hand, Holder was so nervous that he considered resigning his position. He was certain that someone else could do the job better. But it was too late to back out that day, so he went ahead, and ultimately persuaded management to rehire the worker. Afterward, Holder decided that he should stay on as union steward after all. "Maybe I made a difference," he said later. "But that conversation would never have happened if we did not have the union contract."

Stuart Mora asked Holder to drive over from Indianapolis for the meeting with the Earlham workers, and to look for opportunities in the conversation to speak up about his experiences. After the introductions, Mora leads the discussion about how the union supporters should talk to their coworkers. "It's important to let others say how they feel, then you can react to that," he says. He asks the workers and the students how they think the company will respond to the union campaign. Mora uses a red marker to list the likely carrots (small raises, employee appreciation parties) and sticks (cutting hours, switching job assignments).

"What about our response?" he asks. The workers talk about advocating for their colleagues to management. But they wonder aloud what their legal rights are when they speak up. Holder responds with a concise explanation of the protection of "concerted activity," delivering a better and far more understandable summary of the relevant National Labor Relations Act provisions than most attorneys could provide. Then the students are invited to offer their comments. They pledge to engage in a process known as worker "walk-backs," accompanying workers to their workplace the day after an action or strike, which is designed to limit the prospects of company retaliation. They also promise to organize mass action on campus if the company tries to retaliate against prounion workers.

On the white paper stuck to the living room wall, Mora circles one of the suggestions for a response—"Move our co-workers." The best defense is a good offense, he says. The stronger the union is in the workplace, the less chance for any enduring backlash. The current five-person worker organizing committee needs to keep growing, so together they identify some more likely allies. Marc is squinting at the list on the wall, so Anita hands him her glasses. He wears them for the rest of the meeting.

All agree that the lead pizza worker at Earlham is looked up to by his young colleagues, and he is likely to be prounion. Two of the students, who regularly talk with the worker about their shared interests in heavy metal music, will speak to him about the campaign. Several other workers are discussed, too. All are identified as sure to be sympathetic to the cause. But will they be willing to take the risk of openly supporting the union?

James Holder has not spoken much to this point, but slowly the Earlham workers begin turning to him and asking how Marian and Butler workers dealt with different challenges. Holder has been where they are now, and he suggests they not give up on the workers who may be afraid. Holder's experience is that the coworkers are likely to come around as they are mistreated by management and their frustration mounts. "Anger overcomes fear," he says. A few minutes later, Marc applies the lesson when the group talks about a potentially reluctant Earlham colleague. "Hell, she got screwed over just like the rest of us," Marc says. "I don't know why she wouldn't support this, too." (Marc was right. The Earlham/Sodexo workers movement would go public a few months later, with 86 percent of the workers signed up to support the union. As of this writing, the workers are trying to obtain a contract.)

Mora decides to circle back to a topic the company is sure to cite in its resistance to the union. "The dues are $33 a month, but that happens only after you agree on a contract," he says. "Just like at Butler and Marian and IUPUI, we know you can do the math. The contracts always bring the workers a lot more benefit than the dues cost, or they wouldn't agree to them." Mora has deftly led the meeting from the beginning, gently pushing the workers to speak their minds and drive the strategizing, occasionally pulling in the students to offer their support. But, on the dues question, Mora is speaking in cost-benefit prose. James Holder feels called to add some poetry.

"I worked it out, and the cost of my dues each shift I work is about the price of one of them big Pepsis," he says. "So the way I look at is this: If I could buy my manager a tall cold Pepsi every day and be guaranteed in return that he would treat me with respect, I'd do it. Wouldn't you?" Heads nod in response. "Well, that is what the union does for me. And this way, I don't have to give that guy no Pepsi!"

NOTES

Introduction

1. Unless otherwise noted, all quotations in this book come from personal interviews with the author during the period between October 2012 and January 2014.

2. Susan Buchanan et al., "Occupational Injury Disparities in the U.S. Hotel Industry," *American Journal of Industrial Medicine* 53 (February 2010), 116–25.

3. Amy Glasmeier, "Living Wage Calculation for City of Indianapolis," Massachusetts Institute of Technology, http://livingwage.mit.edu/places/1809736003.

4. "Union Membership in Indiana–2012," U.S. Department of Labor, Bureau of Labor Statistics, March 12, 2013, http://www.bls.gov/ro5/unionin.htm.

5. Elizabeth McNichol et al., "Pulling Apart: A State-by-State Analysis of Income Trends," Center on Budget and Policy Priorities, November 15, 2012, 11, http://www.cbpp.org/files/11-15-12sfp.pdf.

6. UNITE HERE is the name of the union formed by the 2004 merger of the Hotel Employees and Restaurant Employees International Union (HERE) and the Union of Needletrades, Textile, and Industrial Employees (UNITE).

7. For example, the landmark United Auto Workers first contract with General Motors that was negotiated in the wake of the historic Flint, Michigan, sit-down strike contained no salary or benefit terms at all: it simply laid the groundwork for the union's recognition. For a discussion of the benefits of first union contracts in the late twentieth century, see Tom Juravich, Kate Bronfenbrenner, and Robert Hickey, "Significant Victories: An Analysis of Union First Contracts,"

Cornell University Digital Commons, January 1, 2006, http://digitalcommons.ilr.cornell.edu/cgi/viewcontent.cgi?article=1250&context=articles.

8. For example, respected labor journalist David Moberg writes that service-sector worker activism could lead to general strikes, European-style minimum standards for particular industries, and a resurgence of the labor movement. In profiling a fast-food worker activist in Chicago in the summer of 2013, Moberg wrote that "she may be a harbinger of new life for the labor movement at a time when even friends are preparing its obituary." David Moberg, "Thank You, Strike Again: How Low-Wage Workers Are Changing the Face of Labor," *In These Times*, July 25, 2013.

9. For examples of this viewpoint, see Zeynep Ton, *The Good Jobs Strategy: How the Smartest Companies Invest in Employees to Lower Costs and Boost Profits* (New York: New Harvest, 2014), an MIT Sloan School of Management professor arguing that service-oriented companies benefit when paying good wages to their workers; Richard Florida, "Building America's Third Great Job Machine," *Atlantic* online, May 5, 2011, http://www.theatlantic.com/business/archive/2011/05/building-americas-third-great-job-machine/238316/, the director of the Martin Prosperity Institute at the University of Toronto's Rotman School of Management and Global Research Professor at New York University saying that the upgrading of U.S. low-wage service jobs will boost the economy and follow the twentieth-century trend of manufacturing jobs becoming more stable and better-paying work; Robert Reich, "How to Shrink Inequality," robertreich.org, May 12, 2014, http://robertreich.org/post/85532751265 (Chancellor's Professor of Public Policy at the University of California at Berkeley and Senior Fellow at the Blum Center for Developing Economies and former secretary of labor, saying that the growing wealth gap is best addressed in part by unionization and better pay in low-wage service occupations that are resistant to global competition and labor-replacing technologies).

10. Information in this book is current as of October 2014.

1. A Campus Union

1. Marlene A. Lee and Mark Mather, "U.S. Labor Force Trends," *Population Bulletin* 63 (June 2008): 7, http://dalmasetto.com/pdfs/US_labour_stats.pdf.

2. Jeremy Peters and Micheline Maynard, "Company Town Relies on G.M. Long after Plants Have Closed," *New York Times*, February 20, 2006, http://www.nytimes.com/2006/02/20/business/20auto.html?pagewanted=all&_r=0.

3. Max Fraser, "Down and Out in the New Middletowns," *Dissent*, Winter 2012, http://www.dissentmagazine.org/article/down-and-out-in-the-new-middletowns.

4 James Madison, "Economy," in *The Encyclopedia of Indianapolis*, ed. David J. Bodenhamer and Robert G. Barrows (Bloomington: Indiana University Press, 1994), 65.

5. Larry Mishel, John Schmitt, and Heidi Sheirholz, "Don't Blame the Robots: Assessing the Job Polarization Explanation of Growing Wage Inequality," Center for Economic and Policy Research, November 2013, 6, http://s3.epi.org/files/2013/technology-inequality-dont-blame-the-robots.pdf.

6. "The Low Wage Recovery: Industry Employment and Wages Four Years into the Recovery," National Employment Law Project, April 2014, 5, http://www.nelp.org/page/-/Reports/Low-Wage-Recovery-Industry-Employment-Wages-2014-Report.pdf?nocdn=1.

7. Drew DeSilver, "U.S. Income Inequality, on Rise for Decades, Is Now Highest since 1928," Pew Research Center, December 5, 2013, http://www.pewresearch.org/fact-tank/2013/12/05/u-s-income-inequality-on-rise-for-decades-is-now-highest-since-1928/.

8. Raj Chetty, Nathaniel Hendren, Patrick Kline, and Emmanuel Saez, "Where Is the Land of Opportunity? The Geography of Intergenerational Mobility in the United States," January 2014, table 4, http://obs.rc.fas.harvard.edu/chetty/mobility_geo.pdf.

9. Peter List, "The Labor Movement Is Brain Dead (And It's Time to Pull the Plug)," North American Employers Group, last updated February 25, 2005, http://home.earthlink.net/futureo funions/id3.html.

10. Josh Eidelson, "Alt-Labor," *American Prospect,* January 29, 2013, http://prospect.org/ article/alt-labor.

11. John Schmitt, "Unions and Upward Mobility for Service-Sector Employees," Center for Economic Policy and Research, 2009, 3, http://www.cepr.net/documents/publications/unions-service-2009–04.pdf.

12. "Big Business, Corporate Profits, and the Minimum Wage," National Employment Law Project, July 2012, 4–5, http://nelp.3cdn.net/e555b2e361f8f734f4_sim6btdzo.pdf. See also Henry Blodget, "Or, McDonald's Could Double the Wages of Its Employees, Not Raise Prices, and Just Make Less Money," *Business Insider*, July 30, 2013, http://www.businessinsider.com/ mcdonalds-could-double-wages-for-employees-and-make-less-money-2013–7.

2. "We Can Win Here"

1. Richard B. Pierce, *Polite Protest: The Political Economy of Race in Indianapolis, 1920–1970* (Bloomington: Indiana University Press, 2005).

2. Tom Marvin, "Community Organizing for the Union: A Tale of Two Campaigns in Indianapolis" (unpublished manuscript, 2013).

3. Audio and video of Kennedy's speech is available at Mohammad Azzam, "The Greatest Speech Ever: Announcing the Death of Martin Luther King," https://www.youtube.com/ watch?v=GoKzCff8Zbs.

4. "Two Nights of Disorder Rack Westside; Calm Restored Saturday," *Indianapolis Recorder,* June 14, 1969, 1, http://indiamond6.ulib.iupui.edu/cdm/ref/collection/IRecorder/id/48469.

5. James Wallihan, "Labor," in *Encyclopedia of Indianapolis*, ed. David J. Bodenhamer and Robert G. Barrows (Bloomington: Indiana University Press, 1994), 106.

6. Elfrieda Lang, "The Columbia Conserve Company Papers," *Indiana University Bookman 1957,* http://scholarworks.iu.edu/journals/index.php/bookman/article/view/3736/3446; Wallihan, "Labor," 107.

7. David Barsamian, "Kurt Vonnegut Interview," *Progressive,* June 12, 2003, http://progres sive.org/mag_intv0603. See also Robert Bussel, *From Harvard to the Ranks of Labor: Powers Hapgood and the American Working Class* (University Park: Penn State University Press, 1999).

8. Fran Quigley, "Are Workers 'Sacrificial Lambs' for Indiana Unemployment Fund Deficit?" *Working In These Times,* January 15, 2013, http://inthesetimes.com/working/entry/14412/ workers_sacrificial_lambs_for_indianas_unemployment_fund_deficit.

9. Former United Farm Workers organizer Marshall Ganz discusses the combination of "biographical availability" (few family commitments) and hopeful nature that cause movement leaders to come disproportionately from the young. That certainly is the case for union organizers, who often relocate to unfamiliar communities to pursue an idealistic goal. See Marshall Ganz, "Leading Change: Leadership, Organization, and Social Movements," excerpted from *Handbook of Leadership Theory and Practice: A Harvard Business School Centennial Colloquium,* ed. Nitin Nohria and Rakesh Khurana (Harvard Business Press, 2010), http://leadingchangenetwork.org/files/2012/05/Chapter-19-Leading-Change-Leadership-Organization-and-Social-Movements.pdf, 5.

10. Parenti's best-known work is *Democracy for the Few* (Stamford, CT: Cengage Learning, 2010).

11. "The Southern California District of the Communist Party," Hearings Before the Committee on Un-American Activities, U.S. House of Representatives, 85th Congress, Second Session, September 3, 1958, http://archive.org/stream/southerncaliforn01unit/southerncaliforn01unit_ djvu.txt.

3. Dreaming of One Good Job

1. "Foreign Born Workers: Labor Force Characteristics—2012," U.S. Department of Labor, Bureau of Labor Statistics, May 22, 2013, 1, http://www.bls.gov/news.release/pdf/forbrn.pdf.

2. Jeffrey S. Passel and D'Vera Cohn, "A Portrait of Unauthorized Immigrants in the United States," Pew Hispanic Center, April 14, 2009, iii, 5, http://www.pewhispanic.org/files/reports/107.pdf.

3. See, generally, Vernon M. Briggs Jr., *Immigration and American Unionism* (Ithaca: Cornell University Press, 2001). Cesar Chavez was among the long line of U.S. labor leaders who expressed concern about the impact of illegal immigrant workers on union activity, even though Chavez would eventually support broad immigration law reform. See Randy Shaw, *Beyond the Fields: Cesar Chavez, the UFW, and the Struggle for Justice in the 21st Century* (Berkeley: University of California Press, 2008), 194–98.

4. Passel and Cohn, "A Portrait of Unauthorized Immigrants," i.

5. Ruth Milkman, "Immigrant Workers and the Future of Organized Labor," *ABA Journal of Labor and Employment Law* 26 (2011): 295, 304.

6. Charlie LeDuff, "At a Slaughterhouse, Some Things Never Die," *New York Times,* June 16, 2000, http://www.nytimes.com/2000/06/16/us/slaughterhouse-some-things-never-die-who-kills-who-cuts-who-bosses-can-depend.html.

7. See, generally, Susan Ferris and Ricardo Sandoval, *The Fight in the Field: Cesar Chavez and the Farmworkers Movement* (New York: Mariner Books, 1998).

8. Milkman, "Immigrant Workers," 302.

9. "Union Members, 2012," U.S. Department of Labor Bureau of Labor Statistics, January 23, 2013, http://www.bls.gov/news.release/archives/union2_01232013.pdf.

10. Immanuel Ness, *Immigrants, Unions, and the New U.S. Labor Market* (Philadelphia: Temple University Press, 2005).

11. Milkman, "Immigrant Workers," 297, 298–99.

12. Margaret Weir, "Income Polarization and California's Social Contract," in *The State of California Labor, 2002,* ed. Ruth Milkman (Berkeley: University of California Press, 2002), 121.

13. For the most part, U.S. law erects a so-called "firewall" between immigration law and labor law. See *De Canas v. Bica*, 424 U.S. 351, 361 (1976). The most notable exception is a 5–4 2002 U.S. Supreme Court decision holding that undocumented workers are not entitled to back pay and reinstatement if they are fired for union activities. *Hoffman Plastics Company, Inc. v. NLRB*, 535 U.S. 137 (2002).

14. Annette Bernhardt et al., "Broken Laws, Unprotected Workers: Violations of Employment and Labor Laws in America's Cities," National Employment Law Project, 2005, 5, 42, http://www.nelp.org/page/-/brokenlaws/BrokenLawsReport2009.pdf?nocdn=1.

15. The ad, entitled "You Should Not Have to Sacrifice Quality for Price," can be viewed at http://big.assets.huffingtonpost.com/news_01f.jpg.

16. "Final Order," *Indiana Department of Labor v. Hospitality Staffing Solutions, LLC*, and its Successors, IOSHA Board of Safety Review Case Docket No. 11–006, May 10, 2012, accessed May 30, 2014, http://www.in.gov/dol/files/Hospitality_Staffing_Solutions(1).pdf.

17. Tom Marvin, "Community Organizing for the Union: A Tale of Two Campaigns in Indianapolis" (unpublished manuscript, 2013).

4. Alt-Labor Hits Indianapolis

1. Amy Glasmeier, "Living Wage Calculation for City of Indianapolis," Massachusetts Institute of Technology, 2014, http://livingwage.mit.edu/places/1809736003.

2. The average weekly hours of employees in retail trade hovers around thirty hours. See "Average Weekly Hours of All Employees: Retail Trade," U.S. Bureau of Labor Statistics, series

CEU4200000002, April, 2014, http://research.stlouisfed.org/fred2/series/CEU4200000002?cid=32316. Increased and more reliable hours are some of the core requests by low-wage workers organizing at outlets like Walmart. See, e.g., Catherine Ruetschlin and Amy Traub, "A Higher Wage Is Possible: How Walmart Can Invest in Its Workforce without Costing Customers a Dime," Demos, November, 2013, 1, http://www.demos.org/sites/default/files/publications/A%20Higher%20Wage%20Is%20Possible.pdf.

3. For an overview of the phenomenon of increased corporate reliance on temporary workers, see Michael Grabell, "The Expendables: How the Temps Who Power Corporate Giants Are Getting Crushed," ProPublica, June 27, 2013, http://www.propublica.org/article/the-expendables-how-the-temps-who-power-corporate-giants-are-getting-crushe.

4. See, generally, John Schmitt and Janelle Jones, "Low Wage Workers Are Older and Better Educated Than Ever," Center for Economic and Policy Research, April 2012, http://www.cepr.net/documents/publications/min-wage3-2012-04.pdf.

5. Melissa Maynard, "With Big Changes, Can Labor Grow Again?," April 15, 2013, http://www.pewstates.org/projects/stateline/headlines/with-big-changes-can-labor-grow-again-85899468193.

6. Richard B. Freeman, "Do Workers Still Want Unions? More Than Ever" (Reporting Peter D. Hart polling 1984–2004), EPI Briefing Paper #182, Economic Policy Institute, February 22, 2007, http://www.sharedprosperity.org/bp182.html.

7. Harold Myerson, "Labor Wrestles with Its Future," *Washington Post*, May 8, 2013, http://www.washingtonpost.com/opinions/harold-meyerson-labor-wrestles-with-its-future/2013/05/08/852192d6-b74f-11e2-b94c-b684dda07add_story.html.

8. Biju Matthew, *Taxi! Cabs and Capitalism in New York City* (Ithaca: Cornell University Press, 2008).

9. See Workers Defense Project, http://www.workersdefense.org/.

10. See Domestic Workers United, http://www.domesticworkersunited.org/index.php/en/.

11. Because of the exclusion of agricultural workers from the protections—and restrictions—of the National Labor Relations Act, the United Farm Workers were able to coordinate broad boycotts of stores selling nonunion grapes. As a result, Cesar Chavez was ambivalent about proposals seeking to bring farm workers under traditional labor law protection. See, e.g., Thomas Geoghegan, "The Man and the Message," *New York Times*, April 25, 2014, http://www.nytimes.com/2014/04/27/books/review/the-crusades-of-cesar-chavez-by-miriam-pawel.html.

12. "Immokalee Tomato Pickers Win Campaign against Taco Bell," *Democracy Now*, March 10, 2005, http://www.democracynow.org/2005/3/10/immokalee_tomato_pickers_win_campaign_against.

13. Vanessa Tait, *Poor People's Unions* (Cambridge, MA: South End Press, 2005), 76–98, 222.

14. David Moberg, "Thank You, Strike Again: How Low-Wage Workers Are Changing the Face of Labor," *In These Times,* July 25, 2013, http://inthesetimes.com/article/15235/thank_you_strike_again.

15. Tait, *Poor People's Unions,* 228.

16. Lydia Saad, "In U.S., 71% Back Raising the Minimum Wage," Gallup.com, March 6, 2013, 2014, http://www.gallup.com/poll/160913/back-raising-minimum-wage.aspx.

17. See Indiana Code § 22–2–2–9.

18. Erin Polley, "Give Hotel Workers a Tax Break," *Indianapolis Star*, August 12, 2011, http://www.indystar.com/article/20110815/OPINION01/108150311/Give-hotel-workers-a-tax-break.

5. The Fight for 15

1. "The Low Wage Recovery: Industry Employment and Wages Four Years into the Recovery," National Employment Law Project, April, 2014, 5, http://www.nelp.org/page/-/Reports/Low-Wage-Recovery-Industry-Employment-Wages-2014-Report.pdf?nocdn=1.

2. "Big Business, Corporate Profits, and the Minimum Wage," National Employment Law Project, July 2012, 2, http://nelp.3cdn.net/e555b2e361f8f734f4_sim6btdzo.pdf.

3. Michael Powell, "Making $7.75 an Hour, and Finding There Is Little to Lose by Speaking Out," *New York Times*, July 1, 2013, http://www.nytimes.com/2013/07/02/nyregion/making-7-75-an-hour-and-figuring-theres-little-to-lose-by-speaking-out.html.

4. Jack Metzgar, "We Are Worth More," Talking Union.wordpress.com, May 6, 2013, https://workingclassstudies.wordpress.com/category/contributors/jack-metzgar/.

5. "D15–Detroit Fast Food Workers Strike for $15," Good Jobs Now—Detroit, May 14, 2013, http://www.goodjobsnow.org/2013/05/14/d15-detroit-fast-food-workers-strike-for-15/.

6. Adam Weaver, "Fast Food Workers Strike: What Is and What Isn't the Fight for Fifteen Campaign," Machete 408, August 29, 2013, http://machete408.wordpress.com/2013/08/29/fast-food-workers-strike-what-is-and-what-isnt-the-fight-for-fifteen-campaign/.

7. Charles Morris, *The Blue Eagle at Work: Reclaiming Democratic Rights in the American Workplace* (Ithaca: Cornell University Press, 2005). But see Julius G. Getman, *Restoring the Power of Unions: It Takes a Movement* (New Haven, CT: Yale University Press, 2010), 300, which argues that formal minority-bargaining agreements violate the National Labor Relations Act.

8. McDonald's Corp.'s annual revenue reported in 2013 was $28.11 billion. "McDonald's Corp.," "Market Watch," *Wall Street Journal*, http://www.marketwatch.com/investing/stock/mcd/financials.

6. Legal Problems

1. Gina Ruiz, "Employers and Hiring Practices Are Targets in Immigration Debate," Workforce.com, June 9, 2006, http://www.workforce.com/articles/employers-and-hiring-practices-are-targets-in-immigration-debate.

2. Steve Early, "Organizing for the Long Haul: Colonizing to the Rescue?" *WorkingUSA: The Journal of Labor and Society* 16 (September 2013): 358.

3. Jeff Swiatek, "Hotel Rally for One of Their Own," *Indianapolis Star*, February 21, 2009, http://www.indystar.com/article/20090221/BUSINESS/902210414.

4. John Schmitt and Ben Zipperer, "Dropping the Ax: Illegal Firings during Union Election Campaigns," Center for Economic and Policy Research, January, 2007, 11, http://www.cepr.net/documents/publications/unions_2007_01.pdf.

5. Thomas Geoghegan, *Which Side Are You On? Trying to Be for Labor When It Is Flat on Its Back* (New York: New Press, 2004), 252, 255.

6. See Joseph A. McCartin, *Collision Course: Ronald Reagan, the Air Traffic Controllers, and the Strike That Changed America* (Oxford: Oxford University Press, 2011).

7. John-Paul Ferguson and Thomas A. Kochan, "Sequential Failures in Workers' Right to Organize," MIT Sloan School of Management Institute for Work and Employment Research, March 2008, 3, http://www.cswj.us/TK%20and%20JPF%20EFCA%20Policy%20Statement%203%2025%202008.pdf.

8. Ellen J. Dannin, *Taking Back the Workers' Law: How to Fight the Assault on Labor Rights* (Ithaca: Cornell University Press, 2006), 5.

9. James Gray Pope, Peter Kellman, and Ed Bruno, "'We Are Already Dead': The Thirteenth Amendment and the Fight for Workers Rights after the EFCA," *National Lawyers Guild Review* 67 (2010): 110, 112–13.

10. See also Julius Getman, *Restoring the Power of Unions: It Takes a Movement* (New Haven, CT: Yale University Press, 2010), 206, 211.

11. *Snyder v. Phelps*, 131 S.Ct. 1207 (2011).

12. *Citizens United v. Federal Election Commission*, 558 U.S. 310 (2010).

13. Getman had previously expanded on these views in a 1984 law review article: Julius Getman, "Labor Law and Free Speech: The Curious Policy of Limited Expression," *Maryland Law Review* 43 (1984): 4.

14. Getman, *Restoring the Power of Unions*, 276.

15. Jane McAlevey and Bob Ostertag, *Raising Expectations (and Raising Hell): My Decade Fighting for the Labor Movement* (London: Verso, 2012), 315.

16. Nelson Lichtenstein, *State of the Union: A Century of American Labor* (Princeton, NJ: Princeton University Press, 2002), x, xiii.

17. Shawn Gude, "Right to Work: A Setback, Not a Roadblock," League of Ordinary Gentlemen, December 16, 2012, http://ordinary-gentlemen.com/shawngude/2012/12/right-to-work-a-setback-not-a-roadblock/.

7. UNITE HERE

1. Julius Getman, *Restoring the Power of Unions: It Takes a Movement* (New Haven, CT: Yale University Press, 2010).

2. Kent Wong, "Interview with John Wilhelm," *New Labor Forum* 14 (Spring 2005): 79.

3. Getman, *Restoring the Power of Unions,* 110–11.

4. Arlen Jones and Greg Hoffman, "Viewpoint: Pink Sheeting and Harmful Organizing Methods at UNITE HERE," Labor Notes, January 8, 2010, http://labornotes.org/2010/01/viewpoint-pink-sheeting-and-harmful-organizing-methods-unite-here.

5. Steve Early, "Organizing for the Long Haul: Colonizing to the Rescue?" *WorkingUSA: The Journal of Labor and Society* 16 (September, 2013): 364.

8. Struggling for Contracts

1. Kate Bronfenbrenner, "No Holds Barred—The Intensification of Employer Opposition to Organizing," Economic Policy Institute, May 20, 2009, 9, http://www.epi.org/publication/bp235/.

2. Jane McAlevey and Bob Ostertag, *Raising Expectations (and Raising Hell): My Decade Fighting for the Labor Movement* (London: Verso, 2012), 222.

3. Tom Marvin, "Community Organizing for the Union: A Tale of Two Campaigns in Indianapolis." (unpublished manuscript, 2013).

9. Wonderful Field, Awful Pay

1. "Employment Projections 2010–20," U.S. Bureau of Labor Statistics, February 1, 2012, http://www.bls.gov/news.release/archives/ecopro_02012012.pdf.

2. Eileen Boris and Jennifer Klein, "Home Care Workers Are Not Just 'Companions,'" *New York Times*, July 1, 2012, http://www.nytimes.com/2012/07/02/opinion/fairness-for-home-care-workers.html.

3. "Report of the Governor's Commission on Long Term Caregivers," 2009, 1, http://phinational.org/sites/phinational.org/files/clearinghouse/Indiana%20GCLTC_part1.pdf.

4. Srikant Devaraj, Michael J. Hicks, and Rohit Ravula, "Home Care Industry Growth in Indiana," Center for Business and Economic Research, Ball State University, January 2012, 15, http://cms.bsu.edu/academics/centersandinstitutes/bbr/-/media/WWW/DepartmentalContent/MillerCollegeofBusiness/BBR/Publications/HomeHealthCare.ashx.

5. "Minimum Wage, Overtime Protections Extended to Direct Care Workers by US Labor Department," U.S. Department of Labor, Wage and Hour Division, September 17, 2013, http://www.dol.gov/opa/media/press/whd/WHD20131922.htm.

6. Julius Getman, *Restoring the Power of Unions: It Takes a Movement* (New Haven, CT: Yale University Press, 2010), 314.

7. Marshall Ganz, "Leading Change: Leadership, Organization, and Social Movements," Harvard Business Press, 2010: 7, http://leadingchangenetwork.org/files/2012/05/Chapter-19-Leading-Change-Leadership-Organization-and-Social-Movements.pdf.

8. Kelly Kennedy, "High Turnover Affects Home Health Care Quality," *USA Today,* February 15, 2012, http://usatoday30.usatoday.com/news/washington/story/2012–02–15/home-health-care-turnover-quality/53109424/1.

9. Candace Howes, "Living Wages and Retention of Homecare Workers in San Francisco," Department of Economics, Connecticut College, June 2004, 23, http://laborcenter.berkeley.edu/homecare/pdf/howes_01.pdf.

10. Trying to Secure a Union

1. Thomas Geoghan, *Which Side Are You On?: Trying to Be For Labor When It Is Flat on Its Back* (New York: The New Press, 2004), 260.

2. Former SEIU organizer Jane McAlevey's chose to entitle her memoir *Raising Expectations,* and she writes, "Organizing, at its core, is about raising expectations: about what people should expect from their jobs; the quality of life they should aspire to . . . expectations about what they themselves are capable of, about the power they could exercise if they worked together, and what they might use that collective power to accomplish." Jane McAlevey and Bob Ostertag, *Raising Expectations (and Raising Hell): My Decade Fighting for the Labor Movement* (London: Verso, 2012), 13.

11. Prayers for Citizenship

1. "A Nation of Immigrants: A Portrait of the 40 Million, Including 11 Million Unauthorized," Pew Research Hispanic Trends Project, January 29, 2013, http://www.pewhispanic.org/2013/01/29/a-nation-of-immigrants/.

2. Rachel Strange, "Born Abroad: Recent Immigrants to Indiana," IN Context, Indiana Business Research Center, Indiana University Kelley School of Business, http://www.incontext.indiana.edu/2013/sept-oct/article3.asp.

3. Paul Taylor and D'Vera Cohn, "A Milestone En Route to a Majority Minority Nation," Pew Research Social and Demographic Trends, November 7, 2012, http://www.pewsocialtrends.org/2012/11/07/a-milestone-en-route-to-a-majority-minority-nation/.

4. "Growth and Opportunity Project," Republican National Committee, March 18, 2013, 8, http://goproject.gop.com/RNC_Growth_Opportunity_Book_2013.pdf.

5. Rachel Weiner, "Reince Priebus Gives GOP Prescription for Future," *Washington Post*, March 18, 2013, http://www.washingtonpost.com/blogs/post-politics/wp/2013/03/18/reince-priebus-gives-gop-prescription-for-future/.

6. Public Religion Research Institute, "Attitudes about Immigration in Indiana," May 27, 2013. On file with author.

7. RTT News, "Indiana Treasurer Mourdock Announces Primary Challenge to Lugar," February 22, 2011, http://www.rttnews.com/1558737/indiana-treasurer-mourdock-announces-primary-challenge-to-lugar.aspx.

8. "Donnelly Takes Stand on Immigration, Border Issue," *Michigan City News-Dispatch*, July 18, 2010.

9. "Fact Check: Mourdock's Friends Try to Hide His Pattern of Extreme Positions," joeforindiana.com, October 26, 2012, http://www.highbeam.com/doc/1G1–306520677.html.

10. John Russell, "Walk from Indy to Anderson Planned to Draw Attention to Immigration Issues," *Indianapolis Star,* November 1, 2013, http://www.indystar.com/story/news/2013/11/01/walk-from-indy-to-anderson-draws-attention-to-immigration-issues/3348433/.

11. See, e.g., Katherine Marshall, "Charity and Justice for All," Berkley Center for Religion, Peace, and World Affairs, Georgetown University, January 4, 2010, http://berkleycenter.georgetown.edu/posts/charity-and-justice-for-all.

12. John L. Allen Jr. "Vatican Must Hear 'Anger and Hurt' of American Nuns, Official Says," *National Catholic Reporter*, December 7, 2010, http://archive.today/PqHN.

13. Gerard O'Connell, "Pope Appoints Archbishop Joe Tobin as Head of Indianapolis Archdiocese," *Vatican Insider*, October 18, 2012, http://vaticaninsider.lastampa.it/en/world-news/detail/articolo/stati-uniti-united-states-estados-unidos-18973/.

14. "Donnelly Statement on Senate Passage of Bipartisan Immigration Reform," Senator Joe Donnelly, June 27, 2013, http://www.donnelly.senate.gov/newsroom/press/donnelly-statement-on-senate-passage-of-bipartisan-immigration-reform-.

15. Letter to the editor, "Story Was Biased Piece on Immigration Reform, Reader Says," *Criterion,* November 22, 2013, http://www.archindy.org/criterion/local/2013/11–22/letters.html.

16. Letter to the editor, "We Need to Enforce, Not Change, Immigration Laws, Reader Says," *Criterion,* October 11, 2013, http://www.archindy.org/criterion/local/2013/10–11/letters.html.

17. Helder Camara, *Dom Helder Camara: Essential Writings* (Maryknoll, NY: Orbis Books, 2009), 13.

18. Rush Limbaugh, "It's Sad How Wrong Pope Francis Is (Unless It's a Deliberate Mistranslation Bby Leftists)," RushLimbaugh.com, November 27, 2013, http://www.rushlimbaugh.com/daily/2013/11/27/it_s_sad_how_wrong_pope_francis_is_unless_it_s_a_deliberate_mistranslation_by_leftists.

19. Zachary A. Goldfarb and Michelle Boorstein, "Pope Francis Denounces 'Trickle-Down' Economic Theories in Critique of Inequality," *Washington Post*, November 26, 2013, http://www.washingtonpost.com/business/economy/pope-francis-denounces-trickle-down-economic-theories-in-critique-of-inequality/2013/11/26/e17ffe4e-56b6–11e3–8304-caf30787c0a9_story.html.

20. Official Twitter page of Pope Francis, @Pontifex, July 8, 2013, https://twitter.com/Pontifex.

21. Laurie Goodstein, "Pope Says Church Is 'Obsessed' with Gays, Abortion, and Birth Control," *New York Times*, September 19, 2013, http://www.nytimes.com/2013/09/20/world/europe/pope-bluntly-faults-churchs-focus-on-gays-and-abortion.html.

22. Max Weber, *The Protestant Ethic and the Spirit of Capitalism* (New York: Routledge, 2001).

23. Pope Leo XII, "*Rerum Novarum,* Encyclical of Pope Leo XIII on Capital and Labor," May 15, 1891, http://www.vatican.va/holy_father/leo_xiii/encyclicals/documents/hf_l-xiii_enc_15051891_rerum-novarum_en.html.

24. Pope Pius XI, "*Quadragesimo Anno,* Encyclical of Pope Pius XI on Reconstruction of the Social Order to Our Venerable Brethren, the Patriarchs, Primates, Archbishops, Bishops, and Other Ordinaries in Peace and Communion with the Apostolic See,and Likewise to All the Faithful of the Catholic World," May 15, 1931, http://www.vatican.va/holy_father/pius_xi/encyclicals/documents/hf_p-xi_enc_19310515_quadragesimo-anno_en.html.

25. Ernesto Cortes Jr., "Faith, Charity, and Justice," *American Prospect*, April 22, 2007, http://prospect.org/article/faith-charity-and-justice.

26. Pope Paul VI, "If You Want Peace, Work for Justice: Message of His Holiness Pope Paul VI for the Celebration of the Day of Peace," January 1, 1972, http://www.vatican.va/holy_father/paul_vi/messages/peace/documents/hf_p-vi_mes_19711208_v-world-day-for-peace_en.html.

27. Pope Benedict XVI, "Encyclical Letter *Caritas In Veritate* of the Supreme Pontiff Benedict XVI to the Bishops, Priests and Deacons, Men and Women Religious, the Lay

Faithful and All People of Good Will on Integral Human Development in Charity and Truth," June 29, 2009, http://www.vatican.va/holy_father/benedict_xvi/encyclicals/documents/hf_ben-xvi_enc_20090629_caritas-in-veritate_en.html.

28. Kim Bobo, "Do Catholics Still Care about Labor?" *America*, August 29, 2005.

29. See, e.g., Brian Roewe, "A New Generation of Labor Priests," *National Catholic Reporter*, August 31, 2012, http://ncronline.org/printpdf/news/people/new-generation-labor-priests.

30. "Remembering Father George Higgins: The Life and Times of a Labor Priest," *American Postal Worker Magazine,* September–October 2002, http://apwu.interactiverequest.com/labor-history-articles/remembering-father-george-higgins.

31. *The Public Papers and Addresses of Franklin D. Roosevelt, Volume One: The Genesis of the New Deal 1928–1932* (New York: Random House, 1938), 778.

32. John Ryan, *A Living Wage: Its Ethical and Economic Aspects* (Washington, DC: Catholic University, 1906).

33. Laura Murphy, "An 'Indestructible Right': John Ryan and the Catholic Origins of the U.S. Living Wage Movement, 1906–1938," *Labor: Studies in Working Class History of the Americas* 6 (2009): 57–68, 71, 79, doi:10.1215/15476715–2008–045.

34. Ibid., 83–84.

35. Ibid., 77.

36. U.S. Conference of Catholic Bishops' "Seven Themes of Catholic Social Teaching," 2005, http://www.usccb.org/beliefs-and-teachings/what-we-believe/catholic-social-teaching/seven-themes-of-catholic-social-teaching.cfm.

37. Adam Shaw, "Pope Francis Is the Catholic Church's Obama–God Help Us," FoxNews.com, December 4, 2013, http://www.foxnews.com/opinion/2013/12/04/pope-francis-is-catholic-churchs-obama-god-help-us/.

12. Advocacy for Citizenship

1. John Shaughnessy, "As Congress Nears Possible Immigration Vote, Church Supports Fixing System Hurting Millions," *Criterion*, September 27, 2013, http://www.archindy.org/criterion/local/2013/09–27/immigration.html.

2. Daniel Gonzales, "Deportations by Federal Government Drop in 2013," *Arizona Republic,* December 27, 2013, http://www.usatoday.com/story/news/nation/2013/12/27/federal-government-deportations-decrease/4216797/; and Suzanne Gamboa, " Drunken Driving, Traffic Crime Deportations Way Up," Associated Press, July 22, 2011, http://news.yahoo.com/drunken-driving-traffic-crime-deportations-way-072604914.html.

3. Gary Langer, "Public Views on Immigration Reform Underscore the GOP's Conundrum," ABCNews.com, April 3, 2013, http://abcnews.go.com/blogs/politics/2013/04/public-views-on-immigration-reform-underscore-the-gops-conundrum/.

4. Kevin Cullen, "Marchers Seek Support for Immigration Reform Bill," *Catholic Moment,* November 8, 2013, http://www.thecatholicmoment.org/archive/2013/11–10/marchers-seek-immigration-reform.html.

13. Contracts on Campus

1. Fran Quigley, "Health Care Costs Pinch Some Airport Workers," Indianapolis NUVO, February 27, 2013, http://www.nuvo.net/indianapolis/health-care-costs-pinch-some-airport-workers/Content?oid=2544034.

2. Comments followed Fran Quigley, "Butler Food Workers Fight for Improvements," *Indianapolis NUVO,* June 21, 2013, http://www.nuvo.net/indianapolis/butler-food-workers-fight-for-improvements/Content?oid=2618554#.U4jAs_ldVCY

3. See Timothy J. Minchin, *Hiring the Black Worker: The Racial Integration of the Southern Textile Industry, 1960–1980* (Chapel Hill: University of North Carolina Press, 1999), 245.

14. Turned Away at the Hotels

1. Cory Schouten, "Indianapolis Seeks $66 Million TIF for Downtown Marriott Convention Center Hotel," *Indianapolis Business Journal*, May 14, 2007.
2. Theresa Auch Schultz, "Whiteco Gives $1 Million to Romney Super PAC," *Chicago Post-Tribune*, February 7, 2012, http://posttrib.suntimes.com/news/lake/10492741-418/whiteco-gives-1-million-to-romney-super-pac.html.
3. Indiana Code § 36–7–15.1.
4. Indyhotelworkers, "Raising Indianapolis: Hotel Workers Rising in Indianapolis," https://www.youtube.com/watch?v=exBtVnZaWUk.

15. Back to the Hyatt

1. Larry Cohen and Richard W. Hurd, "Fear, Conflict, and Union Organizing," in *Organizing to Win: New Research on Union Strategies*, ed. Kate Bronfenbrenner, Sheldon Friedman, Richard W. Hurd, Rudolph A. Oswald, and Ronald L. Seeber (Ithaca: Cornell University Press), 181–96.
2. Nelson Lichtenstein, *The Most Dangerous Man in Detroit: Walter Reuther and the Fate of American Labor* (New York: Basic Books, 1995), 76.
3. Wade Rathke, "A Wal-Mart Workers Association? An Organizing Plan," in *Wal-Mart: The Face of Twenty-First Century Capitalism*, ed. Nelson Lichtenstein (New York: New Press, 2006), 265.

16. "Bring Lisa Back!"

1. Tom Marvin, "Community Organizing for the Union: A Tale of Two Campaigns in Indianapolis" (unpublished manuscript, 2013).
2. Marshall Ganz, "Leading Change: Leadership, Organization, and Social Movements," Harvard Business Press (2010): 9, http://leadingchangenetwork.org/files/2012/05/Chapter-19-Leading-Change-Leadership-Organization-and-Social-Movements.pdf.
3. Steve Early, "Organizing for the Long Haul: Colonizing to the Rescue?" *WorkingUSA: The Journal of Labor and Society* 16 (September 2013): 358.
4. ATS, "Response," October 12, 2013, at 4 p.m., http://talkingunion.wordpress.com/2013/10/10/organizing-for-the-long-haul-salting-to-the-rescue/.
5. "Salting and the Truth in Employment Act," National Right to Work Committee, http://nrtwc.org/facts-issues/salting/.
6. *NLRB v. Town & Country Electric*, 516 U.S. 85 (1995).
7. James L. Fox, "'Salting' the Construction Industry," *William Mitchell Law Review* 24 (1998): 681, 683.
8. *Dexter Thread Mills*, 199 NLRB 543 (1972).
9. *Babcock v. Wilcox*, 351 U.S. 105 (1956).
10. Ibid., at 114.
11. Fox, "'Salting' the Construction Industry," 683.
12. Nelson Lichtenstein, *The State of the Union: A Century of American Labor* (Princeton, NJ: Princeton University Press, 2002), 49–51.
13. Peter Olney, "The Arithmetic of Decline and Some Prospects for Renewal," *New Labor Forum* (Spring–Summer 2002), 11, http://www.d.umn.edu/~epeters5/MAPL5111/5111%20Articles/Olney%20-%20The%20Arithmetic%20of%20Decline%20and%20Some%20

Proposals%20for%20Renewal.pdf. For a recent account of some salts' experiences, see Jane Slaughter, "Millennials on the Joys and Trials of Salting," *In These Times,* February 27, 2014, http://inthesetimes.com/working/entry/16356/stories_from_salts_the_workplace_organizers.

14. Jane McAlevey and Bob Ostertag, *Raising Expectations (and Raising Hell): My Decade Fighting for the Labor Movement* (London: Verso, 2012), 250.

15. National Employment Law Project, "Super-Sizing Public Costs: How Low Wages at Top Fast-Food Chains Leave Taxpayers Footing the Bill," October 2013, 1–2, http://www.nelp. org/page/-/rtmw/uploads/NELP-Super-Sizing-Public-Costs-Fast-Food-Report.pdf.

17. "That Is What the Union Does for Me"

1. See labor historian Nelson Lichtenstein's observations that political mobilization is current workers' best hope in Josh Eidelson, "Alt-Labor," *American Prospect,* January 29, 2013, http://prospect.org/article/alt-labor: "Because the payoff is so little and the amount of energy and risk are so great, collective bargaining per se, whether public- or private-sector, is pretty much a dead end."

2. See Thomas Frank, "The Problem with Thomas Piketty: 'Capital' Destroys Right-Wing Lies, but There's One Solution It Forgets," *Salon*, May 11, 2014, http://www.salon.com/2014/05/11/the_problem_with_thomas_piketty_capital_destroys_right_wing_lies_but_theres_one_solution_it_forgets/. Frank writes: "Turning to the problem of income inequality here in the United States, there is an even simpler solution, by which I mean a more realistic solution, a solution that builds on familiar American traditions, that works by empowering average people, that requires few economists or experts, that would involve a minimum of government interference, and that proceeds by expanding democracy and participation rather than by building some kind of distant and unapproachable global tax authority: Allow workers to organize."

INDEX

Note: Page numbers in *italics* refer to figures.